It wasn't until 1994 when I was recording a song for the movie Blown Away *that one of the engineers asked me to drop in next door to give a listen to his new mix of the* Woodstock *performance. This was the year of Woodstock 2 and I believe they were re-releasing the movie that summer. I did go next door to take a look at the footage and listen to the remix; it totally put me in shock. I had only seen clips of* Woodstock *in the past on TV or in promo reels, but to see myself on a giant screen and hear myself in the mixing-room setting made me very nervous. It was a lifetime experience that I will never forget.*

 Joe Cocker

Woodstock
An Inside Look at the Movie
that Shook up the World and Defined a Generation.

"The book captures the terror, exhaustion, chaos and joy of the century's greatest festival, and, for the first time, tells the story of the fearless, exuberant, talented and revolutionary band of filmmakers who captured it for the world. Anyone who cares about the American entertainment culture should read this account of the making of two of the defining and seminal events of the 20th century. Many voices; one riveting tale."
John Roberts, Woodstock Ventures Financier

"Get ready to take a wild ride behind the scenes of the making of the movie *Woodstock*...an incredible adventure told by the people who became the guerrilla team assigned to this near-impossible task. It is as exciting as the movie itself. This book should be required reading for all film students and certainly anybody who saw the movie, who was at the concert, or who wanted be there. It is the ultimate companion book to the movie, *Woodstock*."
Mike Shrieve, Drummer for Santana

WOODSTOCK

AN INSIDE LOOK AT THE MOVIE THAT SHOOK UP THE WORLD AND DEFINED A GENERATION

EDITED BY DALE BELL

Editorial Associate: ELEN ORSON

Published by Michael Wiese Productions, 11288 Ventura Blvd., Suite 821,
Studio City, CA 91604, (818) 379-8799 Fax (818) 986-3408.
E-mail: wiese@earthlink.net
http://www.mwp.com

Cover design by The Art Hotel
Copyedited by Virginia Iorio
Editorial Associate: Elen Orson

Printed and Manufactured in the United States of America

ISBN 0-94-118871-X

Library of Congress Cataloging-in-Publication Data

Bell, Dale, 1938-
        Woodstock : an insider look at the movie that shook up the world and defined a
generation / edited by Dale Bell.
                p. cm.
        Includes index.
        ISBN 0-94-118871-X
        1. Woodstock (Motion picture)
        PN1997 .W64 1999   99-28969
        791.43'72 -- dc21   CIP

🎥 DEDICATION

This book is dedicated to three people:

Bob Maurice, Producer of the movie *Woodstock*, whose relentless efforts to preserve our artistic integrity were unsurpassed;

Tom Taggart, the mythical "Port-O-San man," whose worldly compassion for the kids at the Festival and in Vietnam symbolized precisely why we fought for artistic integrity so vehemently in the first place; and

Max Yasgur, the farmer whose generational understanding provided Woodstock Ventures a happening space.

☞ FESTIVAL PASS

This icon—the only identification we of the Wadleigh film team received—will lead you behind the scenes of the original Woodstock Festival. When you follow this pass, you'll discover the thinking, the personalities, and the many events never before been revealed about *this movie that almost did not get made.*

☞ INVITATION

Your personal invitation to the preview screenings in New York eight months later. The movie *did* get made, as you will experience here in these pages. And a year later, we won the Academy Award for

Best Feature-Length Documentary and were nominated for Best Editing and Best Sound. Go with the flow! Rock and roll. The odyssey is a trip!

🎬 WOODSTOCK CREDIT LIST 1970

A FILM BY MICHAEL WADLEIGH
directed by MICHAEL WADLEIGH
produced by BOB MAURICE
editor and assistant director
T SCHOONMAKER
associate producer
DALE BELL
photographed by
MICHAEL WADLEIGH
DAVID MYERS
RICHARD PEARCE
DON LENZER
AL WERTHEIMER
sound & music & assistant to the director
LARRY JOHNSON
music advisor/co-ordinator
ERIC BLACKSTEAD
sound recordist
LEE OSBORNE
music mixer
DAN WALLIN
editor & assistant director
MARTIN SCORSESE
editors
STAN WARNOW
YEU-BUN YEE
JERE HUGGINS
production managers
SONYA POLONSKY
LEWIS TEAGUE
location unit supervisor
JOHN BINDER
production secretary
HANNAH HEMPSTEAD
location technical supervisor
MARTIN ANDREWS
location music engineers
BILL HANLEY
ED KRAMER
LEE OSBORNE
dubbing supervisor
GRAHAM LEE MAHIN

film co-ordinator in Hollywood
FRED TALMAGE
music assistant
DANNY TURBEVILLE
additional photography
MICHAEL MARGETTS
ED LYNCH
CHUCK LEVEY
TED CHURCHILL
FRED UNDERHILL
RICHARD CHEW
BOB DANNEMAN
STAN WARNOW
documentary sound
LARRY JOHNSON
BRUCE PERLMAN
CHARLIE PITTS
CHARLES GROSSBECK
JOE LOUW
MALCOLM HART
assistant editors
BETTINA KUGEL HIRSCH
MIRIAM EGER
BOB ALVAREZ
PHYLLIS ALTENHAUS
MUFFIE MEYER
TED DUFFIELD
ED CARIATI
WINSTON TUCKER
ANGELA KIRBY
MIRRA BANK
BARNEY EDMONDS
LANA JOKEL
BILL LIPSKY
JANET LAURETANO
SUSAN STEINBERG
ANITA THATCHER
JIM STARK
production assistants
ED GEORGE
CHARLES CIRIGLIANO
KEN GLAZEBROOK

production assistants (cont'd)
AL ZAYAT
ALICE MARKS
ANTHONY SANTACROCE
thanks to—on location:
FERN MCBRIDE
ALEX BROOKS
HAROLD SMITH
PETER BARTON
RIC BERGER
SUSAN BERGER
RENEE WADLEIGH
GINNY DUNN
ELEN ORSON
SHARON BINDER
ANNE BELL
JEANNE FIELD
CATHY HILLER
MAGGIE KOVEN
FELICITY LYNCH
KAREN LEVEY
ROBERT SOLOMON
JUDY UNDERHILL
VALERIE PERLMAN
NONI WALTERS
VALERIE SANTIAGO
STEVE KRAFT
JOHN MORRIS
STEVE COHEN
CHIP MONCK
CHRIS LANGHART
HUGH ROMNEY
TOM LAW
KEN BABBS
THE HOG FARM
THE MERRY PRANKSTERS
SIDNEY WESTERFELD
MAX YASGUR
thanks to—at home:
BILL GRAHAM
BILL HILLIKER
JOYCE FRESH
BEAU GILL
CHUCK HIRSCH
PETE, GLORIA & HERMAN

NORBERT & VIC
BOB ROIZMAN
MARILYN SILVERBERG
DULCINDA
HART PERRY
processing lab in New York
J&D LABS
opticals
CINEMA RESEARCH CORP.
PACIFIC TITLE & ART
NATIONAL SCREEN
KEM CORPORATION
ECLAIR CORPORATION
CAMERA MART
HANLEY SOUND
titles
CHARLES CIRIGLIANO
color by TECHNICOLOR

"Going Up Country"
sung by Canned Heat

The Song "Woodstock"
written by Joni Mitchell

☕ TABLE OF CONTENTS

PART IV: OK, WHERE'S THE MOVIE?: *THE EDIT*

PART V: AFTER ... 5 YEARS, 10 YEARS, 30 YEARS AFTER

 **FOREWORD**

MARTIN SCORSESE

(Assistant Director and Editor of the film Woodstock*)*

 Woodstock obviously emerged from its historical moment. And one of the things about that moment was that everyone was waiting for a big, defining event that would counteract all the awful things that had happened. There was the music. There was the idea of rejecting the rest of the world and living in a natural state. There was the drug culture. There was the political stance against the government, specifically its policy in Vietnam. And they all came together in this moment. It's interesting that people called it "The Woodstock Nation," because that's what people wanted—to be separate, to have their own community. And for three days, they had it. When I look back at the second half of the sixties, I realize it is the only time I have ever heard people talk about love in serious terms, as a force to combat greed, hate and violence.

What does it symbolize today? What will it symbolize for future generations? Well, what does the Paris Commune symbolize today? What do the New York draft riots symbolize today? They're events from a more distant past, but it's the same past that Woodstock is now receding into. What it symbolizes is that things can happen, incredible events that are the product of many particular elements converging at a particular moment. And those events can't be repeated— look at Woodstock II. But the fact that something new did happen on a grand scale, something that felt like nothing else that had ever happened before, means that something entirely new can happen again, in a way that we can't predict.

Martin Scorsese on site at the Woodstock Festival

Larry Johnson

1

 INTRODUCTION

DALE BELL

(Associate Producer of the film *Woodstock)*

 It seems like yesterday. A group of long-haired freaks, clad in bell-bottom jeans and tattered hair-bands, some sporting cowboy hats, invade the Warner Brothers' lot in Burbank, California, in the early winter of 1970. Tumbleweeds dance in the Santa Ana winds among the vacant sound stages. Tall grass forces its way through the empty tarmack. It looks like *The Day the Earth Stood Still.* Or is it Stanley Kramer's *On The Beach?* We say to each other, "Is this the Hollywood we've all dreamed of?"

Only a handful of security people greet us, wondering who we are. Where did we come from? What are we doing on their premises?! And WHAT, they demand, is that weird gear we're trucking onto their lot? Whutt're editing tables? We know FILL-um, they say. (A western twang to our New York ears.) FILL-um editing machines always go up and down! Not sideways! Ribbing each other at our expense, they tease: "Your long hair is going to get caught in the reels of fill-um! Maybe you'd better wear hairnets!"

From their offices above and around us, Fred Weintraub, Producer, John Calley, World-Wide Production Chief, and Ted Ashley, Chairman, must have been looking on, bemused. Back in New York City, the chairman of Atlantic Records, Ahmet Ertegun, might have been smiling like a Cheshire cat. The boss of all of them, silver-haired and -tongued Steve Ross, might have been clapping his hands in glee.

Not one of them knew then that our hippie movie, *Woodstock*, would pay their salaries, keep their children in school, allow them to take their vacations, and enrich their stockholders; much less that it would finance the rebirth of the once-mighty Warner Brothers studio, revolutionizing the music business at the same time.

Neither did anyone know how our movie would affect the drug culture, the war in Vietnam, the civil rights struggles in the south, or Kent State. How many times since have writers, musicians, commentators, comedians, and politicians invoked the event they experienced only on film, in vain or in glory?

A scant four months earlier—August 15, 16, and 17, 1969, the jubilant days that now live for generations—half a million people had forged a pilgrimage to a tiny spot in New York State. We had trekked along with the largest, most highly sophisticated documentary film unit ever assembled, to record it all. No precedent to guide our efforts. The presence of drugs was a certainty. The crowd could become uncontrollable. Pandemonium? Nirvana? Madness? Peace and Love? Mayhem?

We were fearful that our fifteen cameramen would run out of precious film if the helicopters couldn't land with our mandatory cargo; we were entirely without any financial means, except just enough to purchase raw stock. Everything else was a house of cards built upon promise and speculation and many gut feelings. *(As late as two weeks before the festival, in early August, no one was preparing to make the movie!)*

Bonded together by camaraderie and adrenaline, we fought off claustrophobia, fear, heat, hunger, and sleep. Working from plywood sawhorse tables underneath the massive stage, deprived of food and water, covered with mud and rain, risking electrocution in the windy thunderstorms of Saturday and Sunday, virtually sleepless for three nights, we moved synchronously through our paces, like an army.

Runners assigned to each of the six on-stage cameramen gathered like ballboys in tournament tennis, ready to leap forward when a cameraman needed help or a new roll of film. Loaders beneath the stage, their sweating arms immersed in black film changing bags, loaded and unloaded magazines tirelessly in ankle-deep mud, knowing that one scratch on the emulsion of one film roll could ruin a good day's—or night's—work!

During day-light hours, when we could maneuver among the throng of half a million people, we tried to determine the kinds of stories we would be able to cover before nightfall, for everyone knew that the documentary sequences would be equally as important as the music. We were mindful to keep our eyes out for spontaneous situations and *to film what interested us, to turn off when we lost interest.*

Never before (and need I say, never since despite so many attempts at imitation!) had such advanced technology been married so dynamically, so swiftly, so harmoniously to a vision we filmmakers had developed independently in the tumultuous cauldron of the Sixties. Over the course of a short but turbulent journey, we were thrown together—total strangers and life-long friends—to pool our collective experiences, our skills, our wisdom and our vision, to create for future generations a single, revolutionary memoir. As none of us could truly assess its impact before the movie was released, we were unaware that we were creating a symbol for an age. But driven by the desire to get it right, we managed to record *live on film* for posterity, the single most successful documentary the world has ever known . . . . an icon of this century, *Woodstock.*

* * *

I always considered myself the least likely person to be at White Lake, New York, that August of 1969. Because my head had always been saturated with Broadway melodies interlaced with Bach, Beethoven and Brahms and sometimes Chopin, there was no place for Baez, Butterfield, or—what was that name?—Sly and the Family Stone?

I was busy raising my family—three small sons: Jonathan, David, and Andrew—with my wife Anne in a Victorian three-story gingerbread house on the banks of the Hudson River facing the vast Tappan Zee. Had we inherited the mantle of revolution from former-owner Betty Friedan whose *The Feminine Mystique*, calling for a changed role for women, had been written in our bedroom just six years earlier? We had just returned from spending a year in Washington where I was part of the press corps in public television; this assignment brought me in touch with President Johnson, Cabinet members, and the likes of Ralph Nader. I counted myself a member of the Establishment. I was by no means a "Long Hair" and I had few friends who were. Most of them were more than a little intimidating to me.

In 1965, I had hired Michael Wadleigh (camera) and John Binder (sound), fresh out of NYU Film School, and had given them their first official jobs. They had long hair and iconoclastic minds. But because they were so good,

Chuck Levey

Michael Wadleigh during Sidewalks of New England for Merv Griffin

Larry Johnson

John Binder, partner with Wadleigh in Paradigm Films

and so different in personality from other crews who were walking the halls of educational television in New York in 1965, they quickly received calls from other producers.

Soon, Mike and John were working regularly, traveling the world, meeting other camera crews like themselves, picking up on the new technologies. Natural light, cinema verite, hand-held cameras were being designed in France and Germany; these new cameras could revolutionize traditional 35 m/m news-gathering. So aware were they of the importance of harnessing these innovations in cameras, recorders and post-production gear, Mike and John visited engineers and factories in France, Switzerland and Germany, and explored the application of the equipment to new concepts in filmmaking.

In 1966, adhering to the Aristotelian unities of time, place, and action, I devised a program which would be filmed within one 24-hour day, by 13 cameramen located in 10 different spots between San Diego and London, as though it was *live on film*. On this project, I brought together Mike (by then, "Wads" to my "Ding") and David Myers, the legendary cameraman from the Bay Area who would become our collective mentor.

Yet Mike and John Binder remained close friends who brought their families and friends to our house on the river. Gradually, in the winter and spring of 1969, I found myself anticipating unemployment for the first time since I had been married. Mike and John invited me to work out of their offices on upper Broadway until I could find something permanent.

It was there that I came in contact with a whole new breed of long-haired, ingenious, funny, inventive, passionate, brilliant and sometimes weird people who were to change my life completely. Among them was the very youthful Larry Johnson, almost an alter-ego to Michael, whose spiritual sense of the powerful music of his generation might have surpassed even his technical ability to record it and deliver it purely to another medium.

Our encounters were tentative at first, but suspicion quickly gave way to mutual respect and appreciation. There was no way to ignore these infectious minds, this sense of camaraderie, this philosophical dichotomy, this sluice of energy which coursed up and down Manhattan. After all, we were filmmakers, above and underground, destined to take on the world. By virtue of the extraordinary variety of our work, we were fast becoming the eyes and ears of the thinking, caring populace, in the US and abroad. Our portable cameras had catapulted us to the front lines. Our responsibility was to tell it like it was. And so we were uniquely poised to leap in to action when the festival happened.

From the moment the film opened in March 1970, a scant eight months after the incredible experience on Max Yasgur's farm, I knew that someday, somehow, our story had to be told. Soon after I returned to my home on the Hudson River, I was deluged with requests to talk about my experiences. So as not to forget too much, I took some elaborate notes, gave several talks to students, and recorded the lectures so that at least my family and I would have them for posterity.

Even today, when people discover that I helped to make this movie, I am asked, *What was it like?* My experience was just one of many. I cannot pretend to know how it affected those who were friends first, employees second, and extended family forever. Far be it from me to try to verbalize or to homogenize their experiences.

Nor should I. Far better for me to ask them to talk for themselves.

It was on this supposition that I asked them all to help in the production of this reunion on paper. Each of the eighty-some people we brought to the site has a story to tell: How they got there, what they expected, what they encountered, how it affected them. Couple those on-site with dozens more in editing rooms which stretched from New York to Hollywood, and the extended family expands logarithmically. We would work together, eat together, marry and live together and finally, would grow into maturity, which is exactly where you find all of us right now, talking about our children and grandchildren. We have had reunions, gathering together with our families on those anniversary days in mid-August. How many other film crews in the history of the cinema have kept in touch for 30 years?

But this reunion is different. It permits us to tell our story as film makers, not the story of the festival itself which has already been analyzed and spun to a fare-thee-well.

Most of us were unaware of the attempts by other filmmakers to secure the rights to film the festival. My recent conversations with Ahmet Ertegun, Chairman and Founder of Atlantic Records, and with Porter Bibb, then working as a producer on behalf of Al and David Maysles, have yielded very curious results, for the first time told here. All of us seemed to be as ships passing in the night, unaware of the other's activities until now. Unraveling our little history still holds a great deal of fascination.

These are our stories, mingled with perceptions from some of the performers and others whose work contributed to the success of the movie. In keeping with the tenor of our original times, I think of this project as a *cinema verite* book. To mirror the movie itself, this is also a *multiple image* book. As a *bookmaker*, then, I have tried to minimize my intrusion into the content of others, as though I were a *filmmaker*, allowing objectivity and individual story-telling to emerge.

As a result of this Rashomon experiment, you may be reading sections of our history through different eyes; thus some repetition may be evident. I hope you can tolerate an occasional *overlap*. Think of it as a *double exposure*, or a *long dissolve*! You may also perceive some *instant replay, slo-mo,* and *stop-motion animation.* Allow your memory to collect this accumulated experience a piece—and a personality—at a time. The truth about this movie *which almost didn't get made* emerges.

By pulling all of our collective experiences together, I hope that those of us who may have caused pain to others in the odyssey of making this film will be shown compassion and forgiveness. It's not an excuse to be lured by a mysterious siren, but we were alive in extraordinarily tumultuous times, with a responsibility as documentarians to record them. We might have thought we were exempt from normal society—"The Untouchables"; maybe we had to believe we were, in order to succeed at our craft. But it was an illusion which would haunt some of us the rest of our lives.

Dale Bell
Grand View on Hudson, NY
and
Mission Hills, CA
December 1998

PART I.
A CINEMATIC VISION ABORNING

MICHAEL WADLEIGH: *Triumph of the Will*

 (Interview with Michael Wadleigh, Director of Woodstock, *on the Warner Brothers lot in Burbank, California, spring 1994. With Larry Johnson and Jere Huggins, he re-mixed the sound track, restored the images, and reconstituted 40 minutes to the first release of three hours, to create "The Director's Cut.")*

Q: Did you have any idea back then that it was going to be anything more than a concert, that it would be this big thing we call Woodstock and have a different connotation?

MICHAEL: Absolutely. I mean, you gotta remember that Woodstock started out as a village that was famous as a radical gathering place. That in 1919 in the village of Woodstock, the American Communist Party was started. In the 1920s, all sorts of radicals came up there—socialists and everything else. In the fifties, Allen Ginsberg came there. In the sixties, Bob Dylan, Baez, everybody else. So we really had a sense that we were a continuation of the traditions of that village in making the festival. So we thought we were onto something big. And then, of course, when we got that beautiful farm from Max Yasgur with pastures, and lakes and birdstands and everything, we thought, well this is a place where people are going to want to come. And sure enough, a half million people got there and three million tried to get there. That's what the cops said on the roads.

Q: At the time, though, were you so busy working that you couldn't absorb this, or was it pretty clear right as it was happening?

MICHAEL: I think it was pretty clear right as it was happening. Because 500,000 people you don't overlook. And then also, as a kind of barometer, when we saw the *New York Times* headline—Well, for two days running, we got full-width banner headlines for the *NYT*. So we thought, well, we're going to really be something.

Everyone thinks of it as sort of the seminal event of the sixties generation, indeed, we're called The Woodstock Generation after the festival. But the other interesting thing is that it's like *The Canterbury Tales*, or *Pilgrim's Progress*. It's really a timeless idea where you see kids streaming out of the cities that are so dirty and complex and pollution-ridden and crime-ridden, coming to the countryside. You know, back to the land, back to the garden, to sort of this pristine natural setting that has the lakes and trees and so on, and the innocence of nature. And then you see the sort of cathedral erected in nature, where the wooden stage goes up, where the choirs will come to sing, where the priests will give the sermons, where the jugglers and the clowns will perform.

So I guess really the responsibility of the documentary may be that it might turn into something of a more timeless nature where the general human condition—where war and peace and generation gap, and human rights and so on, our relationship with the earth—can all be looked at within a kind of metaphorical context or construct called Woodstock.

Q: Having been there yourself and experienced the whole thing—literally from start to finish—are there things that the movie doesn't capture? I mean, what does the movie capture and what did you have to be there to kind of be a part of?

MICHAEL: Well, even there, I think the reason for the film's length was that when Thelma [Schoonmaker], Marty [Scorsese], and others and I were editing the film, we never thought we were "editing a film." We thought we were editing an experience, that we wanted to "take you there," you know? So that part of the POV [point of view] that you might miss if it were a brief film, and part of the experience, would be the length of it. So we thought that we really needed a long film to make it more like the surrogate experience.

Q: When you look back at it now, are there images that only come into focus 25 years later?

MICHAEL: Well, the thing that also I keep remembering, maybe because I'm embroiled with it now, are certain performances. Like Jimi Hendrix doing "The Star Spangled Banner." I can transport myself back there to see that man play as if it's like today. I'm not talking about the film. But he was such an incredible musician and had such a oneness about his guitar and his body. It was virtually like he took his own guts and strung them in place of the strings—really playing his own body. I've often thought of that, and of course thought of him as maybe an example of the kind of loss we all feel for the idealism of the sixties which seems to have all vanished.

Q: Overall, this whole picture—how do you describe it now to people who weren't there?

MICHAEL: Well, as Jerry Garcia says in the movie—it was a biblical, epical, unbelievable scene. And it truly was biblical and epical. You had your masses, you had all your essential body functions from eating and drinking, to taking a dump, to what have you. You had your music, you had your entertainment, you had your jugglers, clowns, priests, and everything else there going. So I think more and more people are describing *Woodstock* as an epic. You know, as the sort of left-wing version of *Triumph of the Will*. That it's just one of those larger-than-life experiences, and it really was.

Q: You kind of got thrust into being the guy who did *Woodstock* . . .

MICHAEL: But then I would point out to you that as television journalists, as movie journalists, we have tremendous responsibility. We, collectively, are the most powerful media that this planet has and we're so influential. Take drugs for example. The film seems to be arguing for drugs. And here, 25 years later, we have this disastrous, horrendous problem with hard drugs. So in a way, you have to look at what you did then, look at the situation today and say, well—did I do the right thing?

Q: Responsibility for the Woodstock generation?

MICHAEL: Well, I was raised by two very good parents who instilled in me the fact that you were supposed to step up to the plate and put your ego aside. And I'm trying and I hope I'm it doing now, articulating concerns that a lot of people had.

Part of the richness I think people ignore about *Woodstock* is the richness of alternatives. After all, in America, one of the big things we're supposed to be is the land of individuals. Which means individual opinion, alternatives, you know. Well I think what *Woodstock* symbolizes is counterculture, alternative culture, alternative points of view, alternative lifestyles. Question everything.

The biggest realization—it wasn't so much a look back as a look at a timeless situation. Country Joe's song wasn't really about the Vietnam War, it's about all wars; Joan Baez's song about Joe Hill is about all organizers; "Freedom" and "Handsome Johnny," songs that Richie Havens sings; "Summertime Blues," that there ain't no cure for them because your congressman won't get you a job, and on and on—they're all metaphors. They work today every bit as well as they worked yesterday.

Q: Has it sunk in these 25 years later any deeper, or is it pretty much the same—

MICHAEL: Absolutely. I suppose it went through four basic phases. First was the excitement of becoming partners with the guys who were putting this on— Wow! We're going to do this event. Then the depressive feeling that it would never happen. That we couldn't get the political clearances, that it would just be a great idea that never was. Third, then, the exhilaration of it actually happening and then beyond our wildest dreams with all these people coming. Then fourth, the horrible responsibility which turned into a nightmare of actually getting the film made.

When the rain happened, there were power surges in the electricity, then it knocked out the motors on eight cameras that I had—I mean they were just fried. So I lived in terror that I actually wouldn't have the equipment to finish the piece. And indeed, when Jimi Hendrix plays the last piece of music, we were down to three cameras. That was it.

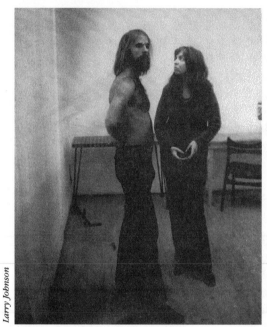

Larry Johnson

Director Michael Wadleigh and Supervising Editor Thelma Schoonmaker consider 65 miles of film.

And then of course you move into the post-coital things of—we made it through *that*, now let's sit down and see what we've got. Working with Thelma Schoonmaker, who I think is the greatest editor that's ever lived, working with her to put the film together on something that's got to be one of the most ambitious films ever made even till today—ambitious in terms of its editing—after all, we shot 160 hours. The finished film is 4 hours long, but with the multiple images, we used 10 hours of film. And 16 to 1, as you know, that's not much of a ratio.

Then it came out and we won the Academy Award. We became the highest-grossing documentary of all time. That was great. And then the downside of it was, for me—my personality—in a way I got too much credit. You know, my partners who put on the event were sort of forgotten and the guy who made the movie which now became the event for millions of people around the world had to become a spokesman for it. And after a while, especially after the sixties ended and the whole country turned to the right, people would literally call me in the middle of the night and ask me, "What does it all mean, where are we going?" And I'd say, "Fuck, hell if I know—give me a break."

2

JOHN BINDER: *OUR EARLY DAYS*

 (After attending NYU Film School with Marty Scorsese, Mike Wadleigh, and Thelma Schoonmaker, John created Paradigm Films with Mike in the mid-1960s.)

A list of unusually talented people had worked with us at Paradigm over the years. It was this gang that Michael called upon to shoot *Woodstock*.

Dale Bell, working with producer John O'Toole, had given us our first professional job at public television station WNET in New York. It was to be a documentary on the "American Communist Party". We hadn't shot much before the powers at WNET got cold feet and O'Toole had to come up with a safer subject. We crisscrossed the country shooting lots of film on the subject of "the vanishing American (hometown) newspaper." We were neophytes when we started, but by the time we finished that shoot we had become pretty good at our jobs.

Thelma Schoonmaker worked for a documentary producer in the city and she hired us a few times, then she started working with us on our projects. Scorsese joined us as an editor often, and also Jim McBride. Thelma edited Marty's first feature, *Who's That Knocking*, which we shot for him. Michael collaborated on McBride and Kit Carson's influential *David Holtzman's Diary*. We all worked together for free on anti-war films when Vietnam heated up, and so on.

Nobody was in the Union. The Union wouldn't have us. Every one of us knew how to do more than one job on a film production. Everyone could shoot a camera, record sound, edit film—some, of course, better than others, but crosstraining and free substitutions were the norm, flexibility the principle. For example, Bob Maurice had come to Paradigm to start our distribution arm when Michael pressed him into service as producer of *Woodstock*. Working with Bob in distribution was Jeanne Field, who worked on *Woodstock* as a camera assistant.

So, we didn't have any permanent configuration at Paradigm. When we needed extra cameras or more people for bigger jobs, we hired them from our expanding pool of acquaintances, or we joined them on their projects. We were like musicians who come together to work on various gigs but don't form a permanent band. Whoever we didn't know from NYU we met this way, including David Myers, Ed Lynch, Chuck Levey and Charlie Peck, Martie Andrews, Richard Pearce, Don Lenzer, Ted Churchill, Peter Barton . . .

Michael was more of a leader than a boss. When he picked up his camera and started moving, everybody grabbed their gear and went to work. Aside from coordination and support, nobody needed much palaver.

It is significant that we had all worked in this semi-independent way because it formed the ethos that made filming possible under the impossible conditions that were to come.

3.

MERV GRIFFIN: *The Freeing of America*

(We refer to Merv Griffin as the "Godfather" of Woodstock, because his innovative assignments to the Paradigm Film team provided them an experimental laboratory for new cinematic technique.)

MERV: Is Michael Wadleigh still alive?

DALE: Very much so. And in New Hampshire. And sends his best.

MERV: Oh, my God. Give him my love. He was such a different kind of guy, for a cinematographer. He was very kind of aesthetic. Almost fragile, but you realized there was a genius there behind that camera. I think the first thing Michael did— when we flew together in that DC-3 airplane I chartered—*Sidewalks of New York*, *Sidewalks of New England*, Aretha Franklin's concert, a Thanksgiving Day show with the kids at my farm . . .

DALE: What do you remember about this merry gang of filmmakers?

MERV: There was some innovation they had in shooting—it was very much cinema verité. I mean Michael was afraid of nothing camera-wise. He wasn't locked in to the moves of the day. In other words, he was very adventuresome behind that camera. I remember we did "Quiet Nights" on a rocky beach where I was walking the rocks, you know, doing, "Quiet nights and the quiet stars," which had been prerecorded by the orchestra and I was singing it live. He was the most awesome photographer.

DALE: He was. Unfortunately he's stopped doing it, the damned fool.

Merv Griffin, the "Godfather" of *Woodstock*

MERV: Has he stopped?

DALE: Yeah. He's writing and he's producing CD-ROMs and he's written screen-plays, but he has not been a cinematographer virtually since *Woodstock*.

MERV: I just recall the time I think he mortgaged his house, his family, his wife's ballet shoes—everything—to do *Woodstock*.

DALE: What did you think about the movie?

MERV: It was fabulous. There never has been a gathering like that. Oh, there've been gatherings—but not with that spirit. I mean it was the spirit, it was the first. To have a memory like that recorded of the first of anything is wonderful.

And of course that was the decade everything—every institution—everything broke down. It was the freeing of America, good or bad. It just took away the reins that were on everybody and the framework that was around everything you did.

My show was a great platform for all the people who protested everything. The show was on nighttime in New York and other major cities, Metromedia. Jane Fonda couldn't get on any television show except mine, because we were syndi-cated, so there was nobody who could say, "Merv, you can't have her on." But she was persona non grata on the networks, as was Muhammed Ali. He was not allowed on. All the civil protests came on my show. The Mailers . . . and on the other hand, we gave equal time to the Buckleys and everybody else.

But my platform was the source of speaking out in America and they couldn't stop me. I had on the first protest by a world-famous person against the Vietnam War— Lord Bertrand Russell, who later ran the Vietnam War Crimes Trial in Sweden. Bob Considine, who was the front-page writer of the then *Journal American* of New York, wrote that "Merv Griffin should be taken off the air for what he's done." And his son was my cameraman, Barry, on the show. And he wrote this piece and I answered him. He said, "We're in wartime and Merv Griffin puts on a protest against America." And I said, "We're not in wartime, what are you talking about? It's a police action, no war has been declared."

DALE: How do you feel about that today, Merv Griffin?

MERV: I feel good about it. It was a contribution. I was the only one ever allowed to go to Alcatraz to tape the Indians, which I did when they took over Alcatraz. My philosophy of the show was that there are many voices speaking in America. Not all of them do you agree with, but you should hear them.

It was happening on my show. Remember the famous one that made the front pages? When the kid—Abbie Hoffman—from the Chicago 7 came on my show and he was wearing what CBS said—(by that time I left syndication and had been on

CBS two years—he was wearing the [American] flag. They said, "You cannot wear a flag as a piece of clothing!" And so they prodded him out of the show with an *electric prod ... [they blooped his picture ...]* and just left me talking to a black screen.

And then when I did the commercial, Roy Rogers and Dale Evans came up in the same shirts for Ford Motor Company! Bob Woods from CBS almost had a heart attack!

MARTIN ANDREWS: *Woodstock*, the Weird Wombat

(Martie began with Paradigm Films as a technical wizard, a function he performed on the movie as its Technical Supervisor.)

There is no doubt that *Woodstock* was the weird wombat wrenched from the womb of Merv Griffin's *Sidewalks of New England* TV special.

Like *Woodstock* (peace, music, multi-image location documentary), *Sidewalks* had a conceptual conception: get Merv out of the studio and integrate his regulars (Arthur Treacher, etc.) with others on location in New England to follow the changing fall foliage. Merv cajoled local-color jokes from Jud Strunk in Vermont. A brilliant Agnes de Mille dance rendition of the Lizzie Borden story was staged in a graveyard for the highbrow audience. Paul Revere and the Raiders provided some Yankee rock and roll on top of the Prudential Building in Boston for the hipsters. There was Aretha Franklin for the Black and Gospel audiences. For general interest, there was the dynamic staging of a Gilbert and Sullivan piece with soloists and choruses on different balconies of buildings in Gloucester, Massachusetts.

Mike Wadleigh

Martie Andrews, technowizard for Paradigm Films, holding up Merv Griffins' DC-3

In turn, *Sidewalks of New England* grew out of the previous year's successful *On the Sidewalks of New York*, which was a similar concept shot by Wadleigh at outdoor metropolitan locations.

The technological innovations of *Woodstock* sprang or evolved from technological innovations in those *Sidewalks* shows. Wadleigh chose to use the newly developed

Eclair NPR 16mm film camera for several reasons. His NPR was the only camera to have survived the documentary he did in the Hindu Kush. Its quick-change magazine minimized the exposure to airborne dust, sand and moisture (rain, snow, humidity) and reduced film-change time.

These 16mm cameras weighed about 20 pounds and were ergonomically suited to hand-held operation in standing, sitting, crouching and even prone positions. Wadleigh would start a shot standing, and as he crouched down (human boom shot), he would press his eye on the 360-degree orientable viewfinder (literally keeping in touch with the viewing image) and with his "eye contact," force the viewfinder around as its relationship to the camera changed.

He, I and others were left-eyed and were enabled by the design of the camera to read the F-stop and focus numbers with the right eye. This was important, because these "wild-eyed hippie filmmakers" had the audacity to change focus and zoom while hand-holding and walking around with these NPRs! Wadleigh's right eye was bad enough that, although he could see the F and focus numbers, he couldn't read them. Thus he had special rings and other accessories made up which he sold to others at cost. I believe that those with the worst eyesight make the best camera operators because, in life, they are looking harder to compensate for their deficiency. Producers, hire cameramen who wear glasses!

These cameras had a minimal noise level at one meter and needed no blimp because the motor's drive shaft directly turned the shutter, registration pin and wedge-shaped claw. The mirror shutter (variable from 5 to 180 degrees) ran on a shaft below the aperture and cut the frame side to side, enabling horizontal pans with less strobe. The reflex viewing area in the ground glass showed what was just outside the film area engraving, so we could compose better as well as keep the mikes out of the shot. The rotating turrets enabled us to quickly remove the zoom lens and go to the 5.9 wide-angle lens while still shooting (losing only a few frames in the rack-over). This liberated us from follow-focusing and increased our mobility.

It is impossible to overstate the effect that this camera design had on the rock-and-roll razzle-dazzle style that persists to this day. This style has been hyped beyond absurdity by MTV with its mandated quick cutting. Such hype has negated the incredible mobility and fluidity we achieved with the technology on the *Sidewalks* show, and later at Woodstock.

The relationship between film equipment and the culture that produced it is noteworthy. The German Arris are precision tanks that can be dropped or even thrown on the floor (*mea culpa*) and still function. The French Eclairs and Beaulieus are high-tech marvels. The Swiss Bolexes are fussy, fingernail-breaking wind-up watches. The Japanese Doiflexes were knock-off rip-offs. The American BNCs and

Panaflexes are reliable beasts that require a curious array of ancillary equipment (dollies, cranes, camera cars, "weightless" rigs) and an army of union personnel to operate them.

Only the young, "uninitiated" hippies could have discovered the capabilities of these technologies. And we were naive enough to actually make use of them. Who were we? We were baby boomers, white, middle-class, male and well-educated (I went to the University of Pennsylvania, where I earned a Master's not just in film but also in the more amorphous Mass Communications).

We were young and typically rebellious, from our Oedipal conflict with fathers wanting us to "grow up and get a job" to society at large. We, in our naiveté, knew it all. We knew that it was time to "get real" with integration. We saw through the sham and lies fed to us by our government about Vietnam. We were rebels with a cause, backed by a phenomenally dynamic, revolutionary and compelling music scene augmented by the adventure of mind-expanding and life-enhancing (we thought) drugs.

We not so much "dropped out" as were locked out by the Union. We "tuned in" to what was going down by reading I.F. Stone, getting together and sharing the messages in our new music. We had long hair, funny clothes and were acutely aware of (hip to) the difference between the bold, adventurous us (hippies) and the status quo gang. We were free radicals who had discovered our own unified field of peace, drugs and music in a world gone mad with greed, ignorance and stupidity.

We weren't rocket scientists (it was only a month before Woodstock that NASA landed mankind on the moon and Ted Kennedy landed Mary Jo Kopechne in the waters off Chappaquiddick). But we did have the new technology—Eclair NPR, lavaliers, shotgun mikes—that could broadcast the sync signal via cordless transmitter to Nagra recorders, those perfect pieces of technology.

Martie to the Rescue

How did I get involved with Wadleigh's *Sidewalks of New England* crew? The Eclair, as innovative as it was, was not the piece of perfection that the Nagra was. What to do? Help! Panic insinuated itself into the equation of filmmakers who were not that far along in experience from the always inadequate film-school education. The now-legendary Ted Churchill came up with the solution: me.

Ted told the powers-that-be on *Sidewalks* that he knew sort of an old guy who had worked on a lot of gonzo films and had some power to stare down and humble adversity. In desperation, they bought it—and the call came in telling me to take a cab to La Guardia where there was a ticket in my name. I was to be flown in, picked up by car, and taken to a place on the Penobscot Bay in Maine.

Ted's incessant energy had gotten everyone pumped up to a state of embarrassing veneration for this "old guy" who, in actuality, had just turned 29. People knew about my connection with Bucky Fuller and I'd just gotten back from a junket in Kenya.

I was able to solve the sync problem by wiring ten 12-volt batteries in series and running them through an antique World War II inverter that was controlled by aligning the vibrating fingers of some kind of tuning fork to give 60-cycle sync. Voilà! We went to the stronger AC motors, which didn't crap out, and we held sync. I was not only home free, I had validated and perpetuated the veneration bestowed on me. I managed to stay half a step ahead of all the oddball troubleshooting and triage tasks that came my way, but that half step seemed to be all I needed. I was on the team, and what a team it was! What a time it was!

It was Merv's show, *Sidewalks of New England*, that assembled the *Woodstock* crew, shook them down and enabled them to develop their documentary style with the Eclair NPR, Nagra recorder, wireless, lavalier and shotgun mikes.

After the show was delivered to Merv, members of the crew came by Wadleigh's production office (some armed with their own personal footage) to re-edit *Sidewalks*. The music numbers on the KEM in a multi-image format became presentations for soliciting rock-and-roll work. It was these presentations that got us the *Woodstock* contract. Finally, the money that Wadleigh made from *Sidewalks* enabled him to tough it out on *Woodstock* to the point where Warner Brothers took it over.

CHARLIE PECK: *The So-Called Sixties*

(Charlie left a career as a television graphic artist to join the Paradigm Films "Merry Prankster" team as a soundman.)

Racial segregation, ecological doomsday, mindless suburban sprawl. Assassinations, police riots, decaying inner cities. Lyndon Johnson and his Techno Wonks and their Disastrous Land War in Asia. And then there was always the bomb . . . the Hydrogen Bomb. With all this appalling crap so sharply in focus, it was hard not to develop a serious attitude problem. For Christ sake, there must be some ideals worth considering that haven't been twisted, co-opted or even completely forgotten about! But *what* were they? *Where* were they? Mom used to say, "Charles, you seem to be marching to the beat of a different drummer." Heck, you bet I was!

Charlie Peck, soundman for Paradigm Films working on Merv's specials

In the 1960s these outsiders got to be a lot more visible. They were dropping out in record numbers, finding each other, and beginning to adopt some interesting new values: honesty, peace, mutual respect—odd notions like that.

Today, they're out there all right, but for the most part, unseen. They like it that way: authors, cabinetmakers, musicians, entrepreneurs, comedy writers, jewelry designers, jugglers, pastry chefs, film editors, genius freelance computer consultants—people who come and go as they please. Go ahead, call them names if you want. They could care less.

And by the way, remember those oddball Puritans who, for moral and ethical reasons, sailed away from England in their wooden ships way back in 1620?

This is very American. It's a part of what makes us so special.

Sexy Media Machines

But our story begins in France. In the mid-sixties the Eclair Company was hard at work developing a revolutionary motion picture camera, the NPR. For the shutter they used the same idea as the German Arri S, a rotating mirror. Below and mounted at a cocky angle was the cylindrical battery-powered motor. To replace it all you needed was one tool, a coin. The lens turret featured a new insert-and-twist bayonet mount. This meant that the lens, usually an Angenieux zoom lens, could be replaced in less than two seconds, with one hand.

But the best part was the camera's magazine/transport system. The sprockets, pressure plate, and film loops were incorporated into each film magazine. That meant that a fresh roll of 400 feet of raw stock, 11 minutes, could be snapped to the back of the shutter assembly, ready to roll, in less than a second.

And all designed and hand-assembled for one purpose: to try to insert a silent hand-held motion picture camera inconspicuously into any interesting real-life situation, anywhere.

And to record the sound along the way, the NPR was designed to work with another European masterpiece, the Swiss-made Nagra III portable tape recorder. Compact, rugged, precise, it was about the size of five bricks lashed together and almost as heavy. The Swiss Army tape recorder.

Oh, but when you opened it up and looked inside, the sight of the motors, pulleys, and electronics was breathtaking. Hand-crafted with not a cubic centimeter of space wasted; parallel colored wires, cute little transistors, all carefully arranged and accented with shiny, silvery, perfectly soldered connections. And it was there in all those unseeable, complex electronics that the engineers at Nagra had really done it. The sound it recorded was rich and pure; crystalline highs, gut-punching lows, almost as faithful as any recording studio in its time. And all there in that indestructible portable box.

The Suspension of Disbelief vs. Belief

As it was with many new developments during the turbulent sixties, the nifty movie equipment from Europe came with a vision, maybe even a responsibility to bring about positive social and political change. By replacing bulky and expensive studio cameras with more advanced portable 16mm systems, what happened in front of the lens would be powerfully and intimately real. In their self-satisfied fashion, the French called it *Cinema Verité*, the true movies.

Vive la différence! A cadre of cinema saboteurs creating a radical subversive film genre. And the folks over at Eclair had done their job perfectly, because as it is with any artfully conceived and carefully crafted piece of machinery, the NPR camera could cast a powerful spell.

When young Michael Wadleigh saw it, he was a goner. He left a promising future at Columbia Medical School and . . . off he went, with his friend John Binder doing the sound, filming a team of mountain climbers up through the snow and ice to 20,000 feet.

According to Michael, "That little 'clair never let me down. Sweet machine. She was a bit hefty but very sweet."

When I saw it for the first time in 1968 at Michael and John's office, Paradigm Films, on 86th Street, my reaction was the same. It was just so SEXY!

"Go ahead, put me on your shoulder. Let's have a little fun, Chèri." . . . Ah Romance. Adventure. CINEMA VERITÉ . . .

She was French, you know.

These hand-held camera people had to be much more than Rock steady. The new Cinema Verité required that they be creative types as well, athletic artists with an eye for detail, and the best of them had a sympathetic concern about other people's lives. This assured that they were always curious, alert. Very important. We tried to be inconspicuous, staying ahead of the action; relaxed, silent, moving; just going with the flow. ANYWHERE.

Chuck Levey, camerman numero due for Paradigm Films on Merv's specials

Too Much the Magic Bus

It was 1968. I was 26 years old and living in New York City when my pal Chuck Levey came to me with exciting news. Messrs. Binder and Wadleigh had convinced America's adorable daytime talk-show host Merv Griffin to get out of his hot overlit television studio and film musical performances in various locations with multiple cameras.

And after I checked it out, I knew exactly what to do. I gave notice at my comfortable job at the Channel 13 Art Department, and . . . off I went.

Ted Churchill, one of three cameramen for Paradigm Films on Merv's specials

26

Ah . . . Adventure, Romance, CINEMA VERITÉ. . . .

The journey was boisterous and arduous and led by our own dynamo mojo, Michael Wadleigh, Ninja *ne plus ultra*. Enigmatic, quiet by nature, built like a wide receiver and with piercing blue eyes, Michael radiated an intense yet benevolent authority, which on this trip demanded that everyone involved find the freedom to EXPLORE.

And explore we did. We had to. Filming with multiple cameras like this had never been tried before, so we had to sort of make it up as we went along, and if confusion, doubt, or exhaustion intruded . . . well, just check out the intrepid Mr. Wadleigh: calm, focused, alert, just going with the flow.

It was challenging because Maestro Wadleigh was always busy choreographing some new multi-camera ballet, shooting from cars, boats, and helicopters. Our irrepressible soundman Larry Johnson called it "The Hully Gully," and Michael's vision soon had the three cameramen (Michael, Chuck Levey and Ted Churchill) literally running circles around the flat, formal, proscenium look of the day.

LEWIS TEAGUE: *The Original Bob Maurice*

(When the Woodstock film team relocated to Hollywood in December 1969, Lewis became our advance man.)

Bob and I were fast friends in high school in North Tarrytown, in Westchester County, New York. The first time I ever got drunk, I was 14 and drank a quart of gin with Bob on the high school bleachers before a football game. In North Tarrytown, Bob lived in a tiny walkup apartment with his French-Canadian blue-collar parents. It seemed that every time I visited them, everyone was screaming and Bob was destroying his collection of jazz LPs by smashing them, throwing them, or stomping on them. He was an extraordinary jazz buff, constantly replacing his collection, only to destroy it again. We shared many adventures, including being chased by the police in stolen cars. He was 16 years old and went to jail for that. Since I was only 15, I went to a youth detention home. When I turned 17, I quit high school and joined the Army. I lost touch with Bob for three years.

When I got out of the Army and decided to go back to school, I somehow tracked Bob down and was shocked at what I found—a guy who had already been in City College for several years, and was passionate about books and learning. He hadn't discarded the blue-collar aspect of his personality, only added to it. He continued to pay his way through college by working construction. He became a professional student, eventually going to college for about nine years. I don't know if he ever earned his baccalaureate, but he certainly became one of the most well read and knowledgeable people I've ever encountered.

I had already introduced Bob and Mike in 1967 when I was running an experimental theater in Los Angeles called the Cinematheque-16. Later I was visiting Mike in an editing room in NY where he was cutting a documentary about Aretha Franklin. He wanted to show me the new Keller Editing Machine he was working on, that allowed him to view three shots in sync with one soundtrack. Since the performance sequences had been filmed with multiple cameras, it helped him to make his cuts from camera to camera.

It was very exciting to watch the multiple images of Aretha singing her heart out. "I'd like to make a concert film and edit it on this machine," Mike said. "And I'd optically marry the images into a triptych."

I agreed that it would be very exciting. "And you know," Mike said, "Monterey Pop made a lot of money."

At the time I was working as an associate producer on *Loving,* a feature film that Columbia was financing, so I guess Mike thought I knew how to produce. He asked if I was interested in producing his concert film. I was, and for a while we made several attempts to either produce our own concert or get the rights to film existing concerts.

At some point along the way, I needed to take a salaried job and suggested Bob Maurice to fill my shoes as producer.

So when it came time to produce *Woodstock,* Bob credited his years on the construction site with giving him the skills he needed. "Working construction. Two guys want to dump their wheelbarrow of bricks in the same spot. The problem is solved by assuming an aggressive stance and saying 'Hey! Fuck you! That's my spot!' Dealing with the studios is a lot like that," he said.

He had the charm and intelligence to make that kind of toughness work.

So when Bob needed someone on the west coast to be an advance man, I'm the one he called.

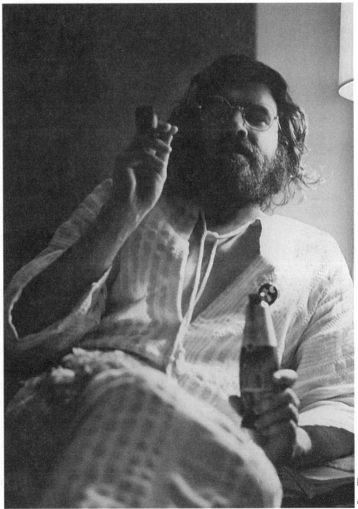

Stan Warnow

Producer Bob Maurie would battle for artistic integrity

JEANNE FIELD: *ARE YOU WOODSTOCK EXPERIENCED?*

(Jeanne joined Paradigm Distribution before coming to the Woodstock site as Production Assistant.)

In early summer 1969, I was in the East Side Book Store across from my apartment at 16 St. Mark's Place and there was a poster with a bird on a guitar, announcing a rock concert called the Woodstock Festival. Woodstock first came into my consciousness as an art community north of New York City and the home of Bob Dylan where he recuperated from an almost-death experience in a motorcycle crash. As he improved he

Larry Johnson, soundman, encircled by Jeanne Field, production assistant

started playing music with a group called The Band and introduced them to his record label, Columbia, who brought out Music From Big Pink. The Band was going to be at the festival and maybe Dylan would be too. There were a lot of bands listed on the poster I'd barely heard of but some names stuck out bigtime: Janis Joplin and the Holding Company, Jefferson Airplane, The Who, Jimi Hendrix, Ravi Shankar, Joan Baez. But who'd heard of Melanie or Jeff something or other. Arlo Guthrie was coming and he was Woodstock incarnate.

Michael Wadleigh owned a VW bus, perfect for this kind of weekend. I began to lobby my new boyfriend, Larry Johnson, to go talk to Wadleigh about going to the festival in August. Camp out, get high, hear music, all near Woodstock. Larry said Wads was into it, so I bought four tickets for Mike, Renée (his wife), Larry and me. Great!

I was a recent hire at Paradigm Films. I'd met Bob Maurice in 1968 at a screening of an independent film and kept running into him at other screenings. Bob had been charged with starting a distribution arm of Paradigm Films and was a regular on the independent film screening circuit. Bob was a pretty distinctive-looking man even by New York City late-sixties standards. Usually dressed in skinny jeans and T-shirt, his most distinctive feature was his enormous head with his large glasses, brooding brows and helmet-like long hair.

Eclair?" and he'd say, "Well it's this crust that has custard and cream in it and choco-late on it . . ." I would say "O.K.,", but that was the extent of my knowledge. I had to try and get a synchronous motor and I didn't know what sync was.

The main thing I remember from that whole experience was that you could think that you knew everything that was going on, but in the meantime some whole other thing was going on.

A lot of it had to do I believe with Mike's personality. He was able to keep a great many balls in the air at once and he was also capable of extreme secrecy. So, he would only tell people what they needed to know. Bob was also extreme-ly secretive. Probably he got along very well with Mike in ways that nobody else could ever get along with either of them, because they were both quite secre-tive and both quite smart.

Stan Warnow

Production Manager Sonya Polonsky seeks out editors

PART II.
A FESTIVAL IS HATCHED

AHMET ERTEGUN: *A Little Secret*

(Ahmet Ertegun is Co-Chairman and Co-CEO of The Atlantic Group, which celebrated its 50th anniversary in 1998. Ahmet founded the company Atlantic Records so that he could devote his life to listening to and loving music.)

DALE: How did Atlantic first get involved with the *Woodstock* project?

AHMET: I was approached by Paul Marshall, a lawyer representing the promoters of the Woodstock concert. [Marshall had recording rights for sale.] I thought there were going to be at least three Atlantic acts on the program. And I thought that if I recorded the concert, I thought I might have three live albums. This was six months at least before the concert. Of course, at that time, nobody knew that it was going to be such a momentous occasion. It was just another rock-and-roll event. So we made a deal for $75,000 with Paul Marshall. He sold me the rights to record the

concert for records and he asked me if I would be interested in the movie rights. And I said, "What movie rights? No, I'm not interested in the movie rights." So then later he couldn't sell it to anybody. So he came back to me and said, "Look—you've got $75,000 committed—give me another $25,000 and I'll throw in the movie rights." I said okay.

DALE: Wow.

AHMET: I had no idea that it would mean anything, but I thought, well, I'll have some footage of three of my acts. I thought maybe Zeppelin would be playing, and I knew that Crosby, Stills and Nash would be on it. We already had

Ahmet Ertegun

a record out. I didn't go to the concert. We didn't have the responsibility of record-ing it. For that money, the promoters were supposed to record the concert and shoot the movie. They kept the rights of making the record and the movie. Of course, after what happened happened, and this became such a huge thing, which nobody expected—we knew as the thing approached, that a lot of people were going to this because it was such a big bill.

DALE: Did you have anything to do with bringing Warner Brothers in?

AHMET: You must realize that I had already sold my company, Atlantic Records, to Warners/7 Arts. But then Warners/7 Arts was bought by Kinney Corporation. When I told them we had the movie rights to Woodstock, they were beside themselves and proceeded to work on developing the movie.

DALE: So, a little history . . . Steve Ross and his funeral-parlor, parking-lot, cleaning-services, car-rental conglomerate—Kinney—had bought Ted Ashley's talent agency in 1967. Together, they masterminded the purchase of Warners/7 Arts, which then bought Atlantic.

AHMET: Yes, Steve Ross and Ted Ashley were partners in Kinney. You know, Fred Weintraub [at Warner Brothers] only got the movie rights because I bought the rights.

DALE: I can't get over it. For $25,000. What impact did the movie have on your artists?

AHMET: Well, all those who were there were delighted, because it was such a his-torical event in rock and roll. It was such a spontaneous thing that nobody engi-neered. I think it was a highlight of the end of the sixties. A high point—a hap-pening—that really was symbolic of the feelings of all the things that had hap-pened before that. You know, Haight Ashbury, Flower Power and all of that. It had all of it going on—sex, drugs, and rock and roll.

It's more than just the music. It was like a spontaneous gathering of people who shared a new point of view about life. It was the culmination of the sixties' revo-lution in music and the anti-authoritarian, anti-establishment feeling that pervaded throughout the young people at that time. I think the song . . . "By the Time I Get to Woodstock"—

DALE: —by Joni Mitchell.

AHMET: Yes, Joni Mitchell—that Crosby, Stills and Nash recorded—I think that sym-bolizes more than any other, the feeling of Woodstock.

PORTER BIBB: *A Fool's Errand?*

(Porter was the Producer for the Maysles Brothers' film company. They almost secured the rights to film the festival, but the deck was stacked against them.)

PORTER: I was working with the Maysles on other documentaries and we thought the Festival was a potentially interesting subject for a documentary. We were looking at music, and through the relationship that I'd developed with Amhet Ertegun and with Ted Ashley—so we gravitated to Warners for the money.

DALE: Now, did you know when you were talking to Ahmet that he had the film rights to Woodstock?

PORTER: No, we did not. Before we approached Ahmet, we had had some preliminary talks with the Woodstock principals. Namely, with Mike Lang. The Maysles and I were basically covering a lot of different ground and not always attending meetings or meeting people together. It was a very fluid situation. And I do not mean to suggest, in any way, shape or form, that there was any dissension. We were just scrambling—the way documentary production companies do when they don't have a project.

DALE: Right. [laugh]

PORTER: And [laugh] so I met many, many times with Mike Lang and the Johns [Roberts and Morris] and Artie [Kornfeld] and David [Maysles, of the two brothers, Al and David], and also had separate meetings with some of the same people at different times.

I can't tell you exactly what was going on because it was fast and furious. My role as producer was to make sure that there was an economic viability here. And Al and David were focusing more on the event, and getting the acts signed up.

I felt that that was a fool's errand, because we were dealing with rock-and-roll acts that had not even committed to perform at a concert.

DALE: Sort of the cart before the horse.

PORTER: Cart before the horse. But David was extremely good at that end of the business, having spent 20 years or more as a documentarian and always aware of getting the rights before he shot. And so, a major effort was undertaken there, and we spent a lot of time with Ahmet, and the answer, bluntly, is that it was never revealed to us that Ahmet had the rights.

DALE: Were you ever negotiating with Paul Marshall?

PORTER: Yes.

DALE: Paul Marshall never told you that he had sold the music rights to Ahmet Ertegun?

PORTER: Never told us.

DALE: And he never told you that he then offered the film rights to Ahmet?

PORTER: No.

DALE: And that Ahmet had turned him down?

PORTER: No.

DALE: Keep going.

PORTER: I would say we were never aware of that. I had, as I said, a business, an economic responsibility as the Maysles' partner, and they had the creative responsibility. And they saw ground-breaking opportunity to make a major theatrical rock film. I saw the economics being covered by the profit of a soundtrack album.

DALE: Well, now, you started negotiating, then, with Ted [Ashley].

PORTER: We had a high level of comfort, despite the fact that we were never even shown a piece of paper, that Warner Brothers was ultimately going to fund a *Woodstock* project. And on the blind faith that documentarians—

DALE: [laughs]

PORTER: —must live by, we just plowed forward and did what we were supposed to be doing as filmmakers. That is, lining up schedules, people, talent, and to the extent of Al's and David's going up to the site several times in the month before the concert, as Woodstock was beginning to break ground and become a reality. . . .

They retained an English crew to shoot some footage, and we began to build a modest file on Woodstock. Perfectly candidly, I was so consumed with trying to get a business deal together that I was paying very little attention to Al and David. They would just say, "We're going up to the country," and they would be gone. Paul Marshall and I were going back and forth between the *Woodstock* people and the Warner Brothers people. As the event became more and more likely to happen, more and more benchmarks were overcome in terms of the size, the scope of the event. The ticket sales, as you know, were originally conceived of as a for-profit paid admission venture.

DALE: Right.

PORTER: But the papers were running . . . *The New York Times*—almost every other day there was news about what was going on. And we were living by the headlines, dealing with the people who we thought were the right people to be

Porter Bibb, who would become the producer of "Gimme Shelter."

Theo Westenberger

dealing with. It became very nervous-making, as we got closer and closer to D-day. Maysles Films did not have great resources. And we were starting to line up a very sizable commitment in terms of crew and equipment, and could hardly have covered that if we couldn't cut a deal with somebody.

DALE: Sure.

PORTER: At one point, we were offered the opportunity to be hired as contract filmmakers by the Woodstock principals. The Maysles said no. They had to be in control and didn't want to be just per-diem filmmakers shooting the thing.

I recollect there was the possibility that there was going to be live or taped television coverage, as well. That made some of us *and* the money very nervous, if they thought what we were going to do was not exclusive.

So I stayed focused on Warner Brothers, and my recollections are not precise in terms of the day-to-day evolution of that dialog, but I would come back after every meeting with Ashley and the business affairs guys and report that we're going to do it with Warner Brothers and they're going to put the money up about two or three days before the event opened.

I had this question put to me by Ted: "What if it rains? You'll have to have a completion bond." And I came back—and this is insane—my answer to Ashley was, "If it rains, you're made, we're made—we've got a whale of a film."

DALE: [laugh]

PORTER: But I spent at least 48 hours calling London and elsewhere trying to find out if we could [both laugh] get a completion bond on this very bizarre event. And that really was a fool's errand. I called every entertainment law firm I could think of on both coasts and in London trying to find somebody to come up with a completion bond, so I could go back to Warner Brothers and pick up what I thought was to be their check. What it was was the most graceful, diplomatic, and conclusive way for Warners to say NO, because Warners knew we'd never get a bond for this thing. But I didn't catch on to that.

DALE: And you're saying this happened in the week prior—

PORTER: In the week prior to the event, by the best of my recollections.

DALE: You came to the Wadleigh offices. Do you remember what you saw and what your response was?

PORTER: Well, I came up there and I was dazzled by this split-screen, multi-screen demonstration. And I just thought, not presumptuously, that we were going to get the money and work something out with Mike. But I had a couple of creative egos, the likes of which I couldn't exaggerate, in the Maysles brothers and I let them try to work out the relationship.

DALE: That's when Mike and all of us decided we could do it all ourselves. But we only had $23,000 in the bank, period.

PORTER: That's $23,000 more than Maysles Films had. When I said Maysles didn't have a nickel in the bank, we had a pretty good business. It was certainly a going concern that we had a lot of receivables, but as you know from your background and experience, the documentary producers are the last people to get paid in any list. And just cobbling together the money to buy the raw stock—not to mention that it didn't ever occur to me that I wouldn't have the money to pay the crew. But needless to say, we didn't get it. Because when I came up empty on the completion bond concept, I went back and realized then how stupid and how foolish I was to be deterred by Ashley in wasting time in going and looking. And it just became obvious that it wasn't going to happen on our end.

DALE: What is amazing, I'm still talking in that week before—

PORTER: And it was crazy on our end in a very negative and depressed way. We were obliged to unhook all of these people that we'd lined up. Because we really believed, up until that last week that we were going to pull it off. And the whole Wadleigh-Maysles confrontation was something that really wasn't even a factor in my thinking because I wanted as much talent as I could get out of the venture and I said, we'll shoot, work it out later. It probably would have self-destructed after Woodstock if we had worked together because Al and David just are not capable of that kind of compromise.

DALE: Nor is Wadleigh or any of us.

PORTER: No.

DALE: I mean in hindsight, in retrospect. There's a part of me that's saying this is the movie that "almost never got made at all."

PORTER: Right. I think that's almost the title of the movie, because it was within a hair's breadth of never happening. And I have to tell you. I was consumed by the way Wadleigh was running the show. Maurice too. I really admired what he was up against and how he was handling everything. Well, you guys made history, too, from the film side. It blew me away. You may remember, I came over frequently during the post-production process, and I saw what was taking shape. It was film history.

MIKE LANG: *IT'S THE MUSIC*

(Mike, the Festival Executive Producer, had responded to financier John Roberts'
advertisement:"Young Men with Limited Capital Seek Adventure.")

John Sebastian, Mike Lang, Artie Kornfeld with technicians on the Woodstock stage

DALE: Think about the movie. Who else was involved in pitching you for rights to make the film? Give me a little timeline.

MIKE: It didn't really happen that way, nobody pitched us, at all. The only people who ever proposed the idea of doing a film were Al and David [Maysles], and Porter Bibb. That was sometime in May or June. We tried to sell it to several studios, nobody "got it" at all. Before that it was just such a mad scramble to put the thing together that nobody was thinking film at all. We didn't even think film until May. And then, Artie Kornfeld [one of the Woodstock Ventures partners] really made the contact with Freddie Weintraub at Warners. Last minute. Once this excitement started to get generated I guess Freddie came in. I don't really remember how Michael and Bob got involved, at that point. The reason that we didn't have the Maysles, I believe, is that we couldn't put the funding in place, in time, and they didn't have any money,

DALE: We didn't have any money.

MIKE: You didn't have any money, I know, but you had volunteered to come in and shoot anyway. And it just happened that Artie made this Warners deal the day before.

DALE: But now give me a timeline for that.

MIKE: That was literally Thursday.

DALE: Thursday before music began on Friday.

MIKE: Yeah. Yeah. Thursday. I believe it was Thursday that Artie called me in the morning and said, "Warners is in." And you guys were already committed to coming in that day or the next day.

DALE: So we had 23[thousand dollars] in the bank by the time we started. That's, I don't know, either more guts than the Maysles had—

MIKE: It was definitely.

DALE: —but it was probably more money than they had.

MIKE: I think so. I had hired Michael Margetts and his partner, remember those guys? [These were two British cameramen who began filming on-site long before we got there.]

I brought them up two weeks before. I just thought, y'know, let's catch this. No matter what happens, if there is going to be a film, this is stuff we're gonna need. They were terrific. They just came, and they were everywhere. The next thing I knew, you guys showed up. I guess we had a brief talk about what to cover, and how to cover and which acts to cover.

British cameraman Mike Margetts at Woodstock before the music began

DALE: Do you remember my asking on the lip of the stage that—I don't think you were there, actually. I think Chip was there, and Steve Cohen was there. I looked at the front of the stage and said—

MIKE: —"We need a platform."

DALE: I looked at Wads, and said, "Wads, it's gotta be this high."

MIKE: Yeah, I was there.

DALE: That was the best thing that you guys did for us.

MIKE: Yeah, I remember that. It was kind of a high stage.

DALE: It was either that or our cameramen would have to work from stilts!

MIKE: Yeah, exactly.

DALE: We sensed—even though we were there, and possession was nine-tenths of the law—in that Friday-Saturday-Sunday era that there was a real evolution of change in the feeling that all of you guys had about us.

MIKE: No. What was going on was, there was so much on our plate to finish that to add one more thing on the back of the crews or anybody else was an impossibility. I mean, as you know we didn't finish the gates, even, or the fences. There was just so much infrastructure that had to be in place, from plumbing to toilets to God knows what. And don't forget we built that site in three and a half weeks, that nobody had the room for anything else. So it was just, "Let them fend for themselves, we can't really pay any attention to this," other than the essentials. And that's really the attitude. It was—I wouldn't say it was an annoyance to have the crews up there, but it was just another thing to worry about. And we had so much to worry about.

DALE: The attitude seemed to change. On Saturday—

MIKE: Yeah. Well,—

DALE: —when all of a sudden, somebody came over from the Green Room, such as it was, the arched green room, with FOOD! Now do you remember that, did you instigate that?

MIKE: I remember. It was just a function of that—it was sort of in the formula at one point, you know, this is something that we have to deal with when we get to it. And that's when they got to it. Things were sort of in gear and rolling, so people could think a little bit broader about responsibilities.

DALE: But that was the time when we said, "I think they realize we're here." By that time, I mean it being Saturday, we knew on stage that there was going to be a deal. Somebody was going to finance it.

MIKE: The deal was in place by then; actually, the deal was in place by Friday. But it had nothing to do with that, really; that was nobody's consideration. It was just, things loosened up enough to pay attention, I think. I remember Artie trying to get the artists to sign releases [laughs] on the way to the stage. Because that's how much we eliminated the possibility of film happening. We hadn't even discussed those rights with the artists beforehand. So we said, "Let's see what, you know, let's get as much as we can on the way in, 'cause it's gonna be harder on the way out, after the fact."

DALE: Was there a point in here while we were on stage, while we were at the festival, when you felt a turning point as it related to us directly? I mean, during the rain, or at some other point, and you said, "My God, I hope they're shooting this, or I wonder, or—"

MIKE: Yeah, Friday. I mean, when we saw the thing start to take form, I remember thinking how glad I was that finally there were people here who were going to document this, because we realized that this was much bigger and much more significant than anyone thought it was going to be.

DALE: So it did, I mean at times you were being interviewed by

Night work on the Woodstock stage

Bill Pierce

this guy, and by my dear friend Greg Jackson, who I brought up to the site; he did the "Why do you think these people are here?"—that wonderful inane question. [Lang giggles.] "Aw, it's the music."

MIKE: I think it was, "What do these musicians have?" Right?

DALE: Yeah, "It's called—

MIKE: —music." [Laughs]

🎥 12.

JOHN MORRIS: *A Nervous Breakdown?*

(Stage Manager at the Fillmore East, and confidant of many of the bands and their managers, John was the Festival Location Coordinator and one of the "Voices" on the albums.)

Dear Tenacious Dale,

My relationship with the movie began when you, Wadleigh and Maurice all showed up the day or two days before, and all I remember is guys in funny cowboy hats, an orchestra ramp for shooting in front of the stage. . . .And then during the festival my amazement that everyone worked so well with us and with the artists.

I remember Renée Wadleigh was something beautiful to look at from my perspective through all the rain, mud and problems. Also Wads, you and Larry, who I must have had in my field of vision for three days.

The most memorable incidents are signing the deal for *Woodstock* upstage with Freddie Weintraub after the festival had begun, and realizing what a limb Bob and Michael, in fact all of you, had climbed out on with no net.

The main remembrance, however, is as close to a nervous breakdown as I have ever been in my 59 years.

The tornado storm that came up on Cocker's set, watching the towers sway in the wind, knowing that there were 300 lb. follow-spots not chained to the towers, being told that 1. Baez was having a miscarriage, 2. Anne, my wife, had fallen and broken her ankle, 3. Cadogan, my dog, was lost and there was a guy with a gun in the audience; all the while the storm grew, we were clearing the stage, trying to get people away from the towers, and we had to cut the power.

Standing on stage with the mike shocking my hand, trying to be calm, and there was Wadleigh on his knees shooting and being some strange connection to reality which is 180° from what it should have been. None of the rumors were true, but all hell was breaking loose and this guy was recording IT.

IT was something in a very strange way that was like a copper wire as earth, a ground, and it got me through.

All in all, the friendships that were so instant with you, Wads, Bob, and Larry carry on to today. We have a line that can be a phone call or just an understanding that we fought that battle together and survived. It's still very strong in our memories but it was a battle we all went through and the respect lasts to this day. With Bob [Maurice], I have a new friendship; he's just an antique dealer, book store owner who I knew from another life, on the condition that when I got calls or did interviews I never mentioned where or who he was now, because he wanted nothing to do with it all.

The overall reaction I have (which keeps getting reinforced by occasional clips of the film on TV) is that the people who met in August of '69, although they don't stay in constant touch, could eat dinner for seven consecutive days and have a great time, based on respect, intellect, and a joy of life.

Best,

John

Bill Belmont, artist co-ordinator, and John Morris, production manager, on stage at Woodstock

Ed Denson

JOHN ROBERTS: *REMINISCENCES*

(One of the four founding officers of Woodstock Ventures, John Roberts financed the Woodstock Music and Art Fair with his inherited trust.)

July 4th, 1969, America's 193rd anniversary. I'm sitting in my apartment on East 85th Street in New York City wondering what everybody else is feeling so good about. Out the window I can see fireworks over the East River, but they give me no pleasure. I'm 24 years old and the possessor of a rapidly dwindling unearned fortune.

Earlier that year I had chosen to finance and produce a rock festival in Woodstock, N.Y. As the expression goes, it seemed like a good idea at the time, and for a while it had been a lark. Ticket sales were brisk. The acts were falling into line, and it had seemed like an easy way to make money, have fun and "do something meaningful" with my life. There had been that little problem with the site in Woodstock, what with the landlord deciding not to rent it to us, but in early April we had found another site about 50 miles away in Wallkill, N.Y. We had gotten our approvals from the town fathers and begun to build the festival. In June it all came unglued. The town got nervous about all the long-hairs and the strange smoky smells that seemed to follow them everywhere. They moved to revoke our permits, and notwithstanding our strenuous efforts, that movement had been successful. On July 3rd they booted us out.

So Janis, Jimi and Creedence were booked to play at a festival that no longer existed. Some 80,000 tickets at $14 a pop had been sold, and about $500,000 worth of work had been done to prepare a site we no longer could use. I was not merry.

History records that Max Yasgur, a dairy farmer in Bethel, N.Y. picked up the phone that weekend and saved our bacon by offering us his land and political protection. The next six weeks were the most frenzied of my life and the most expensive. By August 1st we had sold another 20,000 tickets, but we had also spent another million bucks moving and rebuilding the festival. On average about $25,000 a day was flowing out of my coffers, so I was not feeling particularly flush on August 3rd when Bob Maurice called me to talk about the movie.

We had always thought it would be a nice idea to make a movie about the festival, but it had never been a front–burner item. When you spend your days thinking about Port-O-Sans, traffic jams, food concessions, fencing, security and the ten thousand minutiae of production, moviemaking seems kind of ethereal and unreal. Like everyone else in our group I had seen Monterey Pop and been excited by its energy and spirit, but I also knew that documentaries were not money-making enterprises. To my mind a movie about Woodstock would be more of a keepsake, a filmed record of what I did last summer, and not a venture to charm my increasingly restive banker.

Over the course of the spring and summer we had gone to several meetings with film makers like Pennebaker and the Maysles Brothers, and they had all expressed interest in making our movie. But talks had languished and then died when it became clear that we would have to finance their efforts ourselves. Bob Maurice and Mike Wadleigh had been latecomers to this process. I had seen some of Wadleigh's work and thought it to be original and clever, but nothing I had seen altered my fundamental view that financing a documentary was a sane use of my vanishing resources.

Sunday, August 3rd, 1969 was turning into another typical day at the office. Negotiations with our food concessionaire were turning ugly and it was starting to look like we would have to rebuild their kiosks to their specifications or they would take their hot dogs elsewhere. Given that the festival was scheduled to open in 12 days this was a powerful argument on their part. We were out of leverage.

Around noon I decided to take a break and go someplace where the phones wouldn't ring with Woodstock problems. I walked down to my dad's apartment in midtown. He was out so I flipped on a ball game, and made myself at home. The phone rang. It was Bob Maurice. "How did you track me down, Bob?" "I called every Roberts in the book with a nice address," he said. I should have been more impressed with his ingenuity and determination than I was. Mostly, I was tired and pissed. "Well, you found me," I said. "What's on your mind?" "About 90 grand," he said. "That's what it will take for you to own this movie." I lectured him patiently on the economics of documentaries, concluding with a polite but firm refusal. "You'll have to get it somewhere else, Bob. I'm pretty much tapped."

In the context of so many bad decisions that summer this one looms large. *Woodstock*, the movie, became the highest-grossing documentary of all time with revenues exceeding $100,000,000 worldwide. The soundtrack albums sold over 6,000,000 units also grossing in excess of $100,000,000.

A week later one of my partners made a deal with Warner Brothers for the $90,000. When the smoke cleared they owned 90% of everything, and we got 10% of the profits from the film and about one-half of 1% of the albums. Even those drastically reduced percentages were enough to bail us out of debt when the show lost $1,600,000, and 10 years later we could count ourselves slightly in the black.

It is difficult for me to take ownership of the movie in the modern psychobabble sense of the word. Of course, the festival fathered the film, so I have some causality, but still it always seemed beyond my control or authorship. That weekend in August was such chaos I barely remember the moviemakers, and they never showed up at the crumbling headquarters office from which we ran the logistics, or from which they ran us. It is indicative of the power of film that people would occasionally ask me in future years if I actually attended the festival, since they couldn't remember seeing me in the movie. I remember thinking about the film sometime that week-end, but my thoughts ran to whether there was film in the cameras and whether they could shoot in the rain.

After the festival I became aware that indeed a film had been shot and the instant-ly historic nature of the festival invested the movie with considerable potential. But we had other fish frying—cleanup, lawsuits, partnership problems, an aftermath that consumed the better part of the next year. There was some legal wrangling with Warners over providing artist releases and occasional panicked phone calls from Sid Kiwitt telling me that Bob was threatening to burn the film if he didn't get his way, but as for the quality or nature of the actual product I was pretty much in the dark.

When it was released the following March I was astounded. For one thing it was a technological marvel pulsating with ingenuity and energy. For another it was the first real look I'd had at what I'd wrought. Mostly, it was hugely entertaining, joyous and honest. I looked around for ways to take ownership, but couldn't find any. I consoled myself with a river of royalties.

In my mind the Woodstock festivals of 1969 and 1994 were quite similar. Every gen-eration needs a small taste of anarchy, and the Woodstocks provided it. The movie caught that and much more. What was riveting about that era was the duality of society. While half a million youngsters were at Woodstock that weekend, an equal number were slogging through the jungles of Vietnam. While the late sixties were considered the high-water mark of liberalism in America, in 1968 we elected Richard Nixon and ushered in 20 years of Republican leadership in the White House. Society divided itself politically and temperamentally into over 30s and under 30s, anti-war and patriotic (it would take a few years before most people came to understand that anti-war sentiments or civil disobedience were not nec-essarily unpatriotic stances), long hair and short, pot smokers and liquor users, hip and square, part of the solution or part of the problem. It was not a time of gray complexity.

Woodstock celebrated one side of that equation and it's all there in the movie. An entire generation of Americans sat in dark theatres and thought, "That's just like me and, man, there are a lot of us out there who feel and think about things the same

Amalie Rothschild

View from the Woodstock stage

way." As such the movie was an empowering and validating document. But Wadleigh's achievement was even more impressive. His movie also dignified people on the other side of the equation—the man who spoke so movingly of his son in Vietnam, the Port-O-San worker, and Max Yasgur. All these people were treated with dignity and respect, in essence building a bridge between generations and stressing our shared yearnings. It was a noble film.

PART III.
A FUSION OF VISION AND TECHNOLOGY

DALE BELL: *TRIPPING NORTH*

 Five of us in a car, heading north out of New York City on the Thruway. The time? Early morning, Saturday, August 9, 1969. We are heading for a destination far distant, a tiny town called White Lake. As we speed along the Hudson River, then veer into the Catskills, none of us is aware at the time that this odyssey we are embarking upon will one day catapult all of us, for different reasons, into the record books of filmmaking. Truly, we are on a trip with a destination in the unknown, a synthesis somewhere between vision and technology. Or, perhaps, a potential catastrophe of huge proportions.

Michael Wadleigh, director, Bob Maurice, producer, and Dale Bell, associate producer, make plans five days before the festival

We are a raggle–taggle bunch—Larry Johnson, a world-class swimmer from Florida with an uncanny ear for sound and music, the very, very youngest of us all; Thelma Schoonmaker, a brilliant film editor and old-movie buff from New Jersey who types at speeds in excess of 100 words per minute; John Binder, a rambling storyteller from York, Pennsylvania, college-mate, soundman, and original partner with Michael Wadleigh; Michael Wadleigh, high-school debater and Columbia University medical

59

student dropout from Ohio turned cameraman with eyes in the back of his head, ears to match and stamina extraordinary; Ed Lynch, a cameraman friend of Michael's whom I had scarcely met; and me, a public television producer.

In another car were Bob Maurice, perennial philosophy/religion student at CCNY, construction worker, our chief negotiator; Eric Blackstead, Cornell graduate, music and performer guru; Jeanne Field, who had recently joined Bob in the distribution business; and Sonya Polonsky, colleague of Bob's from CCNY, who was working in production in Michael and John's company, Paradigm Films.

Each of us in our own way was searching for that elusive answer to how to display, or document, that reality which the world generated daily. We had pursued different technologies toward the same end: how to find the truth about what we saw, and how to allow, nay, encourage the cameras to tell the story without the intervention of an outside figure. *Immediacy* was one essential component.

As we approached Max Yasgur's farm, all of us began talking animatedly about what we might encounter, which groups might be performing, how to handle the shooting of the music, how to film the people who would be arriving. Our camaraderie was evolving. None of us had seen the site. We had no idea what we would encounter, for we had only had the briefest of phone conversations with the promoters who were in New York City and who had not yet visited the site themselves! And one of us in that car was even asking: Who was The Who? or Sha-Na-Na, or Jimi Hendrix? (That was me, but I could hum Verdi!)

In cinematic sense, we were pioneers, heading where we knew not, but filled with the sense of the possible.

Boy, these roads were narrow! Barely two cars could squeeze by. And then we were at the actual site, looking down a glen towards a mass of long-hairs scurrying about. Maybe one hundred men and women were working on the construction of the stage. Plywood had been built around it to protect it from the audience. Chain-link fence was on its way up.

Once Mike Lang and others agreed to install a platform in front of the stage, we asked that they create a large, crude table beneath the stage, where the assistants would be able to load magazines. Plywood would be needed in some of the towers, too, so that tripods could be hoisted up and fixed for the longer shots of stage and audience. Our "headquarters" would be under the stage or in the trucks. We would bring sleeping bags, I said, lying through my teeth! Who had money for sleeping bags? Who had money?

We discussed with the stage crew the kinds of lights they would be using to illuminate the performers. Where were the various activities going to be held? Where was the food, the toilets, the medical facilities? How many people were they expecting?

How about the performers—how were they going to get into the area if the roads were clogged? There will be helicopters, John Morris said. (He was one of the promoters/producers). Food and water, and performers would all come in with the choppers. Like Vietnam, someone muttered!

We must have sounded as though we could do it, even though we had no idea that it truly might be possible. Instinct was taking over, not practicality. All we did was ask questions and listen to responses. Yet something was happening. The more we talked, gave advice, argued, probed with the promoters, who at first would have nothing to do with us, the more we began to realize that we were capable of pulling this off, *if*.

It would take a massive effort: untold amounts of gear, of people, of vehicles, of food. The p r o m o t e r s were telling us that they would

Our home away from home near the stage

Amalie Rothschild

have their own hands full trying to supply their own people with enough food when the 50,000 people arrived. We needed our own army.

In the grass overlooking the stage, where none of the promoters could overhear us, we began to plot, among the echoes of the hammering and the boom of the loudspeakers. One critical question remained: Were the promoters going to get the site prepared well enough in advance so there would be something to film? They only had five days before the first music was to begin and there was lots to do. Or would the whole project be a bust?

But that meant that we, too, only had five days! I remember surveying the tiny roads one more time before I said that if we were going to do it at all, we would have to bring everyone up by Thursday afternoon at the very latest. We could not count on working at night, for there wouldn't be any light except very close to the stage.

If the Maysles were thinking in terms of two "divisions," we reasoned, maybe we should too. One group would be in charge of the concert filming, another of the non-concert or documentary portions. Wads and Larry would deal with the picture and sound of the concert. Thelma would act as assistant director. John and I would deal with the documentary portions, and I would be responsible for getting the people and the gear. Bob would negotiate and try to insulate us.

We first talked concert. It would take six cameras, six cameramen, six loaders to change magazines, six assistants to take the loaded or unloaded magazines to and from the cameramen, and six notetakers, each keeping meticulous track of what their person was shooting with which roll, at which time, with which type of raw stock. The loaders would work under the stage, standing on plywood, their hands never leaving their black changing bags. They would have to get a head start on the cameramen so that they could then keep up. An estimated total of 24 people to shoot the music, if they were only filming over eight-to-ten-hour days. But what would happen when the music began at noon and ran until the next dawn??

If there were six cameramen, we would need six 110-volt sync motors and a couple of spares, so count eight at least. Where would we find eight NPR cameras? Some cameramen would own their own, but some might not. Everyone had to shoot with the same kind of equipment, at minimum.

How could we keep sync? If each cameraman started at different times, how would we ever know how to track it? I suggested that we find a digital clock, luminous, which we would mount on-stage at the back. Each time a cameraman started to shoot, he would catch the clock first, then keep rolling.

Since I had given much NET (National Educational Television) work to many of the best DPs in New York and Los Angeles, we ran a list which included Richard Pearce, David Myers, Chuck Levey, Ted Churchill, Ed Lynch, Fred Underhill, Don Lenzer, among others. Where would we find enough assistants, and then the other people?

How could we get them here between Monday and Thursday afternoon? Could we pay them? What? How many people would we need on the documentary side? John Binder and I calculated three teams of camera-sound each, hopefully on motorcycles so they could get about in the crowds. After all, if there were going to be 50,000 people milling around, it was going to be very crowded on this little farm. Each of the teams would have to carry walkie-talkies, all on the same channels, so that we at home-base central, nearby the stage, could communicate with all of them at one time, as though we were *live* again. We would establish some sort of communication with the promoters, keeping up with their activities so that we could route one documentary team to cover a "breaking story."

By the time we had finished calculating, it looked as though we needed about 15 people with cameras, an equal number of bona fide assistant camerapeople, about ten people on sound, six of them to work with the promoters on the concert sound and another four to work on the documentary side. We would need about

20 other assistants who would help to keep track of what was going on. Some people would have to sleep while others worked. Maybe we really needed five more assistant camerapeople and another ten assistants?

Michael and Larry would deal with the music, aided by Eric

Backstage looking towards the helicopter landing zone and the performers' area

Blackstead, who knew many of the musicians and managers. And they all were familiar with the music: how the performers played their sets, which performer had the lead and when it transferred to another player, how long each piece would run—all of this very valuable information for those of us trying to plot out how to cover the music. (Eric would later produce both records.)

A new, young feature director we knew in New York, Martin Scorsese, would assistant-direct with Thelma on the concert stage. They would be connected by headsets to the camerapeople, finding out what each person was shooting, so they could coordinate shots as live television directors would do in a control room environment. Wads would always take the number one position, down front and in the center at 6 o'clock, picking up the lead performer.

David Myers and Al Wertheimer would be the lead documentary people.

After Bob Maurice and Sonya finished their session with the promoters on-site, we left that evening to return to New York City where we would confer again. On the way back, we talked more about what we would have to do. Suddenly we determined we had not counted on one element—the raw stock. We calculated again: There were going to be three days of peace and music. How many cameramen would be shooting the concert? Six! How many songs would we shoot? How long were the songs? How much stock would we need? How much did we have on hand? Would Kodak have sufficient quantity on hand? What would it cost?

How many of the acts would appear in daylight? How many at night? What kind of night stock would we need? Kodak was selling two kinds. How much should we *push* the ASA of the stock? We couldn't determine any of that without knowing how much light the promoters were going to give us on stage. And particularly, how much *white* light? For if all they had on hand were a lot of blue and red gels, we would never see a performer's face clearly, and the whole night shooting would be eliminated.

But if there were going to be 26 groups, and we wanted to film one song from each of them, it would take 26 *times* one 11-minute roll *times* the number of camera-men shooting at that time. And if we wanted to shoot a piece that ran for 25 min-utes, we just increased logarithmically the raw stock requirement by 2.5 times!

Then, what about the documentary portions? Many of us thought the motivations of the people might be even more valuable than some of the music. What would happen if someone was killed? Or if someone gave birth? Hundreds of acres, a craft show, places for children to play, swimming, an art fair. It was to be more than music. This festival was to be a statement to the world about the Vietnam War and about drugs as well. As true documentarians, we had to listen to what they were saying and try to incorporate it into the overall film.

Where were we going to get the money for something like this? How would we get the permission from the groups to be able to film them? Would we need releas-es from the people who would be gathered there, or would the fact that we were filming constitute a release in fact? Was there a precedent?

At 7am on the following Sunday morning, now five days away from the moment we would have to start filming, we met, on the second floor of our offices at 81st Street and Broadway, and made plans.

Wads had $10,000 in the bank. Immediately, Bob and I would try to get money in from Michael's last film in Wyoming. That might add another $10,000. Most would have to go for raw stock, for without it, the whole effort would be lost. We might have to save some for film supplies, like audiotape, gaffer's tape, etc.

We drew up a final list of people, with alternates. They were scattered all over the country, but I had my trusty phone book connecting me to them. We would—I would—tell every cameraman that we would guarantee them only a day's pay at $125, the then going rate. If the project went beyond that, their time would be "on spec"—they might get paid and they might not. Those of us in the room would work on spec, with the prospect of rewards later if we were successful in finding more money.

I would also have to find the gear. Because I had been renting so much gear in the previous five years from camera houses in New York City—Ferco, Camera Mart, Laumic, General Camera—my name was relatively trusted there, too. Perhaps I could tell everyone that I was only renting for a one-day shoot, which was going to occur on Friday? I would have the gear back to them by Monday, I could assure them. But I would also have to pick up the gear early, so that I could get it to White

Lake early enough to be useful. But I couldn't tell them about the actual site, for they would be fearful that their insurance might not cover loss or damage. They could hear the radio adverts just like everyone else! This was a strange form of trust in which I was basically telling a little white lie, for White Lake!! It bothered me, but I saw no way out of the dilemma. We would charge the gear—not pay cash—take the insurance coverage just in case something might happen to it, and then pray.

But how would David Myers get from San Francisco to New York? David would have to charge the plane fare on his own card. Preposterous! No one should ever agree to such terms, not even David!

By this time, we had determined that we probably needed an enormous amount of raw stock—enough to be able to shoot for 175 hours between now and next Sunday night, when the festival would end, if they held to their schedule. And 175 hours translates into 375,000 feet of 16mm film, or more than 900 individual rolls of film, some of which had to be accessible for daytime use, the remainder for nighttime. With 30 rolls to the case, we would need 30 cases, which also occupied a huge space, easily the inside area of a large panel truck. How to get it to the stage in only four days? Where to store it safe from other people and the elements? If it got too hot, the emulsion would melt, as I had experienced in Venezuela several years earlier!

We had a plan. We would spend everything Wads had in the bank. Bob Maurice would continue the negotiations with the promoters, with Eric Blackstead's assistance. Bob would also try to find big money from studio financiers. I would remain in the office day and night until everyone was on the site on Thursday. Sonya Polonsky, who had been working as a production manager for Paradigm Films and already knew many of the people we would be working with, would organize. Thelma, Larry and Marty Scorsese would get to the site as quickly as I could find cars, other people, and gear.

No one had ever done this kind of film before. Less than 24 hours earlier, reality had been a figment of our imagination. Until we had scouted, we knew nothing and feared everything. But contact with the site and the people, and assessing the conditions, gave each of us a deeper sense of confidence which we then passed on to each other by our very energy. One step at a time. If only Bob could make a decent deal with the promoters and their producers on-site, we might have a slightly easier time when we finally got settled.

None of us were over 30 years old. Whoops, that's not exactly right. I was. I was 31. Maybe Bob was my age, too. I didn't know him very well. He was very philosophical, contemplative and always muttering under his long hair and bushy beard while he climbed the rafters like an Indian on a construction site. "Gotta clear out my head," he would say, as he paced back and forth ten feet above the floor. He had a devilish sense of humor and a wonderful twinkle in his eye as he contemplated the ramifications of each of his actions. "I could drop a keg of nails on them from here!" he would conjecture, much to all of our amusement—and distraction!

We knew we did not want to produce "news coverage." We wanted to produce something which would last, which would be different, and which would truly represent the seminal role that the combination of music and lyrics played in the life of the generation of the sixties. Chaos. Assassinations. Malcolm X. JFK. MLK. RFK. Turbulent civil rights struggles. Beatings. Dogs. Water hoses. Fires on crosses. The increasingly hostile generation gap. Drugs, beards and long-hairs. Killing and maiming in jungles halfway around the globe. Political upheavals at home. Wars on poverty. Gender wars as women sought their legitimate civil rights. Chicago riots and brutality. And men on the moon? Huge chasms yawing between government and the people, gaps of faith and trust.

We were politically active then. Anything was possible. We were *doing for our country* just as we had been mandated by JFK to do on that cold, windy January morning on the Capitol steps at the beginning of our decade. Was it because each of us, in our own personal way, had literally or symbolically been "shot at by sheriffs" (like I had been in Mississippi!) while investigating what we perceived to be injustices? Could this festival become our symbol? Now we actually might be on the threshold of accomplishing something significant *on our own.* But how, we constantly asked ourselves, could we produce a film for a general audience—not simply for a music infected group of long-haired hippie freaks?

Sonya and I set up one office with two desks and three rotary phones. For the next four days, I ate and slept in that office, getting only a very few hours of sleep as we assembled the people and the gear, handling the logistics of moving this little band into the Catskills, working the time zones.

Ferco, Laumic and Camera Mart believed my story about the one-day gear rental which had to be picked up on Tuesday, or Wednesday, or Thursday, as the case might be. And oh, yes, it would be returned on the following Monday afternoon. No, I could not tell them where their gear was going. I had to scrounge to find 110-volt motors and four magazines for every NPR. Why did I need a 25-250mm lens? Why did I need three 5.9mm lenses? What *was* this project I was filming?? I began running into myself at some of these houses: when Camera Mart didn't have something I needed, I would quickly call a second place and order the piece. Bob Roizman at Camera Mart would then call me back, asking why I was renting from the very same place he was calling to fill my order! Although I never checked, I am sure I had all the cameras, lenses, magazines, and motors that were available in New York City that weekend.

David Myers *did* pay for his own ticket and was in White Lake by Tuesday night, from San Francisco. Dick Pearce had contracted to film with another producer that week, but when I located him in Hartford, I promised to find his producer another cameraman so that he, Dick, would be free to join us. I gave away one of the cameramen from the Maysles team, Joe Consentino, who called me asking to work on our project. Dick was on our crew!

Other people who had been contacted by the Maysles called, eager to work. Even in the middle of the night, they would want to come by to show me their reels. One cameraman showed me a piece he had filmed with Joan Baez. It shuddered and shook; it was not at all what Wads and I expected from hand-held cameramen. I rejected him as I did others for fear of muddying the waters.

I tried Don Lenzer at the Chelsea Hotel where he always lived. They said he was shooting on the West Coast. I reached Don in Los Angeles, convinced him to get on a plane that would arrive at JFK about the same time as David Myers would land from San Francisco. I would send Danny Turbeville out to the airport to pick up both of them and drive them directly to White Lake with their gear.

Don had recommended that I hire a cameraman friend of his from Seattle, Dick Chew. When I reached Dick, he told me he was getting married that Saturday. I asked him if he could postpone the wedding, come to New York, and help us film this concert. Within three hours, he was paying his own way on an airplane for a salary of only $125 guaranteed for the first day—his ex–wedding day! Could we please get him a camera? Good-bye, wedding; hello, Woodstock!

Al Wertheimer, a Bob Drew–trained verité cameraman I had heard about in the city, would also drive from New York with his converted Auricon camera. Because he was not slated to shoot any of the concert, I approved his unique gear. Jack Willis kindly declined my offer to be a soundman and always regretted it. Joe Louw, who had taken those historic *Life Magazine* pictures in Memphis of three men on the motel balcony pointing to an adjacent building while they huddled over the slain MLK, would drive up to White Lake to do sound and take stills. Martie Andrews made it on one of the early treks, for he had to design and build all the electronics. Marty Scorsese was in one of the early trucks, transporting gear and headsets. He traveled north with Ted Churchill, one of our marvelous cameramen.

My wife, Anne, was able to get her mother to stay with our kids, so she filled our VW bus with food, blankets, and other people—and not our oldest son, Jonathan, much to his dismay—and became one of the assistants on the lip of the stage. She was joined by Jeanne Field, helping Larry, by Fern McBride from NET, by Cathy Hiller assisting her soon-to-be-husband Stan Warnow, by Elen Orson, and by Renée Wadleigh, helping Michael.

At dawn on Tuesday morning, when I showed Bob the high budget figure of $125,000 for the four full days we rightfully were obligated for, he blanched. We had put together only $23,000 from fees due Wads; all the rest was on the come, so to speak. At four in the morning, we simply glared silently at each other. We—he—had to find the money.

As Bob was barking around New York for the financing, I called my father. His boss, Jules Winarick, who owned the Concord Hotel at Kiamesha Lake not far from White Lake in the Catskills, might put up the $125,000. Alas, Jules declined. Later, during one of our New York screenings, he and my Dad came by to acknowledge how dumb he had been to the offer.

Larry Johnson

Anticipating the likelihood that we might all be sleeping out, Bob Maurice had purchased 60 sleeping bags and tied them to the roof of the panel truck he had rented. At the first sign of rain in New York City that night, he had driven the truck up onto the sidewalk underneath his friend's New Yorker Theater marquee. After the rain stopped, he returned to 88th Street and Broadway to start the drive north to White Lake

Mid-day catnap for our crew

in the middle of the night. Of course, the only sleeping bags remaining were those he had secured inside the van! He drove the van down to the office, picked up the Xerox machine and some extra extension cord, and headed north. The copy machine would enable us to distribute song sheets and schedules to individual cameramen and their assistants.

And *The New York Times* kept writing, while radio announcers kept talking: "The New York State Thruway is closed!" Television stations, hiring helicopters, kept sending images of very clogged exits from New York City as seemingly the whole of New York State converged on Max Yasgur's farm. Eventually, we were to learn that those who had predicted 50,000 attendees had failed to add a zero! It was staggering!

The raw stock? I warned Kodak on Monday morning, first call. I told them we would be ordering about 150,000 to 200,000 feet of film on Tuesday and a like amount on Wednesday. On Tuesday, Kodak said they had the 30 cases we required. I told them a truck would pick it up on Wednesday morning. Yes, we knew we would have to pay cash. We knew of the 2% discount for paying cash. It would be just under $18,000. "Fine, Mr. Bell, just send your truck over and everything will be ready."

On Wednesday afternoon, our truck arrived at the Kodak York Avenue pickup station. I got a phone call from my messenger. Kodak had set aside *three* cases, not 30! I screamed! *They, too, had failed to add a zero!* What to do now? No one had ever purchased *30* cases at one time before, they said! 900 magazines??? They didn't have 30 cases in New York!!!

I was in a cold sweat. Everyone was in the process of finding their way to White Lake. Already, some 20 people were on-site, with 20 more to head up on Wednesday. Then 20 would follow on Thursday morning, bringing our total to more than 60, all of whom were willing to do this gig on spec, mind you! And now, *no raw stock to put into the cameras!!!*

Even before the music began, we were about to be blown out of the water!

Break it down into pieces, I said to myself. Don't panic. Take small steps. How much do you have in New York? I asked Kodak. They said they could find another 10 cases by tomorrow. Maybe a hundred thousand feet. In Rochester, I asked? In Washington? In Chicago? In Los Angeles? They would call back. Meanwhile, I sent the truck with the three cases up to White Lake along with a couple more sleeping bags and snacks and drinks.

Between Wednesday morning and Friday afternoon, I did nothing but scour all over the country for raw stock. I bought from rental houses. Kodak found cases in Rochester and Chicago. I found some in Los Angeles which had to be shipped into Kennedy airport. From there, it had to be transshipped to La Guardia where my messenger service, Coleman Younger, also working on spec, would take it off the airplane and transport it to the Marine Air Terminal where it would board a small aircraft bound for Monticello, New York.

Several cases actually took a wrong turn and ended up in Liberty, New York. I couldn't find them for hours! They had to be shipped back to the Marine Terminal before they could be bicycled to Monticello. Another batch was shipped to Monticello, the proper destination, but no one unloaded it. Hours later, it arrived in Rochester, the home of Eastman Kodak, via Albany! Every case would have to land in Monticello, where it would then have to be airlifted—case by case, until Saturday afternoon when most of the last batch arrived with Bob Maurice—on the very same helicopters that were depositing the talent at the Woodstock stage. Remember the choppers in the background on the sound tracks? It may sound like Vietnam, but that's raw stock they're transporting! Not just food and talent.

At one point, before the imports arrived, Michael and the crew were down to their last case, and it was only Friday! Ding, he said to me, what are we going to do? The music was going to begin that afternoon! Wads, I said, we have proceeded on faith—blind faith—to this point. All the people who were coming to help us were flying on trust. We had to extend ourselves just a little bit more, and pray.

I was able to leave New York City Friday afternoon, laden down with foodstuffs I had purchased on upper Broadway. My tiny VW beetle made it to White Lake by about nine at night.

I made my way backstage. Our headquarters occupied the back of a trailer. There was our trusty Xerox copier and telephone. I sat down to inspect my little home away from home and set up shop.

Finally, Friday night came to a close on Saturday morning. Gathering around me, crew members asked what they were to do now? I suggested that they go back to the motel which we had block-booked a few miles away. After all, I was still relatively clean and naive, having just arrived. We could have scrambled eggs and bacon the next morning, I dreamed. As I was starting to try to arrange carpools, I looked around. Any movement at all seemed hopeless. Beneath the trailer lay 4 x 8 plywood slabs which could serve as our beds. I asked how many could sleep on the ground around the trailer. Some hands went up and they began to disperse. A few people took the handful of sleeping bags and laid them out within the entrance to the trailer to deter potential thieves who would have to walk over them to get to our stashed gear. Anne and I felt we could be comfortable on our mattress inside our blue-and-white VW van.

Two crew members had motorcycles. They were confident they could return to the motel and be back at the site by 9AM. At two in the morning, they departed, carrying their camera, sound gear and raw stock, so they could begin filming in the morning on the way in. At seven o'clock in the morning, I picked up the phone in the trailer. It was the two guys. They had just arrived—at the hotel! It had taken them five hours to go four miles! I postponed their arrival back at the site. Two hours later, I called to wake them up. At 10 AM they started back; at 1PM one of them arrived. They had run out of gas, he claimed. From one farmer, they cajoled some gas, but could not use it until they found some oil to mix with it from another farmer. Then they got stuck in the mud. The second guy walked in an hour and a half later. The music had began at noon. . . .

On Saturday night, Wads and I wanted to get a helicopter shot with the stage, the supertroopers beaming down, the car headlights, and the glowing campfires on the periphery of the audience pit. Late that afternoon, the last arriving helicopter (with more of our raw stock on board, thankfully!) said they could be at our beck and call. The eager-to-please pilot said he could take us up for their standard rate of $200 per hour—money that we didn't have, of course! No matter. Wait, I said. Down the hill, I found David Myers back at the stage. He located his camera and gave it to his assistant, who was instructed to change lenses, load the magazines, and meet us at the helicopter field in half an hour. We checked our watches, cross-checked our destination with him and climbed the hill. After half an hour had passed, we couldn't find the guy. David and I crisscrossed the field over the next two hours, one of us constantly returning to the pilot to hold him in place.

Look at the movie. If we had been able to corral the assistant, the camera, and the pilot at one place, the shot would have been in the film. But we couldn't, and like so many other efforts those days, this one got away.

15

OUR ARSENAL: *The List of What We Took*

9	Eclair NPR cameras
11	Eclair constant-speed motors
10	Eclair variable-speed motors
1	converted Auricon 16mm camera
5	9.5 to 95 zoom lenses
3	Bolex cameras
3	Arri S cameras, constant and variable-speed motors
4	5.7 lenses
2	5.9 lenses
1	300mm Kilfit lens
1	25 to 250mm zoom lens
	assorted Bolex and Arri lenses
40	packets of lens tissue
45	85 filters, gel type
11	Spectra Pro light meters
6	Minolta spot meters
4	Wadleigh-designed body braces (pre-Stedi-Cam)
1	Myers body brace
1	tripod with spreader
15	battery belts
50	camera magazines for the Eclairs
25	changing bags
7	Nagra tape recorders
6	ATNs for the Nagras
11	dozen D cell batteries
6	804 Sennheiser microphones with windscreens
5	404 Sennheiser microphones with windscreens
8	headsets
5	PRO-A headsets
6	walkie-talkies
10	Telex two-way headsets
	repair kits and tools
350,000 ft.	raw stock, 60% in #7255, 40% in #7242
10	rolls infrared film, which never arrived

30	rolls of raw stock delivered to the office two days after the festival!
400	rolls of 131 3M 1/4" audiotape
48	empty take-up 1/4" reels
102	rolls of gaffer's tape
6,000	ft. electrical wiring
100	cube taps
1	Lowell light kit with 18 bulbs
60	rolls of 35mm tungsten balanced still film
10	still cameras
3	Grafflex projectors
3	projector stands
	Aretha Franklin, James Brown, and Paul Revere films
1	Dual 1012 turntable
1	JBL amplifier
2	speakers
1	slide projector
	sync cables, camera cables, power cables, mike cables, phone cables
8	cars
5	motorcycles
1	helicopter
3	tents
12	sleeping bags
1	coffee machine with coffee
	blankets
	bars of soap
	water containers
	cold chests
	cooking utensils
	flashlights
	disposable raincoats and umbrellas for the cameras
	rain boots
	first aid supplies
	vaccines
	speed
3	boxes of NoDoze
2	bottles of champagne
1	bottle of rum
400	frankfurters
75	chickens, cut, cooked, and wrapped, then forgotten at the motel
	egg and tuna salad sandwiches
4	vans

1	copy machine
2	telephones
1	typewriter
1	folding table
6	folding chairs
	stationery supplies, pencils, marking pens
	assorted music albums of these performers on stage
1	record player

16

JEANNE FIELD: *I Had Tickets*

 Another media event took place that July in Central Park. As a small lunar landing module settled onto the face of the moon, CBS, ABC and NBC broadcast those first steps on huge outdoor screens set up in Sheep Meadow. Larry Johnson and I spent the night cruising the crowd sharing the amazement at this moment. The U.S. was on the moon but it was still in Vietnam, so overall, we had a guarded opinion of the government's accomplishment.

These days were a big turning point in my life. In truth, the one real reason I had joined Paradigm is that I had learned while I was at Janus that I didn't want to sell movies, I wanted to make them. *Woodstock* was my chance.

I went to Bob and told him. He said no way. He said I had to continue covering distribution for him because he was going to be a producer on *Woodstock* and Joyce had just been diagnosed with a brain tumor. These were difficult times for Bob but it established a real bond between him and Michael. Wads had gone through three years of med school at Columbia University and was very astute scientifically. He became a strong ballast for Bob and they found a solid friendship during these days. Bob wanted to count on me too and he could, up to a point. My own ambition, my stubbornness prevailed. He would not work it out with me to do both distribution and production. He said it was all or nothing. I did what I had to do.

On Thursday, the day before the music started, I rode up to Bethel (the new festival site which had been hurriedly found and built when the original Woodstock site had been nixed by the nearby neighbors) with Van Schley, a friend of Larry's and mine, and Eddie Cramer, music producer for Jimi Hendrix and the guy the promoters had hired to do the on-site recording. The roads were by this time gridlocked and impassable. Eddie slept through Van's hell-bent driving on the shoulder of the road, and drooled all over my shoulder. Thank god for Eddie Cramer though, he was the reason we were shepherded over back roads to Yasgur's farm by one of the organizing team (and one of the most important people at the festival, since he mixed and recorded every moment of music that was played).

We arrived in the middle of the night and the place looked like a construction site. The stage was barely finished. The movable sections, that would have allowed one band to set up while the other played, were nowhere near finished and never would be. Wads was on with his reservation hat and light meter working with Chip Monck to get his readings. The grip truck was parked in back of the stage and the camera magazine loading pit was being constructed underneath the stage. The place was electric.

Returning to the stage in the morning, I was assigned to Dick Pearce, a New York documentary cameraman from Kentucky. A calm professional, he in turn was assigned to Stage Left, on the stage. I pulled cable, kept him in fresh Eclair magazines, listened on the headset for any directions from Marty Scorsese or Thelma Schoonmaker, scavenged food, provided a backrest and other novice filmie jobs. And I was on the stage or on the film platform four feet just below the front of the stage for the next three days and nights.

I remember so clearly the beginning. John Morris convinced Richie Havens he had to be the first one on. They led him over from the performer's area, tables and chairs covered by a large white silk, across the bridge that connected to the stage that looked out on a sea of hundreds of thousands of people. It was so exciting. It was my first film.

My high was interrupted by Steve Cohen, the stage manager, who came over to me and said, "Who the fuck are you and what are you doing on my stage? You belong down there," pointing at the platform. Dick kept on shooting Richie, and I told Steve we were there to stay. You can actually see this event in the movie in the wide shot during Richie's first song (not in the videotape though, because of course they've reformatted it for your TV).

I have to admit that a lot of these three days are a blur. It's hard to say what I remember from the experience and what I saw later on film. High points for me were: Richie H., his passionate singing, his smiling broadly with no teeth; Joe Cocker air-guitaring and delivering "With a Little Help from My Friends";

Director Michael Wadleigh filming Richie Havens and his band, Richard Chew waits his turn

Amalie Rothschild

The Who, with Pete crowning Abbie Hoffman over the head when he tried to grab the mike; Arlo, funny and relaxed, talking to the crowd; Santana, an unknown San Francisco band; holding AC equipment in the rainstorm, realizing we were all lightning rods; Sly and the Family Stone singing "Higher, Higher," with everyone on their feet screaming with them; CSNY warming the stage when we were all shivering in the wet coldness of 4am Sunday morning; Paul Butterfield Blues Band coming on at 5am and getting an exhausted crowd moving again; The Band, playing but insisting that they would walk if they saw a camera or its operator, which meant we all had to peek over the stage lip; Janis's performance, though not one of her best, still gutsball; Grace Slick looking like she had just stepped out of a penthouse suite; Jimi noodling for an hour before hitting on his stirring war motif "Star Spangled Banner."

17

JOHN BINDER: *HOW I GOT TO WOODSTOCK*

(John was our Location Coordinator for the shoot.)

I was in a cottage at Montauk on the tip of Long Island where I had gone with my wife Sharon and my son Josh. I wanted to clear my head and write for a while. I was tired of documentary films, and of living in my partner's shadow. I wanted to go my own way.

Wadleigh called me one morning. I knew he was putting together this operation to film a music festival up in New York state. He'd been thinking about a music film for a while, perhaps on gospel music or one of the fifties rock-and-roll revivals that were appearing. We had just terminated a partnership called Paradigm Films, which we had formed five years earlier out of film school at NYU.

We had started as a cinema verité team. Michael on camera, me doing sound, making our decisions together. He was very bold and dynamic. He made things happen. I was moody and thoughtful. Without me to caution and counsel him, he would have probably gone over a cliff. Without him, I would never have had the adventure of those years.

Our combination had worked well from the beginning. We worked hard for four or five years and gotten as close as brothers. As partners and brothers do, we accumulated a list of irritations and offenses against each other over time. Larry Johnson joined us eventually and replaced me working in the field with Michael. That helped, but eventually we offended each other in irreparable ways. We broke off our partnership. The breakup occurred just as Michael started negotiations to do this film.

Dealing with Warner Brothers was not something he had done before, especially as he scrambled to amass 60 people and equipment with $24,000 in the bank and some credit at the camera rental houses. He came and talked to me about reconsidering, and helping him produce the film. I knew it was another longterm commitment. It was his "thing," not mine. I was determined. I heartlessly turned him down and headed for the beach.

I'd been away in Montauk for several days when he called. He said he really just needed someone to go to the festival site and hold down the fort until he could get there. He said Bob Maurice, who had agreed to produce, and Dale Bell, the associate producer, and Larry Johnson were all maxed out in the city and couldn't possibly leave.

As usual he talked me into it. I would not otherwise have gone to Bethel, N.Y.

The first event of my Woodstock experience occurred as I was driving up the New York Thruway. A state trooper pulled me over. He was a big country boy. I still remember his huge hands and feet. He asked where I was going. I told him to the music festival at Bethel. I had longish hair. He took a step back and ordered me out of the car. He'd been briefed. "There's gonna be a lot of you people coming up here." He made me open the trunk of the car. There was a cardboard box in the trunk. It held a motorcycle rack that you could bolt to the bumper. Some kind of red packing grease had soaked through and stained the outside of the box. When the big trooper saw those red stains he touched the butt of his pistol with his hand. "What's in the box?" I told him it was a motorcycle rack. "What's that red stuff? Blood?" He wasn't kidding. "You wouldn't have a body in there?" I laughed, uneasy with his paranoia. He kept his eye on me as he reached inside the box, half expecting to discover human body parts. When he touched the iron motorcycle rack instead, he looked disappointed. He kept me long enough to run a check on my license. I told him I was going to work on a movie. He asked what movie stars I knew. I told him that we'd filmed John Wayne once. It changed his whole attitude. I often thought of him later and wondered how he felt when the rest began arriving and closed the Thruway with the biggest traffic jam the world had ever seen.

Wadleigh had told me to look up a guy named Michael Lang, an

Steve Cotter

A Woodstock version of a cine mobile

organizer of the festival, when I got to the site. I found him in his headquarters in an old frame farmhouse on Yasgur's farm. People were coming and going. Phones were ringing. Michael was on one of them. I looked around the place. Someone opened the door of an old stove in the kitchen to check on a cookie sheet piled with marijuana leaves that she was quick-drying in the oven. Music was playing loud. There was a record or tape change and I heard Joe Cocker for the first time in my life. I had to ask who he was. As I remember, everyone stopped what they were doing. They ignored the phones for a while and listened. This English guy was not background music.

There were two people there already filming when I arrived, two British guys, the Two Michaels (was everyone at Woodstock named Michael?). Michael Lang had hired or cajoled them into documenting what was going on, at least until Wadleigh's crew arrived. Michael Margetts, the cameraman, had been a fashion photographer in "swinging" London and dropped out from what he described as a highly paid rat race. "I have a rule. I only turn my camera on when I see something that turns me on, and I turn it off when it doesn't excite me. I don't film anything out of obligation."

I didn't contribute all that much to the making of the film. But I think I made one important contribution. When the other camera and sound teams started showing up and asking what was the plan—Wadleigh wasn't there yet; he was still negotiating with Warner execs in New York—I just passed on British Michael's philosophy: Film what turns you on and stop filming when it turns you off. That may not sound like a plan, but it was ideal for *Woodstock*.

Later, a consultant for Warners showed up, an old-school documentarian. Wadleigh was busy, so he foisted the guy off on me, told me to reassure him. I failed. The consultant called Warners and advised them to back out. It was a hopeless situation, he said. There was chaos here and we didn't have any organization at all. He couldn't understand that ours was the perfect response to an uncontrollable situation. He missed the main point of Woodstock and of the sixties altogether.

There was a lot of anxiety as the flow of people kept increasing and reports proliferated that the clogged roads made escape impossible. It scared me. I was talking to someone who noticed my anxiety. "What's bothering you, man?" I said that this was getting to be a bad situation. I, like a lot of people, feared catastrophe. The hippie carpenter I was talking to surveyed the scene. "Anything you can do about it, man?" Obviously there wasn't. He added, "Then why worry about it?" And after that I didn't. I think everyone there went through the same anxiety I did, and most of them surrendered to the situation.

Later I was sitting in a teepee as the sun went down and darkness replaced it. Five or six of us sat in a circle, almost completely silent, passing a joint, exchanging glances and approving smiles, thinking our private thoughts. When the light was completely gone someone stood up and stepped out into the night. The others followed, me behind them. There were lights coming up the hill which turned out to be a caravan of buses. The "Merry Pranksters" arrived. I had heard nobody signal their arrival, yet everyone materialized from the woods, from tents and teepees, and all in silence. I had the distinct impression that communication had become telepathic. The Pranksters spilled out of their buses. The Hog Farmers greeted them with hugs,

kisses and laughter. It was a meeting of the tribes, or as close to it as white dropouts could get. Ken Babbs of the Pranksters and Wavy Gravy stood in the headlights of the lead bus and tossed the I Ching to predict the fate of the festival. The results of the coin tosses were read aloud from the book.

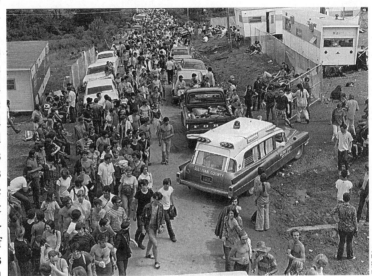

Ambulance into sick bay

Bill Pierce

The omens were good. Everyone drifted off again to their respective nests. I felt that I had glimpsed something that now is ridiculed if it's mentioned at all. It was the other side of the American soul, the opposite of individualism, the Indian side, the yearning to belong to the whole tribe.

A much different moment that I witnessed came on Sunday morning, the weekend of the performances, after the night of the big rainstorms immortalized in the movie. People were padding around in inches of water. Everything was wet. There was a meeting of the festival honchos behind the stage a few yards from the main power box. All the electricity had been shut off the night before in the storm so people wouldn't get electrocuted. Lang and Kornfeld, Chip Monck, John Morris and Steve Cohen were huddled discussing the danger of turning on the power, which could electrocute God knows how many people who were standing in all that water. Somebody said it could be like dropping the hair dryer in the bathtub for thousands of people. Nobody wanted to pull that switch. Some were saying that they had to call it quits, declare the festival over—too much risk turning on that power. In the midst of all this, somebody—I think it was Steve Cohen, but I'm not certain anymore—quietly broke off from the group, sloshed over to the power box, opened it, reached in and pulled the master switch. The power came on harmlessly. The festival continued. Only that small circle of men knew what a disaster Woodstock could have been.

We had a semitrailer sinking off angle in the mud behind the stage with our equipment in it. I was walking through the dark at night and I came across a little cabal of guys in a circle plotting something. I heard a familiar voice prompting the others to come with him to rip off our truck. I ran off into the dark and got two guys on our crew, Charlie Grossbeck and Fred Underhill. We dashed to the truck. Abbie Hoffman and his guys were already climbing inside. One of the women on our crew was trying to stop them. We jumped up and managed to run off all but Abbie and a cocky-looking sidekick who had a very expensive lens in his hand. Grossbeck had already relieved Abbie of whatever he was stealing, but his friend would not let go of the lens. Abbie said, "Let us have it, man. It's Warner Brothers stuff. We'll give it to Newsreel." I explained that Wadleigh had rented all this stuff and the insurance company had canceled his insurance since it was an official disaster area. Warners had nothing to do with it. Abbie bought that but his friend didn't, and we were very close to a fight. Abbie stepped between us. "Hey man," he said, "are you gonna be the first guy to throw a punch at Woodstock?" He grinned, took the lens from his buddy and gave it back. Later that night, Abbie and the rest of the Lower East Side boys stormed the stage while The Who was playing. They were going to take over and politicize this thing. Abbie jumped up onto the stage right in front of Peter Townshend, who clobbered him over the head with his solid body guitar. Abbie fell backwards off the stage.

A few hardy souls remained alive to film Jimi Hendrix when he came on with his "Band of Gypsies" at eight o'clock Monday morning. Jimi was high and searching for something elusive on his guitar. He would start and stop. He'd whisper to his band. They would try again. He wasn't satisfied. The crowd had dwindled to a fraction of the night before. Those that were paying attention at all were shouting out for old favorites. Jimi didn't yield to them. He stepped to the mike and muttered something about trying to "find something here" and then he kept noodling and searching. This must have taken half an hour. I was standing behind Wadleigh on the ledge where he was shooting just below center stage. Hendrix was just a few feet away. He was riveting even if there seemed no rhyme or reason to his musical fumbling. It seemed that he was hopelessly lost in space, would never get it together. What a shame, I thought. The legacy of heroin I presumed, but I presumed too much. Suddenly he found it. The volume increased, slashing notes and exploding chords ripped into the exhausted hungover mud sodden silence of Max Yasgur's farm. Jimi's guitar conjured up every tortured blood-dripping experience of sixties America. I don't know how Wadleigh kept shooting. It raised the hair on your neck.

Energy shot up your spine. The kundalini energy that all those fire breathing hippie yogis were trying to raise in that session that appears now in the film was raised at that moment by Jimi's guitar spitting out the most angry and ecstatic "Star Spangled Banner." I, for one, wept and it still raises a tear when I recall it today.

I didn't work on the film after the shooting phase. I did keep an office near the editing rooms. I was privileged to sit through the hours of assembled footage that showed the work of all the cameras with six synchronized projectors simultaneously. It's too bad that film could not have been magically preserved, too, before it got shaped into the film we see today.

Anyway, during this time I kept in touch with the gang that was cutting it. It may have been after everyone had packed up and gone to Hollywood to finish it, when I got a call from Thelma Schoonmaker. She wanted to tell me something funny that had just happened to her. There had been a great deal of Sturm und Drang among the Warner Brothers executives about what kind of rating this film was going to get. They had to leave in the nude bathing stuff; it was already a famous part of the festival from magazine pictures and such. Thelma had become embroiled in these considerations. It was feared that they might get an X rating from Mr. Valenti's censors and lose a lot of money. (What must have scared them most was some footage of a young man walking along, alone, amid a number of naked people fresh from the lake. I had seen this guy in person when I was with Ed Lynch as he filmed the skinny-dippers. We saw him twice, in fact, hours apart. He was hard to miss and impossible to forget because both times, as he strolled nonchalantly along with the crowd, he had an erection which he made no effort to disguise.) Eventually, the guardians of our innocence and the censor board came to an agreement. A marketing fellow called from Warners. I picture him with a cigar in his mouth and gruff impatient voice. He was a man of few words. He said decisively, "Thelma, [cigar chomp chomp] one hard-on and you get an X."

18

MARTIN ANDREWS: *AH, WOODSTOCK!*

The Call to Arms

The Woodstock Festival had been hyped all summer long on the radio. I don't enjoy being in crowds, so I had no intention of going. I remember the call from Wadleigh which ended with his asking me to bring all the film in my fridge ("the project was somewhat underfunded"). I grabbed all the Background-X (ASA 10), Tri-X, and assorted cans of color, gathered up my location tool kit and was on my way. It was a few days before showtime, so we had no trouble getting there. As much as I wanted to shoot, Wadleigh told me that I was to be Location Technical Director.

I didn't know what that meant, but it sounded pretty important. The job defined itself as we went along. Basically I was grip, gaffer, triage agent and general recourse of last resort for cameramen who still hadn't been around that much. One of the first things I had to deal with was to create a platform for the crew to shoot from in front of the stage. It was still early enough to get scaffolding, which worked perfectly. I pride myself on not over-ordering stuff that never gets used. My intuition is located somewhere in my viscera. I instinctively know how much film or tape I have remaining. I can rewind a cassette tape and stop it exactly where I want to be. This time I did order extra scaffolding—just in case.

The "just in case" immediately became apparent after I had assembled our shooting runway. Where was the press going to be? The extra scaffolding was used for them so they would not interfere with "our" space. My gut instincts had proved infallible again.

Talk to me, Martie!

I suppose that, beyond general exhaustion, the most stressful number I did at Woodstock was to literally cobble together a two-way telex-type system so that the stage cameramen could talk to each other and Marty Scorsese could cue them as to what to shoot. There were wild fantasies about the cameramen dancing together (3 steps to the left, 2 to the right, pause a beat, 3 to the left; bossa nova, tango, merengue, cha-cha-cha). Others didn't want to be encumbered by such a system. I put the project not just on the back burner but actually off the stove until people figured out what they wanted. I had other urgent things to do. This is what I mean by "triage." As the most urgent tasks were completed, the demand for a communication system increased. As showtime approached the demands went from urgent to insistent. "Talk to me, Martie! What's happening with the [communications] system?" I had to do something, or tell them to shove it. "Shove it" disappeared as an option. I talked to Dale Bell.

It was Dale who introduced me to Lee Osborne, who took me to the legendary Bill Hanley. Bill's a dyed-in-the-wool Yankee from Boston. "What do YOU need?" "Well, I'd like—" "No, what do you NEED?" "OK, I need eight headsets with attached microphones, an amplifier and an eight-channel distribution board." "Lee, give him six headsets and an amp. He'll have to work out the distribution himself. I can't give him a whole mixing console. It's too much. He doesn't need it." He was right. All I really needed was a distribution system for audio. It would be similar to power distribution, which I deal with on the mega level. What I required was piss-ant level—I'd just have to make my own. We were less than an hour from showtime. What to do? "Talk to me, Martie! Where's the system?!"

Necessity can be a Mother, all right. Coupled with urgency, the options get narrowed in a hurry. When the festival people built the barrier wall to keep the hordes off the stage, they pile-drove 2' x 8' boards vertically into the ground and evened off the top with a chain saw. I grabbed about a one-foot length of top board off the ground and hustled a handful of nails from a stage carpenter. The layout was simple: six channels into the amp, six out to the headsets. I just had to cobble it together. I thought of connecting all the incoming cables and all the outgoing cables together, but such a Marloilla is notoriously unreliable. "Martie! How long? Talk to me!" Murphy's Law was running rampant. I had to go with the "nail board," not high-tech but strong as an Arri. No need to solder them now. The mechanical connection of wire to nail is all that counts. Final sound check for stage is going on overhead. Bang, bang with the hammer; wrap, wrap with the wire. Cameramen's eyes on me, burning into my hunched-over back. Bang, bang, wrap, wrap. "Talk to me, Martie ..." Richie Havens and his drummer are coming out ... Hook up the amp to the board, thump, thump, thump. I can hear Richie's foot thumping out the rhythm on the stage right over my head. "TALK to me, Martie!" Plug in the amp—thank God—transistors—no warm-up time. "TALK TO ME!!!" "OK, guys, go!" It was on—up and running! Richie's yelling "Freedom" over and over, unaware of its special meaning for me.

The system worked great—except I don't think they really made much use of it to coordinate their shots. It was one of those ideas that are good conceptually, but in reality, the cameramen were too busy riding out their own shots to be bothered with the nuisance. I guess Marty Scorsese used the system to cue them as to which numbers to shoot. It was really more of a rallying point, a catalyst, a flash point, a defining rig that, if done, would justify us hippies working the job, a validation of the producer's having selected the Wadleigh team over better-known competitors.

Another memory that may or may not be true has to do with *Woodstock*'s famous fornication scene. I had field-stripped Ted Churchill's NPR in the equipment truck when I heard this couple discussing where they were going to "get it on." I couldn't abandon my project, find a camera, load it, get a charged battery and follow them. They would have been lost in the crowd before I got it together. So I was delighted when Destiny threw my friend and hero, David Myers, my way. He came into the truck wiping his noble brow in the heat of exhaustion, and was about to recount the vicissitudes of his immediate past when I cut him off, saying, "Pardon me, David, but you see that couple? They were just outside the door talking about where they could go to fuck."

The Port-O-San scene in *Woodstock* would become the same thing. David doesn't just passively record what's happening. David, you are the best—an inspiration to all of us.

The rest is history. We went, we did it, we changed the world! At least there were no more "Talk to me, Martie"s. They were able to talk to each other instead.

![top icon] 19.

CHUCK LEVEY: *The Perfect Job*

 (Chuck was one of the many members of the New York University "Mafia" who brought their talents to the movie. Chuck was primarily a stage cameraman. He would be the only person from the original team to work on the 1998 nostalgic film, "A Day in the Garden," produced at the original site, by Steve Garfinkel. Chuck was then the Director of Photography.)

In the sixties Mike Wadleigh and John Binder had a film company, Paradigm Films. It was the hub for a number of people who were interested in film. Not movies, not commercials—film.

At the time Mike, John and I were married to women who were dancers. They were all members of the Paul Taylor Dance Company. We also lived within two or three blocks of each other. We had kids the same age who all played together. That's how I got to know Mike.

I quit my job at Channel 13 in order that I might get more involved in film, as a cameraman. Paradigm hired me to work on some projects. Among others, a ground-breaking Merv Griffin TV special, during which many of the multi-camera location techniques later to be used at Woodstock were figured out. The crew that worked on this shoot, Mike, John, Martie Andrews, Larry Johnson, Charlie Peck, Ted Churchill and myself, went on to get the *Woodstock* film done.

In July 1969 my then wife and I bought two tickets to go to the Woodstock Music and Art Fair. At the same time, Wadleigh and the group at Paradigm were putting together a package in order to get the job of filming the concert. In that package was film that I as well as others had worked on.

In the beginning of August I was in Philadelphia working on some forgotten project when I got the word that Mike had gotten the gig and I was asked to work on it. Maybe it was you, Dale, who called. I don't remember. WHO KNEW! It seemed like a great job, a perfect job for a 28-year-old film hippie. Where are those tickets now?

I was originally supposed to be shooting MOS (Mit Out Sound) with a Bolex. At that time I did not own an Eclair NPR or anything else. When I got to the stage area, however, I was handed a rented NPR, assigned a soundman (Tom Cohen) and told to shoot whatever I wanted to. Setting up, people arriving, anything that set the stage for the coming concert. (I had arrived three days before the concert was to start.)

On Friday morning (maybe it was Thursday, the day before the concert started— I'm not sure), the first day of the concert, before I left to go shoot at the Hog Farm, I went up on the as yet unfinished stage and looked out and saw a hayfield being cut. Upon returning some hours later I went back up on stage and saw something entirely different. PEOPLE!!! Everywhere. It was staggering. And it was only early afternoon. Something was happening and I was there with a camera. The PERFECT JOB!!!

Santana was the first of the big groups to perform Saturday. The plan for shooting performance was simple. Mike had only assigned us rough positions, zones, to shoot from. That was his only direction. Ride it out. Let it rip. Don't worry about the holes in the stage.

Marty Scorsese . . . I barely knew him. He was trying to do his thing from stage left. He was screaming into the "not-so-clearcom" *trying* to tell me (and I guess other cameramen) what to do. Of course, he couldn't see what I was seeing and because of his chatter I couldn't hear the music, so I looked at Marty and took off my head-set. The beauty of Mike's plan was to hire people who could do it on their own. On or off the stage. Do the right thing.

It rained. Nobody left. Maybe they couldn't. Mud. So I got my camera, switched from the AC motor to the constant-speed battery-powered motor with sync cable, for documentary use, and went out into audience/crowd not knowing what to expect. Everyone was "going with the flow." Mud, use it. Sliding contests happened. The incredible good feelings were not dampened. Being on the stage was, of course, a lot of fun. But, being a documentary cameraman, I was most comfortable "out there." I was out there.

During the filming of the event I had no idea of how the world was viewing it all. Macrovision. Being in the middle of it all, I couldn't see out. The eye of the storm. I don't remember caring. I was having the time of my life. Given the choice, I wouldn't have been anywhere else, doing anything else. Our time had come. I guess that this, later on, would be the only disappointment of Woodstock: our time came and went. What we did there was record a point in time. For years things were either BW or AW (BC, AD) for me. Some things still are. BW I got married, had kids. AW I got divorced.

I've since remarried and had more kids. AW. Life is not linear.

ARLO GUTHRIE: *BEYOND FAR OUT!*

 (Son of the legendary folk musician Woodie Guthrie, Arlo's initial on-film perceptions about the status of the New York Thruway and its police force have since been dwarfed by his view of what the festival and the movie symbolize. The second part of his conversation is in the last section of the book.)

DALE: Did you expect to be filmed when you arrived up there; or did you have any idea at all when you got to Woodstock in '69?

ARLO: As far as my memory goes, I had no idea that they were either recording for audio or filming anything that was going on there. I don't remember seeing any cameras or recording equipment, and so I was surprised, like a lot of other people, when there was talk of a movie coming out, or a record.

DALE: And do you remember—your story conforms to several others, I have to tell you— do you remember what your reaction was when you first saw yourself in the movie?

ARLO: I wished I would have known [laughs] that we were doing a film. I would have been a little better prepared.

Arlo Guthrie singing "Welcome into Los Angeles"

Henry Diltz

89

Woodstock was a double-edged sword for me on the one hand; it was one of those moments that we all knew was historic at the time that it was going on.

On the other hand, I had got there, at least as far as my memory goes, the day before I was supposed to play. And so, I was indulging in all the things that were going on there. I think I had to play on the first day, because I was one of the few people who was able to get in or something like that, and I really wasn't ready to perform in front of anyone. [Laughs] And I was too young to realize that I could have said "No!" when they asked me. Realizing that there would be millions of people who would see me throughout the decades now, I sort of regret not doing that, looking at what was one of the most wonderful and at the same time one of the most ridiculous moments of my life. [Laughs]

Larry Johnson

Director Michael Wadleigh, cameramen Fred Underhill and Ed Lynch on stage

DALE: Your story is a little bit similar to Country Joe's. He had just come up for the ride. He wasn't going to be playing for two days. Just wanted to sit on the edge of the stage and watch everybody else.

ARLO: Right. Right. That's what we were doing. And we were all hanging out and goofing off and having a great time, and I was perfectly willing to forgo any of the pleasures of performing until after I was done playing. Or, I was going to forgo the pleasures of goofing off before performing until after I was done. Which is what you always do. But in this one particular instance I was sort of caught off guard, and had to think of things to say that, at least for the performance, were worthy of being at least paid attention to. And I was lucky to get that far.

DALE: Have people come up to you and said, "Well, the New York Thruway is closed"?

ARLO: For the last 30 years!

DALE: Right! And, "What do you think about the fuzz?"

ARLO: That's right. [Laughs] My kids still get a kick out of that.

DALE: Well, I mean, they are lines that are eminently quotable, I think.

ARLO: Well, that's what I'm saying. Yeah, it would have been nice to have been able to have been more eloquent, you know, but I'm not complaining too much. It's done now, and I'm refusing to regret a single moment of it. I'm so pleased to have been a part of all that. I think anyone who played at Woodstock and who had some memorable moment—whether it was musical, or lyrical, or visual, or verbal, whatever it was—attained a status within the American culture, actually in the sort of global culture, that was beyond anything we ever dreamed of being. I still don't need reservations in restaurants in Italy, or *India*, or wherever, simply because I was at Woodstock. Which is, you know, . . . I'll take it.

STAN WARNOW: *Hapless Documentary Cameraman*

(Stan is the only member of the team—besides Michael Wadleigh—who brought the twin talents of both cameraman and editor to the movie.)

Summer of '69—and oh what a summer it was—the war in Vietnam raged on, men walked on the moon, and then came Woodstock. By this time it had become even more apparent that the Woodstock Festival was going to be a major event. I had decided that unless I was going to be able to work on the film of the festival, I would not go, as I sensed the crowds were going to be overwhelming. But finally I heard that Mike Wadleigh had received the nod. I knew Mike from NYU and immediately got in touch, and much to my delight, was told they could use me as a cameraman.

When my fiancé Cathy Hiller, and I arrived at the festival, the site was a center of feverish activity. A few thousand attendees had arrived already, but movement around the area was still reasonably unfettered, and I got a chance to get the lay of the land. Fortunately, I knew a lot of the people who were working on the film either from film school or previous working situations. On Friday morning there were production meetings and camera assignments were determined. Not being acrophobic I volunteered to man a camera on a stage-left tower for the first afternoon's performance, and thus Cathy and I had a panoramic view of that historic first afternoon. As I was shooting coverage of the vast human mosaic visible from the tower I began to realize that this had become more than this year's *Monterey Pop* and was some kind of cultural landmark and turning point. It's hard to remember now, but at that time young people with long hair and countercultural (for lack of a better word) lifestyles were still considered a fringe minority. Suddenly, here was a manifestation of the fact that this was no longer the case, that by sheer weight of numbers we had entered the mainstream—a fact that was to become a decidedly mixed blessing.

As that Friday afternoon continued, reports of clogged roads and hippies swarming over the countryside began to filter back to those of us actually at the festival, along with the ever-increasing presence of helicopters flying bands and supplies in and out. As twilight turned into night, I made my way down the tower to shoot more close-up footage of the performances.

There was a lot more to the festival than musical performances. For one thing there was waiting between performances for bands to set up. It must have been during one of these waits that we met a stage crew member who went only by the name of Muskrat. If memory serves, he was an itinerant carpenter, a true sixties person who lived day to day, without an official identity (social security number, bank account, etc.). He had signed on to help build the stage and then had become part of the stage crew. Over

Outside In.

Bill Pierce

Bill Pierce

Inside Out.

the three days we had several recurring discussions about the festival, life, love, politics and philosophy in general.

During the day on Saturday, I shot a lot of footage out in the crowds surrounding the stage, both audience and general activity around the festival site. Already having done a fair amount of editing, when I began to shoot audience reaction shots, I quickly realized that it would be helpful in post-production if the editors actually knew what groups were playing and what they were playing. I began scribbling the names of the groups and the selections (if they came over the PA), as the announcements were made. I would then shoot ID slates either before or after the particular selection. Though at the time I could not know that I would be lucky enough to be editing some the very footage I was shooting, the knowledge of which groups were playing and what they were playing turned out to be a valuable resource later on.

Walking around the outer areas of the festival with a shoulder-mounted Arri 16S was a fascinating experience. In addition to photographing activities far from the center of the action, people would come up to me and ask about why I was shooting and I would get a wide range of responses when I told them it was for the official festival documentary. There were a fair number of negative responses, along the lines of, "You're ripping off our culture," and probably an equal number of "Far out ... right on ... where's it gonna be shown" type of comments. But it was later that day, in the backstage area, that I had my one close encounter with what could have been a really ugly situation.

As I was returning to the backstage area to replace my exposed film magazines with new ones, I saw a Hell's Angel type on a Harley trying to force his way past the security detail at the gate to the restricted backstage area. The people manning that particular gate were not security guards, just festival staff who were controlling the crowds. He was threatening to run them down, his gripe being, what made those people in the backstage area so damn special that he couldn't go in there and look around. The bike's engine was running and he was inching it forward trying to force his way into the backstage area. The security people were blocking his way, but I could see the situation was coming to a boil. Had I had film in the camera I would have been shooting away, but for the moment all I could do was observe. Not surprisingly, the guy was probably stoned on something, or some combination of things. It looked to me like things were about to get physical.

Usually I'm a quiet, non-confrontational type of person, so maybe it was the spirit of the whole festival (peace and love!) converging on me at that moment, but before I quite realized what I was doing, I heard myself joining this very heated discussion. Like a fool, I started reasoning with this guy. I pointed out that there had been no violence at all at the festival, and surely he didn't want to be the one to bring it all crashing down. I told him that everyone who was backstage was there because they were trying to do their jobs. Surely he could understand that—he had a job, didn't he? I pointed out that if there were no reserved areas, all of the several hundred thousand people who were there could converge on the stage at will, that the bands couldn't set up or get in and out, or get on stage to perform, and there would be no festival. I remember that I kept coming back to the fact that I was simply there doing my job. Somehow, against all odds, my reasoning finally got to him. I believe we all shook hands and he finally backed up and backed off, and everyone else heaved a huge sigh of relief. And hey, I felt really good about myself. Exhilarated I went back, picked up some fresh magazines and headed back out to shoot some more, my only regret being that I had missed getting footage of a dramatic moment ... But who can say how it would have turned out had I had film in the camera: "Enraged Biker Runs Down Hapless Documentary Cameraman!"

ELEN ORSON: *SUMMERTIME BLUES*

(Elen was 16, maybe the youngest assistant in all of New York, when she joined the staff as an assistant editor; but later she found herself "drafted" into the "army" as an onstage camera assistant.)

It was late July of 1969. I found out through friends that a company uptown needed to hire an assistant editor, and I was looking for work, so I called for an interview.

The day I trekked to Wadleigh-Maurice, I was nervous. Their studio was all the way up Broadway, farther uptown than most film companies, really far from the labs and studios of the Midtown "Film Ghetto." I could assume that this place would be stuffy and uptight, so I did something civilized with my hair and dressed respectfully, fidgeting with my skirt on the uptown bus as I rehearsed my resumé in my head. They were looking for an assistant to "sync the dailies" on a film about a wilderness survival school in the Grand Tetons. I could do that, I was confident, even though I had heard that it was shot entirely without clapsticks.

But the moment I walked into the studio something seemed, well, . . . a bit odd. I'd heard that this company made educational films. But this didn't look like a scholarly place, not at all. There were long-haired hippies. There were women here, working. Editing was one job in the business where women were actually accepted in the workforce, but here there were so many! And young! Doing everything, not just editorial. And the place was a buzzing beehive of activity.

My interview would be with a man named Dale Bell. The door to the editing room was open, and I could see him, sitting there, expecting me. I walked in, shook his hand, and then caught a glimpse of the editing machine behind him, this astounding tank of a contraption that looked like a NASA control room console. This was a Keller, later known as a KEM, and virtually no one in America had ever seen one before. I forgot my lines. I just said something like, "Hi. What the fuck is THAT?" and then lost myself in studying its rollers, screens and plates. I think he liked that, and I think that's why he gave me the job. . . .

But now I had this new job, and although I needed the money, it was summer vacation time and I had been making other plans. Since early summer, New York FM radio had been running ads for a wonderful festival that would take place in Woodstock, upstate New York, in August. It was going to be the largest confluence of rock culture ever held. I wanted to go in the worst way. I had even begun hinting to my parents that I might be "attending a three-day music festival," something like the Newport Folk Festival. But this film was my new priority, so taking off now would be out of the question. Bummer ...

During this time I was 16 and I was still in high school. I worked on films during summer breaks, and at night during the school year. I commuted into the City from New Jersey in my school uniform, and changed at the bus station for work.

Two years before, when I was 14, a whirl of political activity swept the planet, and I dove headfirst into it. My friends were hanging around in the park but I had other ideas. Through my older sister Janice, I became involved with a documentary film company in SoHo. They let us work with them though we had no formal skills, because we had a willingness to learn and we would work for free. We were documenting the student demonstrations and upheavals of 1968; through these experiences I learned to load a camera in a riot, and record sound while being tear-gassed, and edit for three days with no sleep.

Today such a level of independence at that age is practically unheard-of, but this was the sixties and I was a youth. Looking back, I doubt there would have been any way of stopping me.

The Youth Movement and the Disassembly of the Status Quo

There is a quote going around that "if you can remember the sixties you weren't there," which means you were perhaps among the timid who did not inhale or lose your mind in those crazy days. Or it meant that you were on the other side, a lock-jawed mallet-headed member of the Establishment.

In the late sixties, loud rock music was the language, the very embodiment of the young counterculture psyche. It formed a perfect loop and so it's hard to say whether we wrote the words or the words wrote us. The lyrics united us, reminded us, helped us along. And drove our parents crazy.

Perhaps it's also true that if you need an explanation of the sixties, you won't understand anyway. To us, the youth, most of our parents and their values were hopelessly outdated. They were still stuck in WWII regimented thinking after 25 years, and they were absolutely dedicated to the preservation of the status quo. They would say, "Those darn kids don't appreciate the sacrifices we made for them!" And we'd say, "No, thanks." We wanted all Cold War hostility to stop so we could get on with life, liberty, the pursuit of happiness, and justice for all, which had been promised but remained undelivered. We had been raised on the high moral ground. And Superman, and Roy Rogers. We had been *raised* to look for the bad guys.

John Kennedy had given us dreams of journeying to outer space in rockets, and instead, the government was shipping us off in truckloads to Vietnam, and chucking us in front of live ammo in somebody else's war. After some 10 years of this, to believe in the righteousness of the Vietnam War seemed ridiculous and immoral. We were no closer to peace; just the opposite. And our parents kept bugging the boys to cut their hair and register for the draft, because it was the right thing to do. If your country calls, you don't question it.

War, status symbols, racial bigotry, suburbia, plastic values and the whole system had to go. It Had To Go. We sat in, tuned in, turned on, took it to the streets, put it on the line, put it up against the wall—or wherever else "it" needed to go.

The sixties should be called the beginning of a Restoration Period. This movement included restoration of decaying neighborhoods, healthy eating, spiritual consciousness and humanistic values, free speech, art forms, and the restoration of the independent documentary film. The ball started rolling then, even if it took three more decades to accomplish some of these repairs.

Being the Youngest Member of the Crew

As I settled in at Wadleigh-Maurice, the reason for the buzz around the office soon became clear. The producers were working on a deal to film Woodstock Festival. I started to pick up on the rumors in the wind: They were going to film it "on spec."

But this would be the cruel joke: Here I am working for the same company that's filming the Festival, and I'm assigned to a different project. (One that they were scrambling to get finished in case the other deal came through.) And then in the week before the Festival, a recon crew left for the site. My little heart sank, and I went back to my dailies while all around me, World War Three broke out.

But on Thursday I got a call from Thelma Schoonmaker, who had gone upstate. "Elen," she said, "it looks like we're going to need all hands on deck. We need anyone who can help to come up here. You'll get paid for the weekend, don't worry, but we'll work that out later. Can you come up?"

Can You Come Up? Words of Magic. A dream come true. Yes, I'll come up!

That night I told my mother that I had a job for the weekend filming the same festival I had wanted to attend. She had seen the news reports of hordes of people heading for New York State from everywhere, and was not sure I'd be OK. "But we're not camping out, like the crowd, Mom, we have hotel rooms." And when she realized I would be in the company of Adult Professionals, she gave permission. I had spoken to some friends who were driving up that night and I could hitch a ride with them. I packed hurriedly and sped off to meet them in New York for the drive to White Lake.

In the morning I met up with the other crew members at the motel. Some were familiar faces from the studio in the City. Many were not. We wolfed down breakfast and then were ferried over to the festival site. It was the last I would see of my lovely little hotel room, although I didn't know that. But somehow I knew to take my bag and bedroll along just in case.

This was the opening day and workers at the site were literally running to finish in time for the late-afternoon start-up. The production assistants were gathered up backstage, in the area that was reserved for the film crew. Coordinators with clipboards buzzed around. They had to shout over the noise of hammers and saws; carpenters were still building the rotating stage platform! We were asked who could do what, and then were assigned to various tasks. I raised my hand when they said, "Does anyone know how to load magazines?" and suddenly I was on the camera crew.

Underneath the stage, we set up plywood tables and began preparing the artillery for the coming battle. But I had never loaded an Eclair magazine before; I had only worked with Arriflexes. No one had time to teach me the fine points, and this was very critical stuff, so I was re-assigned to a cameraman as his assistant and runner.

The air was thick with pre-show jitters. I shook hands with my cameraman, Ted Churchill, and he looked over his shoulder at the coordinator, sort of to say, "You must be kidding! This 5'3" teenage girl is my assistant?!" I asked him to have complete confidence in me, or something like that. I was at least able to convince him that I had cut my teeth in the Chicago Riots and I could think on my feet. But I think what won him over in the end was not the way I could wrap cable, but that I could give a really good backrub, and that's important to someone who has held 25 pounds of steel on his shoulder for 10 hours straight.

Ted Churchill and I, we were a team. He was given a camera position high atop one of the lighting towers, where a platform had been set up for us to shoot. One of the first scenes of performance would ultimately be ours, a pullback from Richie Havens on the stage to the great sea of people.

We had four magazines, and it was my job to go down and get more film when the first two mags were shot. That would give me about 22 minutes to make it through the crowd, drop off, pick up two more magazines, and hustle my butt back up the tower. I had brought a shoulder bag which was just large enough to hold two magazines, and I could sling it over my back and hoist myself up the scaffolding, a good 60 feet of climbing. Don't look down. Don't look down. I am not afraid of heights, but I'm terrifically afraid of falling. However, I did this all afternoon, through the beginning hours of the concert. The crowd got thicker and thicker until there was no path left to get to the backstage gate. I had to just tiptoe over and through the solid mass of people, lying on their blankets and grooving to the music.

As night approached, a drizzling summer rain began to fall, and they called us down from the tower and repositioned us on the stage. The performances were happening in a steadier fashion now, whereas the afternoon had been a little shaky with many long gaps between acts.

Ted would give me a warning that he was about to run out of film, or I would be standing behind him watching the meter and I would warn him. I waited for the click-chunk-whir sound that meant the last frames had traveled through the gate. Ted would whip off the mag, I would thrust a new one into his hand, he'd slap it on, I'd take the spent one, mark it, and stand by again.

So close to all that fine music . . . the rest of the evening was a blur of satisfying mental bliss, gauzy around the edges. The mist made everything softer and we settled into a work groove, while the rain gently fell, creating the first installment of muddy mud. We had to stop several times while filming, because the humidity made the film emulsion swell, and the film jammed in the gate. Whip off the mag, clean the gate, slap the mag back on.

I remember the Big Storm. That's me in a huge close-up, my long hair whipping with the wind, on-stage in the scene where the storm's hitting. I was holding the AC line to the camera in my hands, looking up at the HUGE black clouds and little spurts of lightning, wondering if we'd all be fried on the stage. Ted was doing a 360° pan of the melée when they were about to cut the power, and he caught me in frame as he came around, and held on the shot. Thanks, Ted.

Bob Campbell

Elen Orson

I remember sitting out the Storm after they cut the power, under the stage with my blanket over my head, a strange calm break in the busyness of the previous two days. Then Marty and another crew member came along and asked if I had an extra blanket, and we all sat there for a while. Just taking it all in, calmly, like we were on a park bench or something. I remember being tired with every muscle hurting. I remember the ride back home in a VW van with a lady from the crew [Anne Bell]. I remember the overwhelming sadness that it all had to end, this giddy, silly, wonderful display of the strength of our ... oneness.

23

MICHAEL SHRIEVE: *OUR WEAPON WAS MUSIC*

(Rock and Roll Hall of Famer Michael Shrieve caused an overnight worldwide sensation with his drum solo on "Soul Sacrifice" as a member of Carlos Santana's band.)

DALE: You were the youngest performer on that stage at Woodstock. What did you see when you went out there for the first time, and what did it feel like?

MIKE: I had turned 19 a month prior in July, so I was young. But everything felt in place for me. I remember thinking when walking up towards the

Mike Shrieve, drummer and the Santana band being filmed by Michael Wadleigh and Ted Churchill

Bill Pierce

stage and then on the stage at Woodstock that it was like standing on the beach and looking at the ocean. And there were people as far as you could see until the horizon. It was nothing like anything I'd seen before. It was a fantastic feeling actually.

DALE: How did you get to the site?

MIKE: We soon found out that the way we were gonna have to get to the site was by helicopter. And so it was all very exciting. We did fly in on a helicopter and it was an incredible sight to see. The interstate was closed and there were cars parked out as far as you could see. Also I think that it's important to recognize—I'm sure a lot of people have explained the mindset at this time. People wanted to change the world, and the music and the culture was the vehicle that people wanted to change things with. So to see the interstate closed and then to fly over the site and see all the people was absolutely incredible. And you realize that this hippie thing had gotten to this point. You felt like it was really peaking and that something was seriously going on now. It was all exhilarating. It wasn't something that you felt afraid of. You felt a part of something larger than yourself.

DALE: Mike, what led you to be a drummer? What was the path that you took as a young person to end up in Carlos Santana's band?

MIKE: I was living in the Bay Area. I was a young drummer, very much into jazz and R&B and not so much into rock and roll as a drummer.

My father listened to a lot of jazz when I was growing up. And the house was filled with music. I just started picking music up that I liked. And I started playing drums in the 8th grade and then got really serious through high school and practiced a lot and got into stuff.

Obviously, the Beatles were happening and this was the beginning of the San Francisco scene. Jefferson Airplane, The Grateful Dead and these kind of groups were playing around and I was very young, but they would come and play down the peninsula, the Palo Alto area.

Jefferson Airplane played once in Palo Alto and I remember going and thinking—looking at Jack Cassidy and Yorma—how does one get like that? What do you do to become that? There's such a great distance from where I am and where they are. Not particularly that I wanted to be them. But the way they dressed and the way that they appeared to be was such a great distance from where I was. I was curious.

I started going to the Fillmore up in San Francisco and seeing such great music. I mean Cream and Yardbirds. And Yardbirds with Jeff Beck and Eric Clapton and Miles Davis and B.B. King and Ray Charles and Charles Lloyd. A lot of good stuff going on. And Michael Bloomfield was the guitar god at the time. And there was a concert going on there called Super Session. With Michael Bloomfield and Steven Stills and Al Cooper. And for some reason I started calling my friends. I was still living with my folks, and I said, "Let's go see if we can sit in," which was absolutely absurd. I don't know why, but I thought about it. That it was even possible. But everybody said no. Everybody said that's crazy. And I decided that I would go by myself, just so that I could say that at least I tried.

So I borrowed my father's car and I went up and made my way up to the front of the stage and pulled on Michael Bloomfield's pant legs and said, "Could I sit in?" And I figured that he'd kick me in the face and say, "Get out of here, kid."

DALE: Right. Kicking sand on the skinny kid at the beach?

MIKE: Absolutely. He was the deal. And the shocking thing was he said, "Well, what do you play?" I said, "Drums." He said, "Well, the drummer's a really nice guy, let me go ask him." And at that point, panic set in and I thought, oh my God, I was doing this to say that I tried. And next thing I know he said, "Yeah. It's okay." And I actually sat in at the Fillmore, which was the Mecca. This was the place that every musician wanted to play. So here I was sitting in with these guys—Bloomfield and Stills and Al Cooper—who were great to me.

Stan Markem, the manager of Santana, and David Brown, the bass player, came up to me and said, "We heard you play and you sound really nice and we're thinking about getting another drummer. We have a band called Santana." I was very familiar with the band, and I really wanted to play with these guys. They were already playing the Fillmore. Well, I didn't hear from them. I saw them once play at a high school in our area and I went backstage and said hello. Met the other guys.

A year passed and I was hustling recording-studio time at a local studio in San Mateo, California, for my own band. As I was walking in the door, the drummer in Santana was literally walking out. They had just had a big fight, a big falling out.

But a couple other guys remembered me and recognized me from that night. They said, "You wanna jam?" So it was a year later. We're jamming in the studio until dawn. They took me in a room and said, "Would you like to be in the band?" And it was just like that.

They literally followed me home to my parents' house in my car. I woke my folks up. I said, "See ya later. This is where I get off." I packed some things and I got in the car with all of them and drove up to the Mission District in San Francisco where I slept on the couch.

And I'll say one thing, although it was a time of peace and love and hippies everywhere, I soon found out that this band was not so much about peace and love. It was more like a street gang. And its weapon was music.

I was very young and very white and here I was living with a black militant, a Mexican, a Nicaraguan, a Puerto Rican, one other guy from down the peninsula, Greg Rawley. So things started happening fast from there.

DALE: Go back to when you went on the stage at Woodstock.

MIKE: It was Saturday. On that day it was Canned Heat and Creedence and The Dead, Janis Joplin, Jefferson Airplane, The Who. John Sebastian played as well. I'm not sure of what the scheduling was supposed to be. We were there hanging around back stage and something happened. They said, "You're going on now, instead of two or three hours later down in the afternoon."

We were very aware that there was cameras. There were a lot of photographers and there was—it's not the sort of thing that you go and check your hair for. We must've been nervous, but as a group we played to each other. We didn't see ourselves so

Mike Shrieve, drummer and the Santana band being filmed by Michael Wadleigh with his 5.9mm lens, Chuck Levey behind

much as performers, but as musicians. And I think that's part of the strength of us being in a situation like that.

We were an unknown band. Bill Graham got us on the bill. If it wasn't for Bill, we'd never been on there. I believe we got paid five hundred dollars to do the gig. Just sort of token money to get on the bill. So yes, we were aware that there were cameras and it was being filmed. Of course, nobody realized the outcome of that.

DALE: When was the first time that you saw yourself in the film?

MIKE: I recall that we were in New York. We had a day off and *Woodstock* was showing. So as a group, we went to see the movie. We had heard nothing about it, except that we were in it. We were waiting in line like everybody else and the prior showing was coming out. People were pointing at us and looking at us. We weren't famous yet or anything. We were a working band with a record out and working really hard.

We went in to see the movie and there we were sitting together. It was unbelievable. It was an unbelievable experience for me personally. Seeing myself split on screen into six times or whatever it was. I didn't know whether to shrink down in my chair or stand up and say that's me, that's me! They picked the best piece, "Soul Sacrifice." We had a tough time that day, because it was hard staying in tune. There were a lot of problems with the sound and I believe that might have been the only good piece of music we played that day.

Seeing myself split up on screen during the drum solo was really something. To see yourself in a big movie theater playing a drum solo. Even today, I cringe when I got so soft and when I left space in it. And then I'm thinking, "Come on! There's over half a million people, keep the beat going!" I was more kind of into this jazz thing and all that. But after the performance, even at the movie theater, the theater burst into applause. It was the most unbelievable experience for us to see that. It goes without saying that clip changed our lives.

DALE: Do you recall what Carlos's reaction was?

MIKE: I don't recall specifically, but I know that Carlos was having a difficult time staying in tune that day. It shows on the film a lot of things about Carlos. It shows his intensity and his passion and his urgency. He was doing his best to stay in tune. As he says now, he was saying, "Lord, please just keep me in tune."

I think everybody in the band was completely amazed at seeing themselves on the big screen, for one. And that the performance came off as something really very special. It captured the band—I mean it was great at the concert. Wow. We were a perfect group for that day. We were a perfect group for that festival. We were tribal. Rock and roll is one thing. There was a lot of great acts there. But we were really tribal and it just works for that many people. It still works, but that sound was very effective.

DALE: You say that clip changed—what did it change?

MIKE: First of all, it broke us as a band internationally. My first clue of that was one of our first trips over to Europe and Montreux Festival. And I took a walk to the local train station to pick up some magazines, 'cause I was always a magazine freak. And I walked in and I see this magazine called *Rock & Pop* and I'm on the cover. And it's a big picture of me from *Woodstock*. I had never, of course, been on the cover of a magazine before, or anything like that. Reviews were coming out and I guess the record was out. Or the film was out, of course. It just broke us everywhere and Santana took off after that film happened.

I remember when I was about 35, I was living in New York and walking down Fifth Avenue and somebody said, "Hey, Mike Shrieve! Man, I just loved your solo in *Woodstock!*" Which is something, of course. I'd be rich if I had a dollar for everyone in my life that I heard that. And the guy looked at me for a while and said, "Look, man, what's happened? You've gotten older!" And I was 35 and it really upset me.

And I just thought, "Is this what I'm gonna be trapped as? Known as the drummer from the *Woodstock* movie all my life?" It really upset me. What I realize now is that the concert meant so much to so many people. To them personally. I meant so much to so many young people who have told me that, "We saw you there with all those guys. All those heavy hitters and you were our age. And you didn't seem to be any older than us and you inspired me to play the drums," and it just goes on and on. And you can't fight it.

Finally you just have to be gracious enough to say, "I'm grateful I was there." It was a wonderful day. It broke the band. There's nothing that I'm gonna do in my life that is more momentous than *Woodstock*. I may do better work. I may play better drums. I may record better solos. None of it matters. It does matter, but it doesn't matter in the big scheme of things. Remember the reasons that you started doing music initially, because you love the music. So just be grateful. Don't be bitter.

![An Aquarian Exposition STAFF PASS](24 icon)

24.

AL WERTHEIMER: *IT SOUNDS LIKE AN ADVENTURE*

(Al's engaging personality and cinema style allowed him to film some of the most memorable documentary pieces in the movie, an honor he shares with David Myers. Al and David were "no longer young" at the time. Both began as still photographers.)

DALE: So June, July 1969?

AL: I was working with filmmakers Mitch Bogdonovitch, Ricky Leacock and Don Allen Pennebaker. They were developing the equipment in order to separate themselves from the soundman; in other words, getting rid of that umbilical cord between the camera and the recorder. The cameraman could reach out with a long lens, and he could go past crowds. But the soundman couldn't. The name of the game was "How do we get cinematographers to be as free as *Life Magazine* photographers?" So there was a technology shift from what was basically using tripod studio camera-type thinking, to portability, where the photographer was free to come and go.

I firmly believe that the more uncomfortable the cameramen and technicians are, the closer they may be getting to the truth. The darker the scene, the more the people will tend to be themselves rather than posing for the camera. This is maybe why you get close to the truth in dark bars.

Part of what I was hoping to get into was to seek out the truth. Well, the truth is relative; it's relative to what your state of mind is at a given point in time, what your background is. Your truth as a cameraman is going to be fitted in with all the other truths of the director and the editor, and in the end your truth becomes part of the blend of their truth. And then the question is, how do you take an event that's three days long, with all kinds of feelings, and then eventually make it into a two-, three-, and four-hour film, which is an abstraction and two-dimensional magic act of what the reality was?

So there you are, Dale. You're calling me up and you're saying, "Al, can you spend three days up here at this bungalow, at the Silver Spur at White Lake?"

And I said, "Well, this sounds like an adventure. I don't know any of these guys—I don't know Mike Wadleigh, I don't know Dale Bell—but it sounds good, and I hope they can pay my fee. Song, music, lots of young people, it's Upstate New York—" I got into a car and next thing I know I was at a bungalow.

DALE: Did you and Wadleigh ever have any kind of a conference about what this film was really going to be about?

AL: No, the only thing I could remember about Wadleigh was that he had very long hair, looked like Jesus Christ, or images of what Jesus supposedly looked like, and he looked at me and I had fairly short hair. And I remember we were already at the site, in this van which we used as a . . . place. All the camera people, we sort of picked our spot. We were trying to get our little space. "This is mine. I'm gonna leave my extra magazines here, my extra batteries there—don't touch it!" Y'know? And we sort of hoped that everybody would respect that.

So then the question was, "What do I do up there?" Mike said to me, "Al, you look like you could fit in, in town. Go see what you can find in town." And I said, "What do I shoot?" And he says, "Well, you figure out what to shoot. Whatever interests you. Stick with it, y'know?" So, he didn't want to give instructions. He was not about to tell me that when I get to town I'm gonna find such-and-such and do such-and-such. So I said, "All right—"

DALE: Did you feel this was off-putting? Was this the kind of instruction you could deal with?

AL: I felt that since I ultimately wanted to be a director myself, this gave me the chance to direct my own little scene. Just keep your ears and eyes open.

So you find this little town is being drained of all its gasoline. There's nothing left in the gas pumps. And then like a herd of locusts, the stores have been cleaned out. Then next thing you know, you get some older people who were complaining about how these hippies don't appreciate what our boys in Vietnam are going through, and you've got this whole argument about the pro- and the anti-Vietnam old people.

Meantime, you'd have some long haired kids going into the store and this is all kind of taking place on the sidewalk. And then the young people would get involved in a discussion with the old folks, and you're just kind of seeing the points of view develop, and you can't pre-conceive this. The dialogue is too good; it would be very hard to script.

And I remember what Bob Drew once told Abbot Mills. He said, "Look, for God's sakes, stay on their faces! I don't care if they're hitting a hammer or they're putting something in a bag. Show me what their emotions are like while they're hitting the hammer." So I said to myself, "All right, Al, slow down, don't be jerky, don't go back and forth, stay with the face. See the reaction. Then go, slowly spin over and see if you can get the person who's talking. And try not to zoom in, focus, zoom back. Try to be smooth, you know?"

Journalist Tom Barry interviewing bathers

So what happens is, you've kind of got one eye through the camera lens, watching your story; and in the meantime your other eye is open, looking for things coming into the scene. So that you can prepare yourself to move off that, to something else.

Originally, when I first got into films, I thought a three-second take was long. I thought a one-minute take was exceedingly long. Then I started working for Bob Drew, and they went through ten-minute rolls. Never stopped the camera. So then I said, "Well, OK. Never stop the camera. That way, at least, you might get a nice chunk of material."

DALE: Tick off for me—what did you shoot? What do you remember shooting?

AL: Well, I shot the scene in town—around the grocery store, the gas station, if it's still in the film. I shot the kids on the side of the road; one said she's gotta go to Guatemala or something, and he was talking. It was sort of a philosophical discussion about this young couple. And she had just come back from somewhere but was going somewhere, and somehow it sounded like she was going to South America.

DALE: In the editing we would refer to—these are "The Two Kids by the side of the Road." Did you do the one with the—

AL: With the farmer and the, uh . . .

DALE: Repairing under the car?

AL: Yeah, uh . . . "It's a shitty mess! I can't get the cows milked . . ." And then the girls would be asking the farmer's wife for a favor to call so-and-so—that's all my footage.

DALE: "Shitty Mess!"

AL: We just decided: have the camera rolling, walk in, and say, "What's going on here?" And then he's able to just give his opinion. Y'know, "How can they just leave cars like that?"

DALE: "Six Ice Cubes Out of the Bag." Was that yours too? You know, the guy, somebody comes in, they want to buy six ice cubes out of the bag—

AL: From the farmer—

DALE: —or from the store owner.

AL: I don't know about that. If it was in town, it was probably mine. But the other thing is the lake. You know, all the stuff around the lake, where I finally got myself a boat and went out into the lake. And shot from a rowboat. People swimming, with the tents on the shore.

And then there was some mounted police I recall, going through. And I said, "Uh-oh. Here comes the confrontation. I smell pot everywhere." You know, pot was in the air. And no—everybody was being very considerate, and everybody kind of properly closed their eyes and there was no confrontation. After that scene, I followed a bunch of nude guys on the road, and I followed them from the rear, and then I sort of stopped and got into an interview with them.

DALE: Did you do "The Woman in the Information Booth"?

AL: Yeah, she's going—she's kind of panicking and she's looking for her sister?

DALE: Right, her sister. They've gotta go to court on Monday?

AL: That's right, that's right. Yeah, that's my stuff.

DALE: What was going on in your head when she's spouting all this stuff off?

AL: Well, she's telling a story. We're all telling stories. I'm telling a story. Her story was one of—she's looking for somebody in these three, four hundred thousand people and she can't find her. And she might be on lysergic acid or something. There was a lot of that going on, and my concern was "What am I getting in the frame?" And as long as it's interesting, hold it.

So when I went to the Information area, I was concerned about "How do I make a little scene out of this?" There are a lot of different faces, a lot of young faces, there are some concerned people, some people are slightly panicky, some people have lost their shoes, somebody's telling a story, they're each telling each other. And just hold the camera steady. Stay on the faces and let the people tell their story.

And then you'd see these helicopters coming in and you'd say, "How bizarre!" I mean, you've got Marine helicopters, and you've got Hippies, and they're not supposed to be in the same scene together, but how come they're here and how come the Media's now here? And then you find out that the road is closed and so now it became a Media Event. It no longer was the individual stories of these people.

I remember when we first went there, there was a fence. And then all of a sudden the fence came down. And then, I mean, how were you going to hold off these hundreds of thousands of people from not coming in? You might as well be generous and let them in because you would have had a riot on your hands if you tried to take them out.

And then, of course, the rain. The Rain. The rain was really a main character in this event. And I was so tired at night, and then there's a point where you don't give a rap.

DALE: Where were you sleeping?

AL: I was sleeping in the car that I had rented to bring up. And soundman Charlie Pitts was also sleeping in the car. And then the next thing you knew, other people were trying to get into the car. And you're saying to yourself, "Now why do I want all these . . . I know it's love, and peace. But I don't know any of these guys . . . and I've got a lot of fancy equipment here and it's my livelihood, and its MY car, and what are they doing sleeping on the hood? And sleeping on top of the car?" And after a while I said, "I don't care."

And so I must have gone to sleep, and dawn came, and I remember hearing these Coke bottles and Pepsi bottles clinking, clinking, so now I was back in business, and photographing. I see these guys doing sort of a Jamaica—what do you call, when you go like this and you try to go below the stick?

DALE: The "Under the Bar"?—You're talking about the Rain Sequence?

AL: Yeah, the Rain Sequence, so I started shooting that and they started to slide, and they start to do a—it was like a spontaneous happening in the mud, everybody was getting—

DALE: Were you afraid yourself, I mean, of the rain or anything else like that?

AL: No. No. I mean the thing was, they were involved; you see, once people are involved, they've got enough on their mind. And then I started trying to get people sliding into me and it was like a happening. Nobody knew exactly what the next move was, but if you just were patient, it would happen. And you could either complain and bitch about the mud, or you could enjoy it. And it was like going back to childhood. Mud pies. And sliding. I mean, here are people taking sticks and bottles, and making music.

DALE: It was as primitive as the first people did with stones and rocks.

Into the woods

AL: Probably. Eventually I wound up on stage and I was doing some shooting, and when I was on stage I was surprised at how close Wadleigh would get in to shoot. I mean, I never saw a guy who would be three feet away from the performers with a camera, and then later on I realized he had a 5.7 lens, or a 5.9 lens, and there was extreme wide angle. So you know, he'd have that real "in-close" kind of look.

DALE: What was for you the most fascinating, the most intriguing thing that you came away from this experience with?

AL: Well, you get caught up in the event. I mean, first it's a job, then you find out it's a happening. Then you find out: How does a town of this many people come and then eventually disappear?

And then, what is happening with the sea of mud here? I mean this was once a field, and now it's nothing but mud with things that were of value like blankets and shoes and bags and that are just garbage. You find that people whose interest is in farming and getting in and out on a road are more concerned about being proper and orderly, while young people who've got nothing to lose—they don't have a lot of property—they say, "Hey, this is wonderful. We're having, uh—it's a happening. It's love and peace."

It's just a question of whose point of view you see this from. You think you have answers and then you find out: Well, there are no answers. It's just various shades of a story.

Had it not been for a technological change at the time, to permit the recording of the event, it would have been a different event on film. It would have been done with tripods; it would have been done in a more formalistic way. There is a certain marriage of technique that goes with the storytelling. Now, we were all experimental in our style. We were sort of "go with the flow" attitude; we were able to capture that 'cause the film industry and the dyes and the speed of the film and the technology of the cameras was such, it permitted us to do it. And getting rid of the umbilical cord—and that added to a certain naturalness. And getting close with medium-wide-angle lenses to the subject gave it a kind of a presence that you don't get if you just take a long lens and zoom it out, and you don't get that texture. So this film had a certain amount of texture.

In my own case, I was always trying to seek the truth with my camera and tell the story of the truth as I saw it, being naive enough at the time to realize: there is really no truth. The only truth we can do is the outer reflections off surfaces rather than what's going on in people's heads. See, the writer can get into somebody's skull; but the photographer has to deal with light and with movement, and with outer reflections. And so therefore we make those things more exciting than they really are when we just look at it. When we're just looking at it, it's one thing, but when you see it through the camera lens, it's another thing. When you look at something, . . . when I look at you, I don't see anything out of focus. You're sharp, the wall is sharp, down there is sharp when I change my focus; but with a camera lens, and certain angles, there's a selective focus you can play with, going from the foreground face to a background face. And then maybe going to a foreground face again. Or hands. And these are tricks of cameras, and tricks of the way lenses see things, and tricks of the way cameramen think.

Al Wertheimer

25.

ANNE BELL: WIVES, SISTERS AND GIRLFRIENDS

(Anne was one of many wives and girlfriends who accompanied their mates to the site to help out as "assistants" for three days of peace and music. Luckily, we left our kids at home for the weekend with GranMama.)

My husband, Dale, asked me to help out with the crew that he was trying to assemble (on spec) to travel up to White Lake and try to film the scheduled music festival. The call went out — all wives, sisters and girlfriends were asked to help.

I started north with a map on Thursday, alone. I found my way upstate New York, but several miles from Woodstock the roads became crowded. I could see long lines of people walking along the road. Then the whole road became full of people. About 15 people climbed onto the outside of my bus, and at least five stood on the rear bumper (it bent very low on one end and remained that way for the rest of its life). We sold it many years later. To this day I always look at the rear bumper of vintage VW buses hoping to find my old van.

Because I had film crew credentials, I was waved inside the gate bringing my human cargo with me. I was told to drive to the stage and park behind it. I looked for Michael Wadleigh and his wife, Renée, but it took quite a while before I found them. After I found them, I never let them out of my sight except to go for food.

That evening I got hungry, so I ventured out of the stage compound. When I finally got to the top of the hill, I could see long lines of people snaking past tables where people were serving a sort of gruel (some sort of hot vegetable-and-oats mixture I think). I don't know how I got a bowl and spoon but everyone got fed. People were sitting on the hillsides all around the little valley where the Hog Farm had set up camp. Bonfires were burning and some people had brought assorted instruments and were playing music, while other people danced by the firelight making lively silhouettes against the night sky. Later I found my way back to my VW bus, climbed inside and went to sleep. The day of the concert Mike assembled the crew, and work began in earnest.

Michael gave me a pad of paper and asked me to keep track of which groups were performing and the titles of the songs that they played. He had a *stage* crew of cameramen and various helpers. Mike and Renée stood on a dropped ledge that ran across the entire front of the stage. I was placed to his left just in front of the huge

113

Amalie Rothschild

Director Michael Wadleigh, his wife Renee Wadleigh assisting him, and Martin Scorsese, assistant director

battery of sound speakers. Directly below us on the ground was the crowd, behind a wooden fence which kept them from overrunning the stage.

That afternoon the first thing that hit me was the SOUND! After three hours of the first performance I felt like I had been through an artillery barrage. It was extraordinary! I was supposed to be writing down the titles of the songs, but most of what I could hear of the lyrics was "yah yah yah." It all sort of ran together. Between songs, I leaned back and asked the crowd leaping up on the fence behind me, and someone or other was able to tell me most of what I needed to know. At twilight, I happened to glance up at the hill and was astonished to see that there was a mass of people reaching back to the horizon. I had no idea that so many had arrived. Everyone was leaping and rocking and waving their arms in time to the music. That night I heard Joan Baez sing "Joe Hill"—her voice so crystal clear, with such depth and purity, it took my breath away. That night she was supremely beautiful.

I can't today remember the order in which the bands performed over the next three days, but they were so different, each one very individual. None of us who were there will ever forget Country Joe's cynical and heartrending lyrics when he sang, "Be the first one on the block to get your boy home in a box." Everafter, when I think about any war and blind patriotism I can hear that song.

When one sat on the edge of the stage as I did most of that weekend, the most extraordinary impression was the outpouring vortex of energy that engulfed us during those 18-hour stretches. The bands were giving it everything they had. It was an outpouring of joy, humor, sex, sadness, love, anti-war and most of all—longing for a better world. We were all very awake at that moment. It was as if the rest of the world just stopped and for that weekend we lived only in the present, and that present was very ALIVE!

The next morning I was promoted. Michael found out that Eric Blackstead and the sound recording crew were keeping track of songs, so I was sent with a few others under the stage and given a lesson in how to load 16mm film into magazines for the cameras. It was a leap of faith on their part because if we made mistakes loading we would ruin a take which could not be repeated, and the film was in scarce supply.

I was assigned to assist Don Lenzer, who would be shooting upstage right, as I remember. His camera was attached to a long cable and he and all the other cameramen were completely mobile, moving about the stage following the performers. With all six men filming at once in sync, the editors were able to show the performers from all angles on a triple split screen. My job was to follow him around dragging the cable, and get him newly loaded magazines as he ran out of film. The cable was very long, and I had to carefully coil it at the side of the stage so that I could take off after him without getting tangled when he moved quickly.

We were in the middle of a performance that Saturday night. My eyes were glued to Don anticipating his every move. He had remained fairly stationary for the first half of the performance—then the band began gyrating in a frenzy of motion. Don took off after them and I began feeding him more and more cable. Suddenly I felt a tug behind me. I whirled around and saw that a Swami was sitting crosslegged on top of my coil. He had his eyes closed and was rocking back and forth deep in meditation or something. I rushed back and sort of tilted him to one side while I extracted the cable. He never woke up.

The next group to play was "Mountain." Leslie West, their lead singer, was a huge colossus of a man—hence the nickname. Don was wearing earphones so that he could hear Wadleigh giving stage directions. Suddenly he threw off his earphones and left them dragging by their wire on the wet stage floor behind him. Someone motioned to me to get the earphones. The order came through quickly: "Don't let the earphones touch the stage floor again—they will short out all the others." At this point I moved downstage right in the shadows, reeling out the cable to give Don some play.

Mountain began to move—downstage—stomping his foot furiously as he kept time to the music. The spotlights moved with him. Don began to move too—upstage behind him and away from me. The cable whisked across to him until the wire to the earphones was used up. In order not to obstruct the audience's view, I took off the earphones and lay down flat on the stage with my arm fully extended holding those earphones off the floor. Mountain and the spotlight advanced. To my horror he paused about three feet away from my head and began a sort of pounding war dance. The spotlight encircled both of us for the rest of the song. I looked up and saw that he had his head tilted toward the sky and his eyes were on the back of the audience. I couldn't tell if he even knew I was there, but I lay there frozen making sure that the earphones never hit the floor.

Wadleigh was all over the performers, moving around the lead singers like a cobra, picking up odd angles and extreme close-ups. When "The Who" were performing, Peter Townshend became annoyed and kicked Wadleigh's camera, causing the eyepiece to smash into his face. Luckily Mike was not hurt badly, but we were all shaken as we watched Townshend stomp and smash his guitar at the finale.

Across the stage behind the performers Dick Pearce's open eye glinted like a cat's as the lights hit on his face. He seemed to do most of his shooting with both eyes open.

That night when we wrapped, I made my way back to my VW van and fell asleep. It was pitch-black. Suddenly I was awakened by the sound of people rapping on the windows and shouting and rocking the car. It had started to rain and they wanted to get inside. I didn't understand what was happening, and terrified, I hid under the blanket until they moved on to the other cars.

In the morning I was sent out of our stage compound with camerman Dick Pearce and Joe Louw on sound. We were told to mix with the crowd and get them to talk about their feelings and experiences. Everyone was young. All were a little damp and bedraggled after spending the night in the field, but they were mellow and happy. The air was warm and the sun was out. The mud games, and nude swimming, and love making were in full swing. No one was angry. It was a magical land, a Garden of Eden of sorts (albeit muddy), no disapproval, no sin, no negativism, no power plays—just fun.

Between sets I took a break to visit the Port-O-San. (Who of us will ever forget the movie's interview with the "Port-O-San man"?) Behind the stage there was still a lot of work going on. Big moving vans with generators and all sorts of supplies were coming and going. There was no line at the toilets because they were for the exclusive use of the performers and stage crews; however, the stench was "out of sight." I had to hold my breath when I entered, and hurry. A new band started to play and the sound was terrific. Suddenly, coming from the adjacent Port-O-San I heard someone shrieking and beating on the wall. As soon as I exited I realized what had happened. A truck had backed up against the other Port-O-San door and trapped someone inside. No one could hear them screaming unless you were in the toilet next to them. I found the driver and had the truck moved, and out stumbled an hysterical person, lucky not to have been asphyxiated. What a way to go!

Sunday was the day of the afternoon storm. We were all on stage when the wind suddenly picked up. This got our attention right away because the lighting towers began to rock. Then the huge tarps that covered the stage began to flap like sails. All of us kept glancing up at the sky but the band played on. After about ten minutes the rain struck hard. Everything was soaked. All the crews were running around trying to cover the speakers and musical equipment. Those who had them donned yellow hooded rain jackets and tried to lash down everything on stage. John Morris took a wet microphone and talked to the crowd

Anne Bell, production assistant, with soundman and still photographer, Joe Louw, and cameraman Richard Pearce

Amalie Rothschild

trying to discourage anyone from running. He told them to settle down and ride out the storm, which they did. He told them we could continue the performance as soon as the rain stopped. The wind and rain lashed down harder, and the crews began moving to find cover, afraid that the light towers might come crashing down on-stage. I found myself underneath the stage dragging several cameras and electrical equipment to safety—or so I thought. The rain began to pour down between the cracks in the stage floor. It was then that I noticed I was standing on a snarl of huge (as big as a man's leg) electric cables. I didn't know if all the power was disconnected, but at that point I crawled under a moving van that was parked next to the stage. I think someone passed me a baloney sandwich and then I fell asleep from exhaustion until the rain stopped and we all went back to work.

Monday morning the audience was a real mess. Everyone was covered with mud and all their blankets and sleeping gear were soaked. The field smelled like a barnyard. Nevertheless they had bonded the way survivors do, and their smiles were triumphant.

I believe I woke up to the sounds of Jimi Hendrix playing "The Star Spangled Banner." It was a wild rendition which seemed to embody our feeling of having survived something extraordinary. A communal awakening to the possibilities that we were young and strong and people of goodwill. That weekend we had come together voicing the desire to create a better world. Peace & Love.

DALE BELL: *THE PORT-O-SAN SEQUENCE*

Saturday afternoon at the festival. Headquarters for Wadleigh-Maurice Productions, Ltd. at the festival was located on a couple of pieces of three-quarter plywood under a trailer to the left of the stage as you faced the audience pit. Our noses assured us that we were not far from a bank of Port-O-San toilets. Class act all around.

David Myers and his soundman, Charlie Pitts, had just returned to our headquarters that Saturday afternoon. As he was getting his gear together, picking up raw stock and audiotape for another run into the crowds, I noticed that a Port-O-San worker had just backed his truck in to clean the many toilets. He got out of the cab and moved to the rear of his truck to unhook the hose.

I approached him with my hand extended in typical Ivy League fashion. He took his glove off and we shook hands. I told him we were making a film, would he mind if we filmed him? No, was his reply. Through diligent training gained at NET on prior documentary shoots, I always knew it was best to ask permission of someone before you filmed them. It eased the relationship, broke the ice. I knew we were never going to get a signed release from all those whom we had filmed; my action was pure courtesy, an introduction on behalf of all of us to a stranger doing his work.

I backed out of the way to beckon in David and Charlie, who by that time had gotten their stuff together and were ready to shoot. David walked in, the red light on his camera indicating that he had begun to roll. Charlie was at his side with his microphone, alas,

Cameraman Dick Pearce, camerman Fred Underhill, soundman Joe Louw, cameraman David Myers, and location coordinator John Binder outside the trailer headquarters at Woodstock.

118

not pointed exactly where it should have been. Never at a loss for words, and one of the most innocent and engaging people in the world, David began his conversation with the Port-O-San man.

Should I say that the rest is history? Almost. As he had done so often before, and as he had always trained the rest of us neophytes, David Myers kept shooting, walking, talking, and moving his camera in and out, anticipating exactly where the image ought to be to coincide best with the words he was hearing or expected to hear. David, the cameraman with the best ears I had ever seen, delicately followed the unfurling of this little vignette, asking those pointed, *double-entendre* questions with his wry sense of humor ever so slightly suppressed behind the constant twinkle in his eye. "Getting a little behind, aren't you?" was David's first little question which prompted all the rest of the quintessential sequence. Both were simply doing the job they came to the site to do: David to document, the Port–O–San Man to clean toilets.

"No," the Port-O-San man replies, just as innocently. And as though it had been orchestrated, rehearsed, and now re-enacted, this *pas de deux,* this duet between David and the Port-O-San man, continues. Uninterrupted by the camera, the Port-O-San man keeps talking with the inquiring man who wants to know how being here, at this site, plays on the man with the long hose. As the Port-O-San man moves from one stall to another, David follows diligently, never losing sight of the overall narrative thread of this extraordinary man in his eyepiece.

Eternally youthful at the ripe age of 55, David was older than the man he was following with his camera. Though born at the outbreak of the First World War, David was far from a man of war. When it came time for him to serve in World War II, this warrior for peace filed with his draft board as a conscientious objector. To fulfill his obligation to his country, which as a New Englander he felt he must, he served as an aide in institutions and hospitals, then planted trees in the forest. He did not believe in killing, even for all the reasons millions went into the Second World War.

The Port-O-San man finishes his task. It hasn't taken him long. His training dictates that he rinse the seats of the stalls with disinfectant. Armed with a long handle, he brushes the liquid around the toilet seats. Now, they are clean enough for the next customer. He knows he will be back again tomorrow. And then, as though feeling the pulse of this multitude, he pauses and releases this simple sentiment born of the recesses of his soul: *"Happy to do this for these kids. I have one here, and one in Vietnam."* Did he truly say that, unprompted, untutored? Did we get it right? Did no one write that for him to say?

I'm not sure, even as I write this 30 years after it actually happened and still feel the chill-bumps up my spine as I listen to the Port-O-San man's pronouncement echo in my mind, whether there is anything more profound in the entire movie. Does it compare to "One small step for man . . ." or "Ask not what your country can do for you …" or "Can't we all just learn to get along?" Was it to capture this essence that we decided to do the movie in the first place?

When this portrait arrived in the editing room, there never was a question that it would find its way into the documentary portion of the movie, virtually uncut. Yet it almost didn't make it, not because of the content but because of the sound.

Fast-forward to mid-February 1970. The Port-O-San sequence takes its turn on the dubbing stage, the place where all the sounds originally recorded on-site are processed, enhanced, equalized, tweaked, manipulated, and/or otherwise balanced and modified to make them snap, crystal clear, out of the speakers. In spite of all the patching of cords, pushing of buttons, sliding of dials, opening and closing of pots, bouncing of VU meters, they could not isolate the dialogue of the scene from all the junk noise in the background. Time was pressing down on us. We tried every trick we had, but nothing seemed to be working.

Wads and I were pacing back and forth on the rug covering the floor of the dubbing stage. The big image was being projected above us. Even at this close proximity to the speakers, we were having extreme difficulty with intelligibility. Neither one of us wanted to lose this powerful piece, this symbol of the universality of humanity. But what to do?

Recalling our use of the bouncing ball over the lyrics in the Country Joe McDonald *"F.U.C.K. Cheer,"* I suggested that we use subtitles to allow the audience to read along while they listened to the words. The combination might make the audience hear better. We looked at each other. The mixers, the editors, all harkened to the idea. So off it went to the title company, preserved indelibly. But this was not the last we would hear or see of the Port-O-San man.

During the screening we had for Warner Brothers, where students and "suits" viewed our efforts for the first time one Sunday afternoon in March 1970, another spontaneous event occurred. Just after the Port-O-San man makes his pronouncement about his son on-site and the other son in Vietnam, the students (I didn't see any "suit" doing this!) leapt to their feet and cheered this man for what he stood for. He became an instant hero, a symbol for all caring individuals.

It was the first of many times this happened.

At the press screening in New York at the Trans-Lux Theater in late March 1970, he appeared in full life, dressed in a suit. A Warner staff person, at my instruction, had located the man (through Fred Dubetski at the Port-O-San company in New Jersey). With his wife and family surrounding him, he made his way into the theater, little knowing what to expect. He had been told simply that he was in the film. Period.

When the moment came for his sequence to appear, I moved from my spot at the back of the theater down the darkened aisle slightly behind him so that I could see his face bathed in the reflected light of the screen. As his story unfolded on the huge screen, I saw him clutch a family member close to him. I also think I saw a tear in his eye. But what remains forever imprinted in my memory is the thunderous cheer that erupted from that packed house as they celebrated his remarks. This warm crowd enveloped him in their arms, lauding his wisdom and compassion.

At the end of the screening, as the house lights were turned on, he was identified for the rest of the audience. Tom Taggart and his family. He stood proudly to receive their welcome once again.

To this day, wherever I have seen the movie, even in London at Leicester Square, the Port-O-San man received a standing ovation, so purely does he resonate. Yet sadly, even this is not the end of this noble story.

Several months after the movie opened across the country, presumably to similar responses, Warner Brothers, Wadleigh-Maurice Productions, Ltd. and exhibitors everywhere were served with a lawsuit pressed by attorneys representing the Port-O-San man and his family. We were charged with defamation of character, ridicule, libel, and he was seeking damages in the millions for what we had done to him before the world. Of course, we were astonished by his action. (It was one of half a dozen suits brought against *the film* for similar exposure or ridicule or whatever.) The suit charged that we had not obtained his permission in writing, that we had filmed him in a demeaning occupation, and that to add insult to injury, we had used subtitles to convey his words, as though he could not talk clearly and be understood.

Our hero had been ensnared by greedy attorneys, perhaps? Apparently, everyone in town knew he worked for the Port-O-San Corporation, but his job classification was labeled "sanitary engineer." No one had ever inquired about a job description, not even members of his family. Once the sequence in the film was exhibited across the country, the secret he had maintained from his family for all those years was now exposed. Apparently, his high school son was ribbed because of his dad's occupation. He was crestfallen; they were shocked that he performed liposuction on dozens of stalls a day. Friendly attorneys *must have* advised him to sue us.

I know I felt very sad at this development. None of us bore any hard feelings towards the Port-O-San man. Although we offered a settlement, the preferred to take the case to court, but they lost.

Other lawsuits were brought by people who thought they had been ridiculed by dint of being included in the movie (the man playing reveille on the bugle from the stage on Sunday morning), or caught unsuspectingly in embarrassing configurations (the man making love in the tall grasses who cocks his hat at a different angle once he has completed his session), yet none of them won.

I—we—regret any inconvenience we caused the Port-O-San man. To each one of us, he was symbol of compassion and we wish him and his marvelous family well. I trust his son in Vietnam returned home safely, but I frankly do not know.

David and Barbara Myers of Imogen Cunningham fame (1998)

Dale Bell

DAVID MYERS: *OUR MENTOR SPEAKS*

 (Dave was the youngest 55-year-old at the site, bar none. His wisdom as a cinema verité cameraman was already thoroughly established long before he flew in from Mill Valley on his own dime. With uncanny laconic simplicity, Dave guided all of us through our paces, leading always by example.)

DALE: Give a film audience an impression of your kind of shooting style.

DAVE: Well, I play off the people I'm dealing with. I play off what's happening and how people are reacting. That's a simple description—within the context of what we want.

DALE: I've always described you as having the best ears of any cameraman I've ever met.

DAVE: Well, listening is definitely the centerpiece. That gives me the clues. And I'm surprised that so many photographers don't seem to pick up on that kind of verbal—sound cues—people's behavior. The emphasis, the way they use language and communicate, is a clue to what's going on.

DALE: Because you listen so well, you could anticipate exactly who in a room or situation was going to speak next or react next.

DAVE: Yes. I go with that. I don't know whether it's a talent or something. But I listen carefully. I do the same thing in effect on stage with rock and roll—when the music is good enough that I go with it. But I take the cues from what's going on.

Body language also. I was once offered a job with the big guru of psychological analysis of people by body language. Raymond Birdwhistle was head of some department at State University at Buffalo. Anyway, Gregory Basin and I did a film about a schizophrenogenic family and I shot a few hundred feet of a mother and a little boy who were in therapy—had some serious emotional thing—and I didn't know exactly what it was either. And I shot this piece, watching them together. And I'd go to the child and go to the mother and it turned out, when they showed it to Raymond Birdwhistle, he did a better psychoanalysis of the mother and child from the visual—from the movie footage—than her therapist had ever done.

There is a certain thing about paying attention. I think it's pretty simple. When you're in the groove on something, you're sort of thinking the way they're thinking—whomever you're dealing with.

DALE: There's a short phrase that you once used as to why you got into motion picture photography after having been a still photographer. Do you remember what that phrase is?

DAVE: Remind me.

DALE: That you *"couldn't shoot stills fast enough."*

DAVE: Hey! That's good. Did I say that? That's good. That's very good. Thank you for returning it to me.

DALE: It's yours. I think I got that 30 years ago.

DAVE: No. What actually happened was that I lost interest in my still photography—things I had deliberately set up—even documentary footage. But the things that attracted me on the contact prints were accidental. Somebody going through frame. And I thought, that looks like movie footage and I think I should be shooting movies.

DALE: Can you remember where you were when we were doing *Woodstock*? Where you were when you got the call? What were your impressions at the time?

DAVE: I figured what the hell. I was loose. Wadleigh called. He said, "It's a loose situation. We'll go, and if there's funding and if there's anything worth shooting, we'll shoot it. Otherwise, we'll have an interesting weekend." And it was my first rock-and-roll concert, for that matter. I wasn't into shooting rock and roll at the time.

DALE: Really?

DAVE: No, I had never shot rock and roll at the time—in my memory. I'm so nervous having to admit this. But it sounded like, what the hell. And I liked working with you guys—and you were being honest about it, so I thought I'd take a chance too. We, of course, had no idea. I remember going up there and I was either in the same car with, let's see, Lenzer—Lenzer at least—and we went to a motel about ten miles away. We left all our gear there, except for the cameras, of course. And we thought we'd be back that night. And that was about four or five days before the concert. We never came back, of course, until we picked things up on the way back to New York. But I did take my two essentials, a toothbrush and a little ground cloth.

DALE: When you came to Woodstock, was there any sort of shared vision that you got—was there any sort of exchange about what to do?

DAVE: Not that I recall. I was thinking about that the other day. In fact, I said to Michael, "I'm very grateful to you that you had that little meeting beforehand." Everyone was sitting there on dry grass, and chatting about who does what. And the first thing he said was, "Go ahead, Dave—do your thing. Go ahead." And I just got up and walked away. I never even knew what planning there was. And it was exactly what I wanted; he must have read my mind.

I didn't have a big urge to shoot rock and roll at that time. I really wanted to go out and see what this interesting and really quite significant mass social situation—what was it all about and what was happening. And I was grateful to Michael for turning me loose. I went back once or twice and shot a little bit on stage, but it really wasn't—it was difficult and it wasn't the way I would like to work where I could wander around. The only way you could cover that stuff was to have a lot of cameras and rather limited individual camera movement. And it just didn't get me.

DALE: When Wads and I designed this part of it—we said okay, we need these people to do the docu side, these people to do the music side. You probably got the first call because we knew if we could entice you to get there, other people would follow you.

DAVE: Oh, you're talking about your planning ahead of time.

DALE: Yeah. This was the Saturday before. Maurice was really handling much more of the negotiations with the festival people. And Wads and I were insisting on the lip in front of the stage.

DAVE: Very smart move. I think I must have shot a little rock and roll before that because I thought that was the best move you could make. Good for you. You made, not a runway, but a shooting platform that was completely across the stage, but maybe 3 or 4 feet below so you had access.

DALE: Where did your curiosity take you?

DAVE: My simple thought was to get out there and see who's here and what's happening and start relating to the vibes. It was really my only thought. It was amazing because I must have walked at least 5 miles lateral distance out around and there were little—actually, the atmosphere in some of those little mini-festivals was actually charming and touching. You know, there were a couple of family groups that camped together and they could hear the music and they would dance there and the little kids would dance. It was a different atmosphere from the happening down there on the big hillside.

DALE: Go through what you considered some of your stronger pieces were.

DAVE: Oh, the hairdresser. It was serendipitous, but it wasn't necessarily a strong piece—it was simply happenstance. But, by the way, that piece—that thing I did shooting the couple going up in the tall grass and making out and then getting up, the guy turning his hat around. I was cued into that by a black still photographer—a *Life* photographer—and I don't remember what his name was. *[Joe Louw, who had taken the photographs on the motel balcony in Memphis of the Martin Luther King assassination.]* I had run out of assistants and I was changing my own magazines up in the semi and we're looking out in the back and he said, "Look at that guy, I think something's going to happen." And I looked over, and I agreed with him so I just threw the magazine on and began shooting that couple. I shot the whole thing on one magazine—11 minutes. In the middle of it, they got farther away and I left the camera running and pulled the magazine off and slapped another one on and I changed the lens —there was a long zoom lens on there—and then they went back and finished the deal. At that time, we had this instruction for the lab that said "Save tail" and I wrote it in big letters on the outside of the can. That was the other lawsuit besides Port-O-San. They tried to get me to go to Toronto and I was going to Samoa at the moment so I gave them a little deposition.

DALE: Well, I know that we helped you a lot in the post-production of that because when we asked the optical house—we asked them to "bracket" it. Shoot it in focus, semi out of focus and more out of focus because we knew that something would happen. And when we looked at the three versions delivered by the optical house, we knew we couldn't use the one that was in focus because we knew we would be sued if we put that out, so the big debate was between Bracket #2 and Bracket #3 and we finally opted for Bracket #3.

DAVE: You did? That's why it was out of focus! You never told me. Do you remember why he sued? He was a hairdresser in Montreal and he thought he would lose his clientele if they found out that he'd been throwing it to a lady. You never heard that? The lawyers told me.

DALE: You worked up at the information booth, didn't you?

DAVE: I thought the phone-home people were more poignant, more interesting to me. I heard a lot about people losing people.

DALE: You were up in a helicopter. Describe that.

DAVE: Well, it happened that I was very interested to do it because I had walked so much of the terrain and seen all of these groups and I wanted to see the overall. But first I thought I couldn't shoot it because the only access I had to shoot out of the helicopter was like an old GM car with the flip window and I just had to squeeze the lens out that little slot. I couldn't take a door off. So I happened to have a 10mm lens with me which I never used anymore, but I had it there and so I put that on and I was just able to get it out there and get a clear shot. I hope it was a clear shot at least.

Even though I had walked over so much of the terrain and had seen the venue from so many angles already, it was almost breathtaking when you got up there and looked down. And even from altitude I couldn't get the whole thing in one frame. And of course, it's better not to. Coming over from one quarter or another, coming down over where the crowd just seems to go on forever and you end up crossing

Bill Pierce

Make love, not war

the stage, well that's more impressive— more interesting.

DALE: Describe your recollections of the Port-O-San sequence. You started shooting over his shoulder and your first question to him was ...?

DAVE: He was dealing with extraordinary diligence with the problem at hand. He was scrubbing these toilet seats around and around—sloshing disinfectant here and there and just working away and I realized he was a very sincere, honest, dedicated worker. And I said, just as a way to lighten it up a little for my own sake, "You're getting a little behind on your work, aren't you." He says, "Oh, yeah. Gotta keep it nice for the kids. Got a son here and a son in Vietnam ..." and it went on

Bill Pierce

Communications central

from there. I liked him, he was a nice man.

DALE: You had the instinct to stay shooting; somehow you knew there was somebody else. Do you remember that?

Bill Pierce

Appeals for vegetarianism

DAVE: Yeah, one of the other—there was another Port-O-San next to it or something. And we sort of ran out of conversation with Mr. Port-O-San and I was aware of this other Port-O-San building next to it, so I thought I'd drift over there and see what happens. And an honest-to-God, certified, flipped-out character came out—with his eyes crossed and clouds of ganja—and he says, "You want a hit?" And I said, "Not right now."

DALE: "I'm working," was your line.

DAVE: Yeah, "I'm working." And that made sense to him. If you have to work, Jesus, you have to put it off.

DALE: Tell me about some of the others. It's Monday morning, you're at the back of the stage with Hendrix.

DAVE: Well, of course, I was completely blown away by Hendrix. It was like the distillation of the music and the whole political—we haven't talked about that—but the whole importance of Woodstock. With McNamara, the emotional part relating to Vietnam and to the division in the country over Vietnam and between the young people who were the idealistic citizens fighting LBJ and the generals.

I mean, they knew it was wrong and they also knew they were in danger, personally. Their lives were in danger, in the sense of disruption at least. And it was completely wrong. Hendrix just made a distillation of the intense emotions that really were at the heart of the Woodstock trip to me. And I think a large percentage of the people there.

At any rate, when he finished, I think they left the tape playing back over the empty stage. I had been watching it from backstage, then I went up on the stage and the last thing you saw of him was that huge crowd there and he was playing, and the next cut is my shot of the sun shining over the stage—it was sort of a visual intensification of that distorted guitar at the end there—and there was an empty stage and only a few scattered people where there had been hundreds of thousands.

And then I went out and photographed people, the few remaining people, the two nuts eating watermelon with a hunting knife, eating in the mud, and the girl with the parasol who was just tripped out and walking around in circles with the parasol—and some others, I wish I could remember them all. But it was very interesting to me. I did shoot that with a bug-eyed lens which distorted it, but we all felt distorted. We felt we'd been emotionally put in a different place by the whole experience.

DALE: Did we glamorize, glorify drugs?

DAVE: No way. By the way, I went briefly into the tent, into the overdose tent, and it was pitiful. That's all. They were just stupid. Stupid. The interesting people never got in there. This was just a dumb minor contingent. They had nothing to do with the emotional context of the whole festival. The drugs were a minor subtext.

DALE: What about Wavy Gravy—you said he was important.

DAVE: He was important. He was very important. I met him again recently and he is still a charming and amazingly productive and ethical person, but at Woodstock he was a lifesaver, literally to me. I was filled up on Wavy Gravy's oatmeal, his free lunch. But his emotional contribution to the festival I thought was important. You remember at times there was a situation that could have gotten more emotional or more destructive and they would just put him up there and he would talk to the crowd. He was just a great influence. He's got a charming and patient way too. He didn't invent himself for *Woodstock*. He came from some kind of idealistic community that he'd organized in Arizona somewhere. He lives in Berkeley and he has a wonderful summer camp among other things where he gets kids out there and exposes them to things they never saw. He's just a fascinating guy.

DALE: What about Nixon and Wadleigh?

DAVE: Yeah, Nixon and Wadleigh got along great. I took over (from Wadleigh) on Nixon's second presidential bid. Wadleigh had started shooting with him and—Wadleigh with his wildest hippie mode—he and Nixon had a splendid rapport. They got along very well—and when I showed up—

DALE: This had to be 1968.

DAVE: I spent three weeks with him. I don't know where Wadleigh went, but he was sorely missed by Mr. Nixon. We didn't get along too well. All he could ever say to me was, "Oh, I see you've got your longshoreman's cap on today," or something like that. Wadleigh had long hair then. Oh, yeah. He was a wild man. It was very interesting that somehow they had something—Nixon's relationship with Wadleigh was strictly personal friendship!

DAN TURBEVILLE: *KEEP FEEDING EACH OTHER!*

(Another member of the Cornell "Mafia," Danny was summoned to the site to help translate music to cameramen. His work on the movie would eventually lead to work on the album with Eric Blackstead, producer of the two albums.)

It sounded like a great idea. I had just graduated college in June, and was kicking back at home in New Jersey with no immediate plans. Drive upstate and help my college band mate Eric Blackstead work on a film of a music festival? Yeah! Eric had the gig as musical director, and the bands were big names. Things were happening fast and I was needed in New York City tomorrow. Sounded like an adventure I wouldn't want to miss!

My gig was to liaise between the entertainers and cameramen, helping the latter become quickly familiar with unknown subject matter.

Astounding to think about it amidst today's culture, but no one filmed rock groups then. Only Pennebaker had made a film out of music. My understanding of music and the groups' stage presentations could really make a difference to the quality of the finished film. To boot I would meet some of my heroes. This was a good match.

Our pal Brooksie (Alex Brooks) was flying up from Mexico to take a look at financing the film because to date, no one else had money for this "risky business." At least my expenses were covered. We were leaving tomorrow. My first job was to drive my car to Kennedy Airport, pick up cameramen and drive to a place I'd never been, a town named Woodstock.

It was so unexpected, that stage in this setting. It seem larger than any barn ever built and so very open, nothing would be hidden. From 100 yards out, I identified Bill Graham, who never spoke below a shout and never shouted without moving some part of his body.

Peter Townshend was surly when I interviewed The Who before their set. Although no one said anything, I got the sense it was because they were waiting much too long before they played. Thirty years later I read in a newspaper article that he was just coming off drugs at Woodstock and had little patience for all that were around him. Rashomon.

Tim Hardin was so smacked out he had to be physically guided from back to the front of the stage to his microphone to sing. We all used drugs, but this was not how anyone I knew wanted it to be. It was the saddest moment of my experience watching this gifted interpreter going down. Tim's wrenching despondent interpretation of "If I Were a Carpenter" was as pure and timeless in his way as was Joan Baez's inspiring and soaring performance of "Swing Low, Sweet Chariot," hours later in the crisp night air. Unscripted and unrehearsed, I believe these two artists presented for us the quintessential lows and highs of existence. I believe they unwittingly played out the thought-provoking dilemma of humankind as it is examined in all the great literature. Until this moment I have never mentioned this observation, that the concert and the movie presented us with incredible dramatic theatre.

There was nothing in the rock-and-roll lexicon to describe Crosby, Stills & Nash. I hadn't seen any of their previous bands live but had heard all their records. As the cool light mist lashed gently through the red, white, and blue stage lights shining down upon David Crosby's fringed jacket in the 4am morning slot, it seemed that we would listen to their harmonies for a lifetime.

Henry Diltz

Graham Nash and David Crosby singing "Judy Blue Eyes"

If you had told me, as I jumped up and raised my hands into the air with 500,000 others when Sly and the Family Stone vamped and paraded on stage with the energy of ten USC marching bands, that several years later I would meet Sly in his experimental West Coast recording studio and be talking to a man descending into drug hell, I would have told you to smoke another one, Jack.

Jimi Hendrix changed the way every guitar player reached for their ax and, after Woodstock, changed the way American kids heard "The Star Spangled Banner." I was one of those kids. He took psychedelia out of your dreams and put it in your face: "Hey man, do you think?" How could you not question your government's policies now? He did it all without effort. Swaying turquoise beads dangling from a light buckskin jerkin, fine jewelry and strength, his eyes looked right into your brain, speaking powerful truth after truth if you read the bones.

Amongst those of us who remembered Woodstock, were there, wanted to be there, were in some way touched by it, there is a camaraderie. This was one of the most deliciously productive periods for rock-and-roll music, a common denominator for youth everywhere. Only a few world events since, such as the destruction of the Berlin Wall and Tiananmen Square, have produced the same euphoric "Keep Feeding Each Other!" utopian sensibility. This total lack of pretense, and desire to enjoy living, shows itself every now and then in my life through unexpected kindnesses and unsolicited appreciation. It always surprises me, knowing what I know about people today.

Music Assistant Danny Turbeville

29.

ALEX BROOKS: *Have $100K, Will Travel*

(In our wild scramble to find money to make the film, we contacted everyone we knew, including "Brooksie," also from Cornell's Cayuga Lake, and his trusty trust fund. He was Eric Blackstead's buddy—part of the Cornell "Mafia.")

After a crazy year owning a nightclub in Managua, Nicaragua—it was August 1969 and I was 24—I was hanging out on the Jardín (plaza) in San Miguel de Allende, Mexico, just north of Michoacan. I was only "thinking about" returning to the States.

About 9 one evening, I was helping some new friends from Iowa City buy some blankets, when my brother came hurrying toward us. The Hidalgo Hotel had received a long-distance call with a message to call New York collect. This was a big deal for the little Mexican pensione, and the hotel family had all turned out to watch when I returned to the Hidalgo. The phones were fairly primitive in the Guanajuato mountains and there was worry that an eventful call to New York City would not be possible.

Miraculously, the call went through to my Cornell buddy, Black (Eric Blackstead, *Woodstock* album producer-to-be), who was wheeling and dealing in a movie production office on Broadway. An excellent blues guitarist and singer, Black had been hired as music director for a documentary film to be made of a gigantic rock concert north of New York City. Although I'd been on the road for several years, he knew I had some money socked away and he wanted me to help them out. The Wadleigh-Maurice production company didn't have enough cash to buy the film for the three-day event. They didn't want to sell out to a big company like Warner Brothers. They wanted to have absolute control of the artistic content of the documentary and my investment of $100,000 would keep the production "in the family."

I was skeptical in that little hotel lobby with the Hidalgo family milling excitedly about. That $100K was the grubstake for my next nightclub and this all sounded a bit overwhelming. Black started reeling off the names of the bands that were to appear—Janis Joplin, The Band, Hendrix, Country Joe, Sly, Butterfield, Richie Havens, Joan Baez and so on—music heroes all. Danny (Turbeville) and Doc (Dave Robinson—Cornell pals who had played in my club in St. Thomas, V.I., in 1967) were on the team, too. He said, "At least come see the show." I was sort of hooked.

Never being one to pass up an adventure, I said, "OK, I'll be there." This was Tuesday night and the festival started on Friday! A third-class bus left for Mexico City at 2am. I started throwing my clothes in my knapsack, and was on my way.

I met Black in a crummy office building. The rooms of Paradigm Films looked like they belonged to a destitute Mike Hammer. They immediately pitched me the concept for the film—a mammoth documentary (possibly 10 hours long) which would define our generation. Their equipment included a German editing machine, which could synchronize up to three different images of the performances for a unique look in documentary history.

Larry Johnson

A producer, Dale Bell, gave a calmer, more practical impression, explaining that they only had enough up-front money to bring film crews from L.A. or to buy the unexposed film. As of that time, they had no film. Warner Brothers had evidently offered to finance this, but then THEY would own the film. I got a subtle feeling that Bell didn't think that would be such a bad idea.

Associate producer Dale Bell with producer Bob Maurice, sorting it out, or trying to.

The other producer, Bob Maurice, was pacing around the office, muttering and waving his arms. This guy seemed to be the most uncool and unbalanced executive I'd ever seen. Perhaps he recognized my skepticism and thus unwillingness to invest. It was immediately apparent that this project was much larger than the likes of us could pull off. Also, it seemed that Warner Brothers would have a lot deeper pockets and could get the finished feature into distribution a lot better than I could. I said I'd have to pass on buying into the film.

The last leg of our drive to the site was by a dirt road that wove through the now-famous resort community and then leafy woods and small fields, until bursting out at the bottom of the hilly field that belonged to Max Yasgur. The first thing I saw was a big old crane, manned by a tie-dyed hippie. He was finishing the light towers astride the stage, which was also in the final stages of construction; 4 x 8s of plywood were being passed up by hand for the surface of the 16' high stage. A few desultory hippies were building a plank fence across the front of the stage. This was to be the fence that encircled the site. I could tell, that fence was never going to make it around the site, even if they worked all weekend. Not many tickets were going to be collected at this event.

I checked in at the Butler Sound truck where Black was stationed. Gaffers were not arriving from California, as anticipated, to run the electric and communications lines for the film crews. I was given some tools and wire and a rough map of the stage and towers and I got to work. (I had done some wiring in my nightclubs.) From a central box beneath the stage, I ran Romex cable up both towers and to four points along the front of the stage, using baling wire to secure it to the risers. The union electrician who was installing the circuit box was shaking his head at the arrangements but was good-natured about the half-assedness of the entire proceedings. Once I had installed the receptacle boxes, he turned on the juice and, to our amazement, THEY WORKED! With some helpers we dug a trench out into the middle of the field to the mixing board and left it for the audio team to fill. Mission accomplished, I met some of the Hog Farm folks who had been building the fence and we cooled out together.

The rest of the film and sound people arrived early in the morning and we did a lot of unloading and unraveling. Rumors swirled about various aspects of non-completion of the stage, the fence, the roof and almost everything else. I followed one of the hand-held camera crews with extra film, and there was a now historic moment. When John Morris announced to the show's young promoters that it would have to be a free concert, there was some weeping, which I believe was edited out of the film. It seemed like the end of the world to them and I was glad I'd held on to my $100K.

My spot was on the platform across the front of the stage where the film crew and photographers operated from. I carried film canisters, Nagra recorders, cameras and duct tape between the trucks in back and the cameramen. After the rain started that evening (during Joan Baez's set?) my ungrounded electrics caused a bit of a buzz to pass through the metal risers but, as far as I know, no one got any bad shocks. Arlo Guthrie and Joan Baez hung out with us on the camera platform to see if the rain would abate, but it just kept coming and the show was stopped. That Upstate rain has a different smell and feel than the tropical kind and it made me feel at home, rained out and all. Getting out of the site was now impossible, so that night, I found my 4 x 8 up under the stage and slept in relative dryness.

The morning dawned and the rain had stopped. During the night, a muddy couple of flower children had crawled onto my plywood bunk to sleep. We talked about the amazing scene a while, then they split for the Hog Farm breakfast. Fortunately, the film team had coffee and doughnuts, which really hit the spot, AND my clothes were almost dry! Looking out on the field was something else again—during the night, their numbers had doubled and it really became an enormous mud party in the milky morning sunshine.

Jefferson Airplane

Eavesdropping on John Morris while he was figuring out what to do as various problems and crises arose was a special treat and insight to what really was happening. Decisions were made out there on the deck of our mighty stage-ship cruising in the roiled sea of our audience. (There were even flapping tarps, high above, to suggest the galleon illusion.) If anyone is responsible for the successful journey of the Sailing Ship *Woodstock*, it is John. He knew all those band people by their first names and had what they wanted. When the snafus were piling up, he improvised a way to apply the oil. Chip Monck's and John's calm, deep voices had a great influence in keeping everything cool.

We knew WE had a tiger by the tail as the bands were having trouble getting to the site due to highways being clogged. It was known on stage that they had gotten the National Guard to send some helicopters, but the crowd didn't know. The Vietnam War was at its height and everyone knew the chop-chop-chop of their rotors from movies and the news. From beyond the hills, we heard that sound steadily increasing until three Hueys in phalanx appeared above the crowd, aimed at the stage. Quiet settled over the throng as heads turned to watch those dark machines coming in low and fast. Many of us felt like we were Mekong villagers for a moment. Were they going to open fire? Quickly, Morris got on the mike and announced to the crowd their purpose, and cheers erupted out of that moment of doubt.

Then the helicopters started arriving with the bands and still the audience swelled as Country Joe McDonald did his impromptu opening for Saturday's entertainment. About this time, Danny, Black and Doc started taking me along to interview the bands before their sets. All of them were both elated and awed by the size and intensity of the audience that was looking down at us.

Canned Heat played one of the greatest sets I've ever seen and the looks on their faces said everything about the power of music. Pins and needles ran up my back as the swelling crowd and bands interacted. What a great time to be HIGH! As the helicopters roared in and out behind the stage, ferrying rock-and-roll heroes, someone commented that this was OUR Flower Power L.Z. (landing zone) of the Vietnam War.

We were raving for PEACE!

Straw-like, long hair under a sweatband, Wadleigh showed no fear. Sometimes in a white peasant shirt (Mexico!) and sometimes bare-chested, he was a dynamic part of the festival we saw. It took balls to do that and those close shots are a big thing in what makes the movie bold and personal.

Wavy Gravy and Chip Monck, "Feeding Each Other"

At some point, it became an ordeal to turn around and look at the audience. Many people on the camera platform mentioned it—800,000 eyes, all of them SMASHED and looking at You! It gave me this drifty feeling, like I was going to float away. Good stuff, all right! I sat for about 10 minutes at the back of the stage, drinking with Joe Cocker just before he went on, both of us marveling at the crowd looking back at us. He said he really needed some fortification to face that throng. As he left to go on, he gave me a wonderfully limp English handshake and said, perhaps he'd fortified a little TOO much. As I watched him sing, he certainly WAS loose, howling and playing his air-guitar.

I got to sit with Janis Joplin and share her bottle of Tequila Crema, talking about Mexico. Like everyone, she was amazed by the crowd. I got the smile of a lifetime from her as she walked out on stage.

Sly and the Family Stone were my favorite performance of the whole show. They were so loose and funny before they went on, I camped out between some cases and stared. They had FUN and steps and routines and blew that soggy crowd away. I think they were one of the best visuals of the movie, too. Melanie played a great set but we missed shooting her. Her song, "Lay Down Candles in the Rain," might have been the most relevant song of the concert, a casualty of not enough film.

Towards the final dawn, Monday morning, I was running on autopilot. Coffee and that Smoke were all that were keeping me on my feet. I was hauling coffees and sandwiches up the towers to the camera crews and it's a good thing I was immortal in those days. Jimi Hendrix was to be that last act and we had saved a lot of film for his set.

The sun came up and we were going to take a breakfast break during the next-to-the-last act, called Sha-Na-Na. Nobody knew who they were, except that they had something to do with the Columbia University Glee Club.

WOW! When they hit the stage, coffee cups went flying! Bleary-eyed and amused, the entire film team said, "We'd better get THIS!" The band's brazen energy got us right up to speed and the hand-held crews got what is another high point of the film.

After a pause, Hendrix arrived at the back of the stage as high as The Himalayas. His eyes were as big as peyote buttons and the call went out for "Valium." Once he settled down a bit, he motored right onto the stage and took off with everyone running to catch him. Jimi Hendrix was such an imposing figure with his incredible guitar licks, he turned the place to butter. Power, Power, The Bonneville Dam! When his guitar neck moved, the crowd moved. All of us on stage were pushed back to the edge. Even Wadleigh, who had had his hand-held camera in the faces of all the greats that weekend, was pushed off onto the platform. Finally, it was a time of introspection and contemplation. Relief was also a common emotion on stage. We had been a part of the historic cultural-social event of our time and LIVED!

The sound track and records did come out well (as did as the film!) and I'm very proud of them, considering what they had to work from. Black was the first of the Players to make money from *Woodstock*, and he earned it. A few years later, royalties in hand, he visited me in St. Thomas where I had another club. After an afternoon of piña coladas one day, he left a check from Atlantic Records for $82,000 at the Morningstar Beach Bar. When we went back the next day, Bobsie the bartender had it for him. (He didn't think it was real anyway!) It occurs to me that being a Player in the *Woodstock* Family changed their lives forever. Whatever fame and/or fortune came their way, they couldn't put on The Suit or kiss the corporate butt again.

30

HART PERRY: *One Very Additional Camera*

 (As the youngest cameraman, Hart seized golden opportunities, then and later on in his life. His fascination with the process of motion picture photography led him to create pixelation, one frame at a time, from one of the Woodstock towers.)

I was a film student at Columbia University when I heard about the Woodstock concert. I was interested in attending the concert as a fan, and member of a rock band, but had made no actual plans to attend. What held my interest at that time was to develop abstract expressionist ideas in film. I had a Bolex camera and was developing my film, printing it, and animating it. I needed an optical printer to put my film together. As I called around New York filmmakers in pursuit of a cheap optical printer, I was given Michael Wadleigh's number.

I called him up, made my case about an optical printer and he replied that he couldn't help me. He did ask me whether I could shoot for him on the Woodstock concert. Of course I could shoot. If he had asked me whether I wanted to be a musician, painter or filmmaker, I would not have been able to give him an answer. But I could definitely shoot rock-and-roll. Shooting gave you the best seat in the house. He told me to bring my camera to Bethel, New York, a day before the concert.

I loaded up my gear into my girlfriend's Dodge Dart and we started to hit heavy traffic en route to Bethel. A lot of people were walking because traffic was backed up and cars were parked haphazardly. We made our way to the stage and asked about the filming—Michael Wadleigh had sent us. I met Michael, reported for duty. He sent me to Dale Bell to take care of business—the salary was $125 flat. Fine with me.

There was a meeting scheduled with the cameramen at the side of the stage. Michael explained his strategy for covering the concert. At that point his company was producing the film on spec. I quickly realized that I was the youngest and least experienced cameraman. So did Wadleigh. My assignment was to get shots of the crowd. There was a tractor trailer where the film equipment was stored and where I could get film. When a huge crowd assembled, we knew that we were recording history. From that point until the festival was over, almost every waking moment I saw through a lens which I tried to keep in focus and at the right F stop.

I climbed up on the scaffolding of one of the speaker towers and set my camera up on a tripod. I proceeded to shoot single frames for several hours. The shot appears on one of the screens in the film. The crowd in the back looks as if it were in real time because the people did not move over the time I was animating the crowd. Avenues of people surfing like a stream appear in the animation. These avenues were not apparent in real time. Just the people in the front of the crowd were animated. I also did shots with dissolves made in the camera of people in the crowd, including some topless women.

I found that being the least important cameraman had some artistic advantages aside from being assigned to the crowd shots. When it rained, the cameramen huddled in the truck. I was instructed to go out into the rain to see if anything worth shooting was happening. I got some of the classic mud slide footage.

One memorable stage moment was The Who's set. I had a good shot of Abbie Hoffman's acid ranting to the crowd in the middle of the set. Suddenly Pete Townshend's guitar came into frame, whacking Abbie in the back of the head. He scampered off the stage and climbed over the barricade which separated the crowd from the stage, and disappeared. My negative feelings about this gratuitous violence were mitigated by their powerful performance.

Another moment was Jimi Hendrix's performance as the sun was rising. My shot was a master of the stage from the crowd. At one point I started to run out of raw stock. Here was an historic performance and I would not have the film to record it. My girlfriend had left a while ago to get more stock. She was nowhere to be seen. I zoomed in on the stage to see if I could spot her. I forgot that the camera was rolling. There she was, dancing and sharing a snort with somebody. I didn't realize that I had filmed the scene until I saw the film.

My only gripe with *Woodstock* is with my credit. I got a "special thanks" rather than "additional camera." A number of my shots were used in the film so a "special thanks" is an inappropriate credit, even for the youngest and least important cameraman on the *Woodstock* film.

31

DON LENZER: *A Vision for Antonia*

(Don wasn't in his usual place at the Chelsea Hotel when I found him. Don's peripatetic camera work had taken him to California just prior to Woodstock. Luckily, I was able to bring him back so he could count this as one of the many seminal events of the sixties he had particpated in and document-ed for the world.)

We were up high, very high, maybe 12 feet, though it felt like 20—Richard Chew and I—high up in a tractor trailer looking down at the countless sleeping bags that were half submerged in the mud below; in the distance about as far as the eye could see, 300-or-so thousand rain-drenched spectators. But our eyes were drawn at that instant to the mud below. I've often thought of that moment and many others connected to the events of those few days that took place nearly 30 years ago. Lately it's become an exercise in memory, and the truth and fantasy of it are not always easy to separate. I'm not sure any more if it was Richard or I who said it as we stood up there on the second day of the festival, but one of us said, "One day when we look back on this, I guess we'll be happy we were here." How little we imagined then the enormous impact those events would have on our lives.

Thirty years ago. I'm astonished at how fast the time has gone by. It's not such a long time in big historical terms, but it's long in terms of a man's life, my life. But the exercise of remembering is an interesting one, a little game I sometimes play with myself. And I even felt a little guilty spending as much time as I did reflecting on it. Its importance seemed to pale next to the Civil Rights Movement; next to Vietnam; next to the way a generation of German youth was trying to deny the legacy of fascism and the Holocaust; next to the events of May '68 in France; next to the coup in Chile that with the help of our government crushed democracy in that country. I realize, though, that Woodstock was both a real and complex event as well as a mythic presence in the narrative of my generation. It was the biggest free gathering ever of peace and music, ecstatic community and solidarity. But it was also "hip capitalism," bad trips and a muddy, debris-strewn disaster zone. And no matter what other young people had gone through in other times, this was part of our reality, and I think it's not a bad exercise to try to make some sense of it.

I was in California, my native California, when I received a call about shooting at Woodstock. I'd just finished producing a film for public TV about student radicals at Stanford University and had never even heard of the festival plans and really wasn't in the mood to return to New York to work on some pop music film. It just didn't mean much to me at the time. I loved the music, particularly the San Francisco and British varieties, and I'd been excited and somewhat influenced by D.A. Pennebaker's *Monterey Pop*. Even when my girlfriend told me I had to do it, that it was going to be the biggest music festival ever, bigger than Monterey, bigger than the Isle of Wight, I remained unmoved. But I was impressed by the prospect of getting together for a multiple-camera shoot with a good many of the heaviest documentary cameramen (and in those days they were all men) in the country. Although competition was a value on which we didn't place a premium in those days and the feeling of camaraderie was truly great among those of us who were relative newcomers, I'm sure I wanted to come up against the "top guns."

There's something you have to understand about that time that seems to have no parallel with the present. It's not that we were any more ambitious than young filmmakers are today. But there was something in the air then, something that led us to believe we were part of a great transforming force in the life of our society and culture. And the music, which was new and completely exciting, had a lot to do with it. We were engaged as cinematographers, not merely in describing it but in interpreting it—in a matter of speaking, in "playing visual rock and roll." That was terribly important to us.

Except for one, the cameramen who shot at Woodstock were all relative newcomers. The one exception was a man by the name of David Myers with whom I drove up to the festival from New York. I'm stunned to think that David was only a few years younger then than I am now. It seems like only yesterday that we were driving to Bethel together and that David a couple of days later shot what was arguably the most famous and best scene in the film, the one with the Port-O-San man. David, I understand, is a healthy 85 now, which only means that time flies and that you better live it well if you have the good fortune, and from everything I hear, David has. I remember him talking a lot on the drive about his wife, Barbara, who's an artist and was a model for the photographer Imogen Cunningham. The wonderful black-and-white image that I later found of Barbara as *Savonarola's Look* in a Cunningham monograph will be etched in my mind forever.

I remember being on the stage a lot, filming a lot of performers and being connected to what was going on, feeling a part of it, of the music, in a way I rarely have since. It started out hot and never let up, right there next to Richie Havens, his foot filling the frame, beating out a rhythm that seemed never to subside. Anyway that's the way I remember it. It was easier for me there on stage than to make forays out into the crowd.

For David Myers, I think, it was just the opposite, and he captured some of the most wonderful moments of the film out there. I remember him telling me that the only performer he really longed to film was Janis Joplin. I wanted to film her too, but when I got the chance, the electric black-and-white images of her great performance in Pennebaker's *Monterey Pop* were so lodged in my conscious that I think I was inhibited from doing anything really original, was trying too hard maybe to compete with someone else's work rather than becoming fully engaged with what was going on, as I most often did when I was filming on stage.

I think I chose to wander most of the time through some of the more bucolic spots during the moments when I was offstage rather than wade into the crowd. I remember in particular floating on a pond in a rowboat with the young soundman Bruce Pearlman, filming the now famous nude bathing scene. I remember feeling a little uncomfortable with our intrusiveness. And when I heard people call to us to join them in the water, I became really concerned that they wouldn't accept our friendly refusal, but would simply pull us and our camera equipment in with them. But that fear was never visible in the images we captured that day, images that became almost iconic of the spontaneity, naturalness and freedom of a whole generation.

Everything seemed to coalesce in Jimi Hendrix's performance at the end of the festival. And it also seemed to inspire me to capture some of the most incredible footage I've ever shot. By the time I heard the first few bars of his brilliant, twisted "Star Spangled Banner," I was totally involved, at one with the music and performer.

I was on automatic pilot. It was the "zen art of cinematography," and I was finding visual equivalents for the music that would surely re-create for future spectators the amazing experience, my experience, of being there, and they'd have the most privileged seats in the house. There was one problem, though, and it was a big one. No one would ever see most of the incredible footage I shot of Hendrix's performance because I was so into it that I didn't realize I had run out of film long before he had finished playing.

My seven-and-a-half-year-old daughter, Antonia, loves rock and roll. She hasn't seen *Woodstock* yet, but I think she'll soon be ready for it and I'm looking forward to her response. She's heard about it, though, from my wife, Bettina, who was a sixteen-year-old in Germany at the time it came out. She tells us that seeing the movie as a teenager was one of the things that drew her to America, and therefore is partly responsible for our finding each other and indirectly responsible for Antonia coming into the world. That's a powerful connection between *Woodstock* and the two people I cherish most. I don't know whether it's completely or even partly true, but it makes a good story and I like to believe it and I like to tell it to my daughter.

What I do know for sure, though, is that the idea of Woodstock is very much alive for those of us who were there and for many who only heard about it or saw the movie. Surely it represented a "vision of fulfilled desire" that stood in such contrast to the boredom and flatness and competitive isolation of so many of our parents' lives. It was a vision of something—dare I say it?—snappier, more colorful, more erotic, more generous, more equitable, more morally worthy of us, that I hope will animate some future generations, perhaps even Antonia's.

Don Lenzer

Antonia Lenzer waiting to view Woodstock

32

JONATHAN DALE BELL: *MY PARENTS BECOME . . . DIFFERENT*

(At the time of the Festival, my son Jonathan was eight years old. I wanted my family to enjoy this outing. Maybe, I thought, all three of the kids might be able to come up to go camping! Maybe the film team would not be working too hard, right? We couldn't film everything after all; just here and there, RIGHT? Maybe we will all have a fun picnic? But another part of me knew better. The three boys would have to stay home.)

About a week before my parents left for Woodstock they sat us down to have a talk with us, explaining that they were going away for a while and that Grandmother was going to come and take care of us. I think we were all a little worried and bewildered. We promised to be good and obey the basic rules of survival and mind our Grandmother, which was pretty easy to do. They kissed us goodbye and left for WOODSTOCK.

We were so happy when Da and Mommy returned, since an eight-year-old kid can only go so long without his Mommy. She was smiles, hugs and kisses and we all ran to her at once, holding on, not wanting to let go. I think she was wearing some different clothes that I'd never seen before. Pretty soon after that there were a lot of new or "different" clothes added to the wardrobe.

The guise that comes to mind was a pair of bells as in bell-bottom jeans tied with a leather fringed belt with beads woven into it and a white tank top with a black silk-screen peace sign in the middle of it and her head topped with a macramé headband. My father's entrance was also dramatic in that he too had changed in some way in less than a week's time. The one item I remember particularly he wore around his neck: a set of beads made from wood, some in the shape of skinny black thread-spools with tan cylinders in between them. I asked him about them and he said they were "love beads."

Suddenly a whole new style of music began to infiltrate the Bell household. Some of the most notable new bands for me were The Who, Crosby Stills Nash & Young, Santana, Jefferson Airplane, Jimi Hendrix, Sha-Na-Na, and Sly and the Family Stone.

I've since seen the film at least a dozen times and listened to the albums well over a hundred times. I still get that visceral feeling of being there, even though I wasn't. I would play the three LPs constantly, and knew how to sing all the songs and all of the dialogue including the stage announcements: "Alan Fay, Alan Fay . . . would you please come to the information booth, please, your friend is very ill . . . please come to the information booth, man, it's a bummer, please . . . " When I was in high school some of my friends and I made up a fictitious student named Alan Fay and had one of our buddies from another school enroll as him, so we could enjoy the announcements over the school PA system searching for him when he failed to show up for class. "Alan Fay, please report to the principal's office." "Oh yeah, we just saw him at lunchtime." We kept that joke going for a long time. I think he almost graduated with us.

Dale and Anne Bell with Jonathan, David and Andrew after Woodstock

PART IV: OK, WHERE'S THE MOVIE?

33.

THELMA SCHOONMAKER: *OVERWHELMED BUT UNDAUNTED*

(On site, "T" and Marty Scorsese were Michael's Assistant Directors. "T" took over as Supervising Editor as soon as we returned to New York with our nearly 900 cans of exposed raw stock. She would guide all the editing, then follow through with the exhibition of the film in some of the foreign theaters.)

DALE: What was the process that you and Michael went through, as you had 160-odd hours of stuff to deal with?

THELMA: After we got over the exhaustion of filming at Woodstock, the first thoughts we had were how to make it all work—how to intersperse the documentary footage with the concert footage. Finding a way to project the work of all six cameramen on the stage simultaneously was terribly important, because we had committed ourselves to using multiple images in the final film. We felt if we could see all the cameramen's work on a particular song at the same time, we would begin to get an idea of whether or not putting multiple images up on the screen would work. I guess it was Larry Johnson who figured out that we could start off six projectors at one time with one switch and they would stay in sync.

Larry Johnson

Director Michael Wadleigh, Editor Martin Scorsese, and Supervising Editor Thelma Schoonmaker, with a little help from W. C. Fields

149

I think we were all a bit overwhelmed by the amount of footage we had shot and the enormity of the work that had to be done to make it into a film.

Martin Scorsese and Michael Wadleigh had hoped to be able to direct the many cameramen on the stage through headsets, and plan concerted camera moves at some dramatic moment in a song. But for some reason the cameramen were getting loud squeals in their headsets, and you would see them ripping their headsets off simultaneously, which effectively put an end to any attempts to plan camera moves.

The high humidity and rainstorms caused us tremendous problems because the moisture caused the magazines holding the film to jam frequently. You would see a cameraman rip off his magazine and call out for another one. His jammed magazine would be passed to me and I would give it to the incredible group of people we had loading magazines under the stage—pregnant wives, children, old friends, all organized by John Binder. Another freshly loaded magazine of film would be handed up to me and I would get it to the cameraman. But by the time he got that magazine on and started shooting again, there was no way to know where in the song he was, if you were trying to sync the dailies. We were unable to come up with a common sync device at the beginning of each song and so every piece of film had to be synced by eye. This was a huge job. We had three crews syncing dailies in New York 24 hours a day—including the midnight-to-dawn shift, the graveyard shift. This meant that the editing machines were never still.

I remember that Marty tried to sync up the Grateful Dead footage, which had so little light on the stage that it was almost impossible to see. He struggled and struggled to find some sync points, because he loved the group and wanted them to be in the film. But eventually the low light level and the chaos in the footage defeated him. Brian De Palma remembers coming to the editing room and watching Marty desperately trying to find some sync point, and laughingly telling him there wasn't even an image there, and that he should stop.

The logistics of dealing with all the footage were so great, that I don't think we really had an idea of what we had until we got a little bit further into the editing. Then we realized we had something special—that we had vividly captured what became, historically, a unique event. As the editing progressed, and we began interspersing the performance footage with the documentary footage, we felt that maybe we had come up with almost a new form for this kind of event. It was incredibly exciting.

I don't know, apart from *Raging Bull*, whether I'd ever been as excited on a film as I was on this one. You could feel that the film was going to have a powerful impact, even though the Warner Brothers executives didn't understand that. It was a battle to get them to understand that the film would have an audience. We knew it; we could feel it very strongly.

DALE: How did you and Michael work together?

THELMA: Michael and Marty and I, in the beginning, would screen the endless miles of dailies and decide who we would assign to cut a particular song. We had three editors working with us: Stan Warnow, Yeu-Bun Yee and Jere Huggins. Marty was editing with an assistant, and I was mainly responsible for editing the non-performance footage—the footage of all the cameramen we had out in the field shooting their brains out while the crew clustered on the stage was trying to film the performances. Marty left the film rather early on to go and bust into Hollywood. From that point on, Michael and I supervised all the editors. I also cut several performance numbers, among them Richie Havens, Joe Cocker, Ten Years After, Country Joe and the Fish, and I worked with Wadleigh on The Who and Jimi Hendrix. There were several groups that were dropped from the film, and I worked on some of those. But mainly I concentrated on the documentary footage. Wadleigh and I were constantly running edits with the editors and discussing changes.

DALE: How did you regard the performances?

THELMA: Getting the performances on film was a great feat. I think one of the reasons the movie *Woodstock* is remembered so intensely, is because the performances were recorded with some theatricality—they weren't just "covered" as sometimes happens in a situation that is so uncontrollable. It was a nightmare for us on the stage, because we had done no negotiating with the groups, who were arriving by helicopter to perform. Backstage Eric Blackstead and others were frantically trying to get the groups to allow themselves to be filmed, which wasn't easy at such short notice. In some cases, we never did get their permission.

Director Michael Wadleigh twisting to get an angle on Taj Mahal

Bill Pierce

151

I knew nothing about the music that was being performed. I had lived a good deal of my life in the Caribbean. But Wadleigh and Scorsese and Johnson were steeped in the music and they would consult, and if they had information about which songs were going to be sung, decide which ones to film. I was just madly dashing around trying to keep magazines loaded and begging Chip Monck, who was lighting the stage, to give us enough light for a good exposure.

So it was critical that Wadleigh, Johnson and Scorsese had such enthusiasm for the performers and the music. Wadleigh had an unbelievable ability to make a camera move at exactly the right time in a song, because he knew a particular chorus was coming, or a powerful lyric was about to be sung. He would time his zoom in or out, or his decision to move from one performer to another, so that we got some very dramatic moments. This takes enormous patience and skill, and excellent judgment. If we hadn't had his powerful image—basically an up angle from the front of the stage, *Woodstock* wouldn't be the film it is. He was bent over that camera, looking through the lens for almost 24 hours a day for three days. It was a superhuman effort. I really don't know how he did it.

Sometimes Wadleigh would jump up on the stage and move around the performers, and it was on one of those occasions that Pete Townshend of The Who kicked him off the stage. We told all the cameramen to stop filming, and then gradually, as The Who became engrossed in their performance, we started filming again.

All in all, the experience during the filming was rather nightmarish for me. Wadleigh would be looking through his lens and screaming, "Get us some light!" and Chip Monck would yell back, "I'm lighting for those people out there!" (He didn't understand that an important act like Janis Joplin would have to be dropped from the original film because we couldn't get a good exposure. She was lit with beautiful red light which worked for

Henry Diltz

Ted Churchill captures John Sebastian

152

the audience—but not for us.) Members of the audience would come flying over the fence separating the audience from the stage. They would be in various states of ecstasy and were dealt with beautifully by the security people, who were basically people like themselves. Someone watching the film crew said it was like watching Geronimo and a few Apaches holding off the U.S. Army. Just looking over the fence at half a million people was rather frightening at times.

Some of the performers at Woodstock never made it into the cut: Burt Sommers, Melanie and Butterfield Blues Band, which did a lovely number. We edited them, but there was so much other good material we couldn't fit groups like that in the movie.

Sometimes we had good multiple-camera footage and other times not. For example, Joe Cocker had practically no footage at all. We had Wadleigh's beautiful camera and one side angle, and sometimes an image from the rear with the gathering rainstorm evident in the sky. But we didn't need much, because his performance was so strong, and Wadleigh really knew how to shoot it.

The same thing was true of Richie Havens. We had hardly any footage on him, because he was the first performer at the festival, and many of our cameramen weren't shooting yet. The first person who edited the sequence just kept cutting to anything if they ran out of shots, almost like a newsreel way of editing a sequence. So one of my jobs was to correct that and try to give the performance power using Wadleigh's camera and a few shots of the drummers in the group. Wadleigh was standing right underneath Havens and decided to shoot right up into his toothless mouth. Many cameramen might have shied away from that angle, but Wadleigh knew that the intensity of the singing validated the tight close-up. He knew that after the first shock, it wouldn't matter that Havens didn't have any teeth.

By the time the dawn came on the third day and we had been shooting for three days with no sleep, I thought we had all gone mad when Sha-Na-Na came out doing a doo-wop number. I had never seen them and didn't realize that they were fondly recalling another period. I just thought we had all been without sleep for too long and were beginning to hallucinate. Then Jimi Hendrix came out and played that incredible set and I still wasn't sure we weren't hallucinating. The light had changed from the blue of dawn to a white morning light. It was one of the most stunning moments of my life. Even though he was working with a group that wasn't up to his standards, Hendrix performed with great assurance, and I was completely mesmerized.

After that beautiful ending to the festival, we had to pack up all the equipment, because there was no place to leave it safely. Exhausted beyond belief, we did it somehow. People were trying to steal our equipment as we tried to pull ourselves together enough to pack it up.

I think I went out in the field with Dick Pearce for a bit, filming all those battlefield images. Finally we came back and we got into someone's car and started driving back to New York. We had been wearing the same clothes for three days. We were covered in mud. We stopped at a restaurant to get something to eat for the first time in three days, and I'll never forget that Wadleigh was so tired, he crashed headfirst into his plate of spaghetti. He just passed out. He was so out of it that we couldn't get him to give us the keys to the car for a long time—finally he gave them up.

Later on, I came to enjoy the experience in retrospect, but not while I was there, I have to admit.

DALE: You guys were trying to create the sense of three days. Two nightfalls.

THELMA: Oh, definitely. Of course, we open the film with the building of the stage and we closed with the battlefield images of people walking across this landscape which had been devastated by having half a million people on it for three days, which worked so beautifully when intercut with "The Star Spangled Banner" being destroyed by Jimi Hendrix on stage. So yes, we definitely had a chronological conception.

DALE: Talk about the documentary stuff. When I talked with Tina [Hirsch], for example, she said that when she came up to apply for work, there was never a question in her mind about wanting to work on the performance. She was interested in the people. What fascination did you find in the documentary side?

THELMA: Well, we had asked to come up to Woodstock some documentary cameramen we knew and admired, like David Myers, and some we didn't know at all. David was great at wandering around the audience and laying down what was happening in a nonjudgmental way. He let the movie audience make up their minds about what he filmed.

And Al Wertheimer's fantastic interview with the young woman in the information booth will always be one of the best things I have ever worked on. Most of Al's stuff was marvelous.

David made very unconventional choices about who he chose to interview. He just had an innate sense of who would be interesting. And his interviewing style was perfect. He would have conversations with people, not interview them. For example, the way he began his conversation with the man cleaning out the Port-O-San: "Getting a little behind on your work, aren't you?" This completely disarmed the man, and made him open up. Towards the end of the scene, Dave said: "It's great of you to be doing this for these kids." And the Port-O-San man said: "I'm glad to do it. One of my sons is here and the other is in the DMZ." You couldn't have asked for more—the Vietnam War resonated throughout Woodstock Festival and the film.

These documentary cameramen were completely unsupervised. They would come back at night and tell us what they thought they had gotten. We were so freaked

Amalie Rothschild

Young guns Joe Louw, Maggie Koven, Dick Chew, Mike Wadleigh

out by trying to keep up with what was going on on the stage, that we just had to trust that we would end up with good footage. Which we did, thanks to them.

DALE: How did you orchestrate the multiple images?

THELMA: The footage determined for us which numbers should be multiple-image. It was obvious that the Ten Years After footage lent itself to flashy multiple-image manipulation. Sometimes I just took one camera's footage, had it duplicated flipped over, so that it looked as if there were bookend images of Alvin Lee.

But the carefully constructed sequences like The Who and Jimi Hendrix were more difficult to edit. It took a lot of experimenting and juggling of the footage so we could get the most theatrical feeling from the performance.

And of course, if there was no light on the performer (like Janis Joplin) there was no footage at all in the film.

Scorsese, who is a great editor by nature, did some wonderfully witty multiple-image editing with the Sha-Na-Na sequence. After he left the film, we didn't change that piece very much at all. It's a wonderful little jewel of a scene.

The same was true of the Santana sequence, which Scorsese blocked out before he left. Wonderful. Stan Warnow finished the sequence, but Scorsese had done some significant things first.

And Wadleigh had a very strong conception for The Who material. Slowing down the footage at times and freezing the frames were all his ideas. Pete Townshend destroying his guitar is a great moment in the film.

Wadleigh also had a very strong conception for the Jimi Hendrix number. First of all, he shot it so brilliantly. Imagine having the presence of mind to let Jimi Hendrix go out of frame when he crouches down playing his guitar and holding and letting him come back up into frame—after you have been awake for three days! Most cameramen would have followed Hendrix. But Wadleigh just stayed put, gambling that Hendrix, when he did come back up, would be framed correctly in his lens. He also framed Hendrix with the towers and crane behind him in such an interesting way. Then he came up with the editing concept which was brilliant. By the time Hendrix came on the stage, as I have said, I was a vegetable. But Wadleigh still had all his artistic faculties fully at work. Phenomenal.

DALE: There were a batch of accidents, of accidental inventions.

THELMA: Accident is a very important part of filmmaking. Scorsese, for example, loves it when something unexpected happens on the set that he can incorporate into a film. An accidental juxtaposing of images can often create something you don't expect. For example, one day we were getting ready for a screening, and I wanted to have two images up on the screen when Gabe Pressman is interviewing Artie Kornfeld up on the stage. So I quickly snatched the footage of the couple making love in the grass behind the stage, because it was the right length, and I thought it would compositionally work well with the interview footage. When we screened it, everyone started laughing, enjoying the odd juxtaposition, and we kept it from that point on. But at the moment, I don't think I realized how effective the combination would be.

DALE: Describe our entry into Hollywood.

THELMA: Our experience finishing the sound on the film on the Warner Brothers lot was very interesting. We arrived at the studio, a bunch of long-haired New Yorkers (mostly), and met the people who were going to mix the film for us. They had been working in the studio system for years, and we must have alarmed them. We had never seen four mixers on a sound board before: one doing the dialogue, one doing the effects, one doing the music and one swinging the tracks across the wide screen. That was a whole new idea for us.

They must have thought we were completely mad. But gradually we began to form friendships with some of the people we were working with.

At first, they were shocked at the volume we insisted on for the musical numbers. The head of the sound department at that time was George Groves, and he had mixed the first sound film [*The Jazz Singer*]. And here he was watching Joe Cocker screaming out lyrics at a music festival attended by half a million people. He told us that we couldn't record our mix at such a high level, that it would never reproduce properly in the movie theaters. But we insisted we could. He took me aside at one point after watching Joe Cocker writhing up on screen and said, "You know, you shouldn't make fun of spastics."

But the knowledge and artistry of the sound crew was invaluable to us. My favorite experience was with Ed Sheid, who had worked on many, many films during his lifetime. He was about 60, I think, and we must have seemed very strange to him. He was the sound effects editor assigned to the film, and kept asking me to let him put in studio sound effects for the storm sequence, among other things. "Oh, no!" we said, horrified. "We're cinema verité filmmakers, and we only put up on the screen what we actually filmed." "Oh, come on," he would say. "Let me put a little *Land of the Pharoahs* wind in the storm sequence and some lightning bolts from *Gone with the Wind*. I would resist and resist, but finally he took me down to his little editing room, which was a concrete cell with no carpeting on the floor. His upright Moviola clattered deafeningly, but with incredible speed he slapped pieces of track into the Moviola and then showed me how his effects would improve the storm sequence. Eventually, we agreed, and we became friends. I remember that he would dress very normally during the week, when his boss was around. But on the weekends he would wear a different-colored sock on each foot. Maybe this was his way of showing us that he could be a bit of a free spirit too. By the end we all had a great time. And Dan Wallin, the music mixer, did a great job, even though he had cotton in his ears the entire time.

The studio in the meantime told us they had no intention of releasing the film in the version we were mixing. They wanted us to shorten the film. All during the editing, they had said to us, "You have to get the film out quickly or people will forget about the event. It's just a news event," they said, "why are you fussing about it so much, spending so much time and money on complex editing—just get it out!"

But we knew we had something special and so there was a constant tug of war going on during the mix. Our producer, Bob Maurice, and Michael Wadleigh did what they could to keep the studio at bay.

When we took the film—in its original version—to the press screening in New York, things were very tense in the back of the theater where the studio executives were huddled in one corner, and Michael Wadleigh, Maurice and I were in the other. Once the film began to run there was an amazing reaction from the audience. People started dancing in the aisles. And it was clear that the film was affecting people in the way we thought it would.

Suddenly, someone tapped me on the shoulder, and I jumped because of all the nervous tension. It was Ted Ashley, the head of the studios. He said, "Okay, you're right. It does work at this length." It was a huge relief. The film was eventually cut by the studio, but at least it got its chance in the first release.

34

TINA HIRSCH: *People Are Always Fascinating to Me*

(Tina's sense of organization and detail, coupled with her good penmanship, placed her squarely at Thelma's right hand, the assistant editor in charge of the "documentary" material and the "room.")

DALE: Do you remember how you ended up where you ended up?

TINA: I remember it very well. I got a call from Sonya. Thelma Schoonmaker explained to me that the movie was going to be divided in two parts during the editorial process: one part was the documentary section, which was basically the story of the festival and the people who were there, and the other was the music section, which was to be the cut musical acts. She asked me which part I would be interested in and, of course for me, there was just no question. I was much more interested in the documentary section, the event and the people who were there, than the performances. I was much more interested in finding out why the people were there, who they were, what they were like and what they were thinking. People are endlessly fascinating to me.

Assistant editor Tina Hirsch

Larry Johnson

I actually saw every frame of documentary footage because one of my jobs, probably one of the most important jobs I had, was checking sync on everything, wherever sections of picture and track had not been matched, it was up to me to figure it out. I had a great time trying to sync up things like someone splashing in the water or a dog barking. I had to create the rhythm in my head from seeing the picture and then seek it out on the sound track. I got to be pretty good at it.

DALE: What was it like working with Thelma? What were you being asked to do?

TINA: Thelma gave me a lot of autonomy in the cutting room. My job, in the beginning, was to check sync on everything and to figure out a coding system for the documentary footage. Later on my job was to keep things organized and running so that Thelma could concentrate on editing. Basically, that's an assistant's job. Sometimes you get to sit with an editor, but most frequently you don't.

DALE: Can you describe the screenings?

TINA: Let me go back and describe the first screening I ever witnessed. One morning I came in and found a note on my bench, left by Michael Wadleigh, saying, "Please put this film together according to my list." Beneath the note was a yellow legal pad with three columns of numbers. One column was labeled "A," one "B," and one "C." In each column was either a set of code numbers or the word "black." I was to put the footage indicated by the code numbers in either the A, B, or C reel and black leader in the other two. Sometimes the film in the A reel would overlap the film in the B reel, and the B would overlap the C, but basically there was film on one reel at a time as I wound it through the synchronizer.

I had just finished assembling the footage when Michael came in and said, "Great, let's run it." The screening room was set up with three projectors, each pointed at a single square in the center of the wall. Rather than three separate images, you would see the images on the three reels overlap, so that when an image came up on the A roll and ran for a while, the film would come up in the B roll, overlapping it, giving you the impression of a dissolve. And then B would dissolve to C. They wouldn't always dissolve; sometimes they'd overlap for quite a while—you know, in a long-lap dissolve or a bi-pack of some sort. As we watched, the Jimi Hendrix sequence, virtually the same as it is today, emerged from those projectors. All figured out on paper by Michael, who had never really cut anything before—at least that's what I'd been told. He wasn't able to physically cut the film, but he was able to conceive this wonderful sequence in his head. I was amazed that he could put it down on paper and it would play as a sequence. A wonderful sequence. It was "Purple Haze" and then it went into "The Star Spangled Banner." He cut the end of the movie—all on paper.

DALE: You were selected to go to California. What was your impression?

TINA: Oh! God, I loved California. I remember everything about the first day. I remember the date, December 7th, 1969. I remember coming on the plane. I remember seeing a very early Woody Allen movie, *Take the Money and Run*. I remember it was out of sync and I complained to the stewardess. I remember arriving in L.A. It was warm and sunny and just so beautiful. I remember we—"we" meaning Sonya and Miriam Eger and I—drove directly to our house on Genesee, changed into shorts, and drove to Cafe Figaro, which was very hip at the time, very L.A. We had a fabulous lunch, paid the bill and then walked outside. We were freezing. By then, it was four o'clock and it was very cold. Coming from the East, we were not used to L.A. weather. In the middle of winter, it can be 80 degrees at noon or one, and go down to 60 by four, and then 40s at night. It was quite a shock. We ran home and got dressed again. That's what I remember of the first day.

DALE: Was there any feeling, on your part, as we came to California and brought the first KEMs to California, of the theoretical revolution we were implementing in the movie capital of the world?

TINA: No, I had no sense of that, because in order to see that, you have to be older, you have to have experienced change yourself before you can recognize it. I had only worked on Moviolas with arms [to hold the reels], but I started to have an idea that it might change things, when an editor I'd worked with the year before in New York, Bud Smith, came to a screening of the film. While he was walking around the cutting rooms, he spotted his first KEM. He asked what it was and I showed him how it worked. I remember him calling me a couple days later and asking, "What do you do with the little trims? Can you run the little pieces?"

DALE: In Hollywood here, describe what you felt was your daily life. What was it like being here?

TINA: Most of the stories I remember center around eating. We were on per diem for the first time in our lives. So, when we first got here, we made it our business to have breakfast, lunch, and dinner—all three meals. We would get up in the morning and drive to the International House of Pancakes and have these huge breakfasts early in the morning, and then go to work.

Another thing I remember is the group dinners. Stan Warnow was newly married and his wife Cathy wanted to cook for all of us, so I remember coming home every once in a while to a home-cooked meal. And I remember that when I left early to take an editing job in New York, I threw myself a farewell dinner at the house. I made shrimp curry. It was the first time I'd ever made it and the first time I'd ever tasted it. It's still one of my favorite meals.

I remember that we really had a great time living together, living in *Woodstock*. We worked very long hours, but we really were like family.

DALE: Were you a member of the 107th Street Bowling League? What was that about?

TINA: That was about Sonya's birthday party, January 20th. We all went to a bowling alley. I guess the joke was, Sonya Polonsky was of Polish ancestry and therefore, must bowl [laugh]. So, her party was held at a bowling alley and we all got these T-shirts that said "the Sonya Polonsky 107th Street Bowling League." I had that T-shirt for a very long time. That was a great party.

I was just remembering another thing about my going back to New York. My last day on the job I was sent over to Warner Brothers studio, which was the first time

I'd been there. Basically, we were non-union people and really couldn't work on the lot. We'd worked in an office building at Yucca and Vine. So going to the lot was very special to me. And I remember going into this screening room to screen the blow-up of The Who doing "Tommy," you know, "See me, feel me, touch me, heal me . . .," to make sure it was in sync and that the blow-up was okay. I sat in this dark room all by myself with this huge image in front of me. It was the first time I'd ever seen it that big. And heard it that loud. And in stereo. It was fabulous. It was as if the music were inside me. It was probably one of the most exciting moments I've ever experienced in film. All the way home on the plane, I kept wishing I could hear that music. I wanted to be in that music again. It had been such an amazing experience for me.

JANET LAURETANO SWANSON: *A FACTORY ASSEMBLY LINE*

(Janet was symbolic of the many people who joined the assembly line of syncers who worked around the clock for weeks, painstakingly marrying picture to its respective piece of sound. Luckily for her and many others, Woodstock served as a launching pad for some dynamic careers in documentary film-making over the years. Among them were the very resourceful and patient women in film who dominated our editing team.)

I had a very minor role in the making of *Woodstock*, but on a personal level it was the beginning of my "career path." I was an assistant editor, age 23.

I had been working all alone in a dingy editing room on the East Side on Friday, and on Monday I entered the chaotic world of the *Woodstock* post production offices. I was scared but excited. My job was to sync up dailies on two concert performances, Sly and the Family Stone, and Country Joe and the Fish. I had done syncing before but never anything as challenging. There were shelves full of rolls of film and rolls of magnetic track and the process of getting the two elements together in a cohesive order was daunting. There were virtually no slates. The camera crews were shooting madly but there was no reference to where in the performance they were.

When I got there someone had already organized the rolls of picture and sound into performances. My part was to put the two together. I was in a small room with two other syncers, Mirra Bank and Barney Edmonds. We were working on 16mm upright Moviolas with headphones for eight hours a day. It was like a factory assembly line. The process was all done by eye. I would look at the picture and try to figure out where they were in the song. Sometimes it was obvious; you could tell if it was a beginning or an end. And sometimes the cameraman would shoot straight through. But lots of times there were little short bursts of picture and it was a slow process of trial and error to find where it went with the audio.

Country Joe's performance was in the daytime so at least I could see what was going on, but I recall Sly and the Family Stone performing at night, which made it harder to see. Sometimes flashbulbs and light changes helped syncing one camera to another. There were new camera takes for each performance and the cameras had to all be in sync with each other as well as with the audio. My memory is fuzzy but I must have been working on a double-headed Moviola, now that I think of it.

My job lasted three weeks; that's how long it took to sync up multiple cameras of two performances (to give you an idea of how painstaking the procedure is).

The most awesome day for me was the first time I had to present "my work" to the editors. I entered the dark screening room and sat on the floor. The creative team was in there, having spent most of their days and nights in that screening room, I suspect. I had never been involved in such a large project with so many people before and it was frightening to me. The only person I remember was Thelma Schoonmaker, called "T." The projectors started up and there were all the reels rolling simultaneously. The upshot was that things looked pretty good as far as the syncing went and I got a few notes of where sections were out by a frame or two. I was relieved and simply proceeded to correct the mistakes and that was that for my job.

Once in a while I will mention that I synced dailies on *Woodstock* and the young newcomer to the business will say "Wow." My 19-year-old son thinks it's pretty cool.

MUFFIE MEYER: *WORKING WITH MARTY SCORSESE*

 (Like so many people who entered our world, Muffie, as assistant editor, represents those who were able to build on their Woodstock discoveries.)

Woodstock was my first professional film job after getting out of NYU Graduate School of Film & TV. I was 22. *Woodstock* was a seminal experience for me. It was while working on *Woodstock* that I really learned what editing was.

Brian De Palma, who was a friend, told me that they needed people to sync up (match the film to the sound) on *Woodstock*. After a brief interview, I was hired and began work immediately.

I was handed a small roll of 16mm film and a huge roll of 16mm sound. When I put the picture up on the Moviola, it turned out to be an interview with the Maharishi. There were no slates, no indication of how to match the several hours of sound with the ten or so minutes of picture. The cameraman had turned the camera off and on numerous times, so there were many takes. One of these little one-minute bits of film would find its sound match somewhere in the hours of sound. This was a daunting task under the best of circumstances. It required the ability to lip-read. This was a skill for which I somehow had a knack. However, in this case, the Maharishi had a heavy Indian accent, which made his lips very hard to read. But it was far worse than that: he sported a bushy mustache that totally covered his top lip, and a beard that pretty much masked his bottom lip! I was tenacious: it took two weeks to sync up about ten minutes of film (a job that under ordinary circumstances might have taken an hour).

At a certain point, I was asked by Thelma to stay and work on the editing of the film. She indicated that I should think about what kind of money I wanted. I spent the weekend debating with myself about whether $150 per week was too audacious. I was still debating on Monday, when Dale pulled me aside, told me that they didn't have a lot of money, and asked if $300 a week would be okay! Okay? It was a fortune! Far more than any of my friends made. A real job and real money: I marveled at my good luck!

At NYU, I loved editing. I edited my own student films and those of several of my classmates. When I began to cut on *Woodstock*, I was assigned to work under Marty Scorsese. (At this time, Marty had directed a few shorts and a feature, *Who's That Knocking?*, which I had seen and loved. He was not yet the well-known director that he would become.)

Picture the scene: a large room with shades pulled down to keep the daylight from reflecting off our picture screens. Three huge KEMs in one room, with numerous other editing tables, rewinds, reels, bins, etc. Different groups were being worked on by different editors at each of the KEMs. Some people worked with earphones, but mostly we all tried to keep the volume down, attempted to focus on our own tracks, and tried not to go mad.

My first task was to edit Sha-Na-Na, a fifties revival group. I had never heard of them before. They wore gold lamé and sideburns—way before *Grease* and *Happy Days*. They were fabulous and very funny. Six cameras "covered" the stage performances. (The KEM editing machines had three picture heads, so we could watch three of the six on-stage cameras at one time.) I picked three cameras and cut them together, choosing the best angles for any given moment. For example, when one guy was singing the lead, I chose the camera that was on him. Then when two other members of the group did the "do-wahs," I chose the camera that shot a close-up of them. Then I put up the other three cameras, and added in the best angles from those cameras. I showed Marty my cut of the song. He was extremely nice and indicated that it needed a little more work.

For the next two days, he sat next to me and made suggestions: "Try it here ... what happens if you cut there. . . ." In a gentle, collaborative way, he told me exactly where to make each cut. And all of a sudden, one day, I got it! It was a revelation! In a flash, I understood that editing was about rhythm, not merely finding "the best angle." I understood how you could use the rhythm of editing to create a "build," to create a climax, to create a kind of closure—in short, to create (even in a funny, three-minute, fifties song) an emotional experience.

Although I only "half-knew" it at the time, it was easily the most important lesson of my professional life ... one that has obviously been expanded upon and has grown with experience, but one that lies at the core of everything.

PHYLLIS ALTENHAUS SMITH: 30 YEARS AGO! HELP!

(Phyllis was one of several apprentices who worked with the assistant editors, keeping track of all those hundreds of boxes over the course of three moves, the last to Hollywood.)

Before my *Woodstock* experience I worked in the music business...I had just completed a six-month film-editing apprenticeship and heard about the filming of *Woodstock* ... and managed to have an interview with Thelma Schoonmaker. I was hired. I was thrilled; this was THE event of the year.

That first day of work was raining, raining, raining. I arrived in the loft-like cutting room and I remember the hundreds of boxes of film that had to be sunc *(or synced, or sunk, or sinked—or sunq!)* up. I was confused, excited, scared and completely overwhelmed—this was my first editing job!

The rough-cut screenings were fantastic—so exciting. We would all crowd into the small screening room—which had a few couches, some chairs and the floor to sit on. It was breathtaking to watch Jimi Hendrix so close—all the acts were fabulous to see this way.

From my film-editing experience I always thought that the rough cut was the best version of any film. When I think back and remember working side by side with Marty, Thelma and Michael—how great that was!

ELEN ORSON: *THAT SYNCING FEELING*

 (From the youngest person on-site with our crew, Elen then continued her role as assistant in the editing room.)

Back in New York, the studio went into a deep Zen mode to prepare for the onslaught ahead. Thelma Schoonmaker had devised a beautiful system for logging and organizing the film, and this became the bible, the template which all syncing editors followed. It took us days just to prep the footage for developing, there was so much film. The cans of exposed negative were sorted in huge stacks on the projection room floor by stock type, by performance, and by cameraman, according to the labels which we assistants had taped to the magazines. All of this information would be crucial to the syncing process, and it followed the numbered rolls as they were printed and distributed to the editors.

As people caught up on their sleep, others were being hired. The call went out to hire all editors in town who could sync documentary dailies. There was a steady stream of eager people arriving at all hours for interviews, because by this time, word was out that this was a massive project, and the concert event had drawn so much attention on the news.

Three shifts worked around the clock. I worked at night. I got to learn all sorts of things from the more experienced editors, in the relative calm of the evening shift. (I remember lots of philosophy with Stan Warnow, Larry Johnson and Yeu-Bun Yee over dinner breaks. I remember Thelma being everywhere at the same time, but she always had time to stop and say things like, "Brown mascara looks good on you.") I think there were something like 94 people on the crew during the height of the syncing frenzy. Most were young; wild hair on the men, long skirts on the ladies. Professionals, but hippies nonetheless. Our boss was the weirdest-looking one of the bunch, with the big Indian hat and ice cream in his beard. The Warner Brothers executives would come by for preliminary screenings; we'd all look out the window at their limos pulling up downstairs. They'd walk in, wearing their three-piece wool suits in August, looking around at all of us, furtively commenting to each other something like "Yeee-eeech" and we tried not to stare at them. This was years before the term "Suit" entered the vernacular, but we would have used it if we'd known it. Here they were, on our turf, and they were the ones who looked strange. Mars meets Jupiter.

Some sadist in command decided that for my first sync job, I should take Ravi Shankar's material. There were no vocals, no lips to read, no flashy rock-and-roll moves, nothing to establish a point of correspondence. Just five people sitting calmly making many, many hand movements . . . oh, and sometimes they would nod to each other. Or smile. I do not know if this was given to me as a test, to see what I could do (or not). Or maybe they knew that because of the rain and the general difficulty of shooting on the first night, the footage would not be complete and it wouldn't matter very much.

Alas, we were 15 years away from having a reliable system for sync by time code, which is pretty much automatic. This was like slashing your way through the jungle with a machete. I don't think anyone has ever eyeballed that much footage, before or since.

Later I got to sync up Tim Hardin, Sweetwater, Crosby Stills and Nash, and more. As an act would be completed, everyone would gather for these monster screenings to see what we'd got, on six synchronized projectors. We had to check our work, it's true, because you couldn't run all six rolls at the same time on the Keller. And Michael, Thelma, and Marty had to see what they had to work with. But the room was always jammed with interested and curious people sitting on the floor (who should have been syncing), sometimes rock stars who came in for a visit, sometimes studio executive types, all digging the music and cheering on the great camerawork. Toward the end of a number, sometimes, the cameras would all start running out of film at the same time and the leader would come in on one, then two, then three or more of the projectors. Everyone would hold their breath and wait to see if any camera could manage to slap on another magazine in time before the last one ran out. . . . Big cheer for the victorious!

A combination of happy accidents brought us all together, but were they? (Accidents, I mean.) We were hippies, but we were also extremely well-trained and disciplined documentarians. From the director on down to the lowly Hippie Chick, we all had a great desire to get it right, not to leave it to the network guys or the Big Studio guys who may or may not understand its value in society. The film had to be made by young hip people who would not interpret, or misinterpret it, but allow it to flow through their hands.

It is truly boring to write the word "I" over and over—what "I" did, what "I" thought. But I'm still so amazed I was there in the first place; it's almost as though this happened to someone else. And I'm amazed that the endeavor in which I found myself was so complex and so profound, its images are still fresh a full 30 years later. Memories worth cherishing. I hold on to fragments and souvenirs. And the lasting friendships.

People react strongly when they learn that I was on the crew of *Woodstock*. The first thing they say is always "Wow!" A part of history. "You were on The Towers?!?" And then they ask if I had any of the Brown Acid . . . little do they know, there was no time for acid, aspirin, food, or anything; just work, and stand by to work more. But the romantic notions are firmly implanted, by the film itself.

MIRIAM EGER: *I Was an Outsider*

("Fresh off the boat" from Israel via London, Miriam became another assistant editor who went the distance because of her patience, diligence and organizational skills.)

The first time I heard of Woodstock was when I arrived in America and began looking for a job. I was born in Hungary in 1944 in a traditional conservative Jewish family, who managed to survive in Budapest through the war into the beginning of the Communist Regime. We immigrated to Israel in 1949 and grew up in the foundling state. I served in the Israeli Air Force and then worked for a degree in construction engineering and drafting. At the age of 25, I decided that I needed a change. I traveled with a friend to Paris to study French but got stuck in the May student revolution of 1968. Everything was on strike, so to pass the time I decided to take a trip to London where I decided because I knew a little bit of English and liked the city a lot, I would tried to find an excuse to stay there. I heard about the London Film School where you can apply without having a college degree, decided to go for it and was accepted.

I had just started in London School of Film Technique and met Jeffrey Eger, an American. Jeff was the first hippie I had ever met, and with long hair, boots, and beads, he reminded me more of an American Indian. The word hippie was not yet a part of my working English vocabulary. We got married in the second semester and by the end of the year, we decided that being a married couple and having our parents continue supporting us through another year in school would be too much of a luxury. We wanted to start working. We got on a boat to New York, hoping we had enough background to get some jobs and continue our studies while working with a hands-on job experience. Arriving in New York, being swept up by my in-laws into highways, tunnels, and turnpikes was my first remembrance of America. I was culture shocked and depressed. I started to go from one independent film-maker to another looking for jobs, but having no diploma or union card, my prospects looked pretty dim. Then somebody told us about a new film that was looking for assistant editors that could be just about anyone, non-union, and with little experience.

I remember going into a big main office building in New York and being greeted very warmly, by Sonya Polonsky—the first person I met from the *Woodstock* team and until today my best friend. Then I was interviewed by Thelma Schoonmaker

OK, WHERE'S THE MOVIE?

who later joked that she didn't understand anything that I was saying and didn't think I understood anything she said. Amazingly enough, I got the job.

I was assigned (on 80th St.) to assist Stan Warnow, one of the editors. The best way to describe Stan was like a big grumbling teddy bear who always appeared a little serious, a little angry at the world but very patient, dedicated, and a great teacher who occasionally let me put my two cents in, whatever it was worth. Also we were experimenting with the new equipment—the KEM editing three-screen table, and learned the ins and outs of how to use it. I was taught how to synchronize and spent most of the days rewinding and watching Stan working on the various pieces. My only direct contribution to the film, and I could be wrong, was one day Mike Wadleigh wanted to screen the Joan Baez piece and Stan Warnow wasn't there. I had to put the two edited pieces together, and decided to do a very long fade-in and fade-out between the two reels. Nobody said anything but I think that piece stayed in the final cut.

The whole hippie scene at the time, as well as the Woodstock festival, was very strange to me. I didn't understand the Vietnam War and anti-war movement because I had been raised in Israel and had just been through the war of 1967. To me, war was a heroic thing. The music was also totally weird to me. Until then, I had only listened to jazz. The first long-haired person I met besides Jeff in London, was the group of people I worked with on *Woodstock* starting with Mike Wadleigh, who to me had the ultimate look of Jesus Christ (Superstar).

There was also gruffy-looking Bob Maurice and Dale Bell, who was a cleaner-cut version, but also with jeans, boots, long hair. It took me a while to become a part of this scene. I was an outsider and everything was new to me—starting with the entire culture, its music, and its cause. I didn't even know how to smoke grass. It was fascinating to me. After spending a lot of time working with Stan on various bands like Santana, Country Joe and the Fish, and Joan Baez (who was the only one I had ever heard of), and also listening to the other pieces of music during the various screenings, I slowly began to appreciate and like the music and the people. I really got into it.

The next phase of the project took place just before Christmastime in Hollywood, California. My first observations of L.A. and Hollywood were the huge numbers of cars, and no people on the streets. We were assigned three rented houses. The one I was in was with Sonya, Tina, and Phyllis. The three rented houses had identical rented furnishings. I thought it was so funny that we went from house to house and saw the same furniture, not to mention the white and pink imitation Christmas trees sold in supermarkets. Since no one drove a stick-shift vehicle, I was the designated driver of a large van, even though I had never driven a van. I managed, after taking some pieces off of our fence.

For Christmas, the spouses came for a week, and we planned a big dinner. Jeff and Cathy, Stan's girlfriend, and the rest of the spouses were in charge of the dinner because we were all working. The spaghetti sauce as I understood later was spiced not with oregano or basil but with marijuana. The ceremonial cooking of the spaghetti involved taking numerous strands of spaghetti and whipping them against the wall. By the end of the meal about fifteen of us were sitting on the floor of the living room, listening to music, singing, and falling over each other in hysterical laughter.

The one other party I remember was a party in the "executive" house where Michael, Bob, Dale, and Thelma lived. It had a swimming pool and I remember we dove off the diving board, some of us without bathing suits.

🎥 40.

STAN WARNOW: MUSICAL RHYTHM AND EDITORIAL RHYTHM

(Stan shared performance editing responsibilities with Jere Huggins and Yeu Bun Yee.

By early September I was back in New York, totally broke and eager to work. The idea of working with all that concert footage on what would clearly be a major film was immensely appealing; I began to make inquiries.

By the time I called, I was told they had everyone they needed for the time being. I wasn't about to give up, so I began to drop by the editing rooms on an almost daily basis, ostensibly to see if my footage was available for screening, but more importantly to try and become involved in the editing. Finally, after about five or six visits, Thelma finally gave in.

Was I willing to work at night, Thelma asked? I was willing to work on Mars at that point, so I finally had a job . . . syncing (SINK-ing) up the concert footage—a giant musical jigsaw puzzle—along with four or five other people on the graveyard shift, 9pm to 6am.

I would be given a pile of film and sound (mag track) for the group in question. Sometimes, but not usually, there were rudimentary notes, like "We think we didn't start shooting till the third song, and shot every other song until near the end, when we shot three in a row, we think." I would then plunge in—could this footage be the beginning of that song? No? Well how about the next song, or maybe the lab printed the camera rolls out of order and what I think is the beginning is really the middle of the set. It was a tedious process, but satisfying in that puzzle-solving kind of way. In addition, as I've always loved music, immersing myself in these classic performances as part of my job was just fine with me.

Some nights I would work for hours, and not get anywhere—and others, I would lock onto the right material almost immediately and be able to sync up an entire act in one night. As time went on I began to learn little tricks . . . such as using the flash bulbs going off as sync marks to align one camera's footage to another. The silver lining to the graveyard shift was that those of us working all night together formed a special camaraderie that can only be shared by people that have undergone some trying and difficult experience together under adverse conditions.

Finally, around the third week in September, there was enough material that had been sunc up (past tense of sync—OK, OK, I know there is no such word in the dictionary, but almost every film editor uses it) to begin cutting. There must have been 20 people who had been working on the syncing, and naturally all of us wanted a shot at actually cutting the material. I was given mine after a few days. I sat at the KEM editing table, with a fair amount of trepidation that always happens when I start a project.

I began reviewing the footage of the musical act I had been assigned (again after almost 30 years I really can't remember which one it was). I was looking for a way in—a structure, which in many ways is at the heart of editing documentary footage. Of course in some ways editing a performance is easier, because one has the progression of the music as a guide, but nevertheless I felt that it was important to have a concept in mind before I began to actually cut. And in the case of *Woodstock* there was the additional challenge of editing for three screens.

KEMs represented entirely new technology and enabled us to approach the editing process in a more modern and streamlined way. In fact, this is one of those cases where the technology we were using helped determine the creative content. If it wasn't for the fact that we had these systems, we probably would have ended up with a very different-looking final product.

I must have spent a day or two looking at the footage and then taken the plunge and started cutting. After a few days of work I was ready to show Mike and T my first cut. To my immense relief they liked it. They soon gave me another one to try, and I began to feel like I might be on my way to a full-time editing job.

There were definitely awkward aspects to the whole process, as clearly everyone wasn't going to get to be an editor. The whole thing was reminiscent of going out for a high school athletic team, where a whole lot of people try out, but only a limited number make the final cut. I don't remember if there was a moment of formal designation where I was told I was now an editor on the film, but by mid-October, it was quite clear that I had the job. At around that time I was assigned a full-time assistant, Miriam Eger. She was of immense help, in what was a very complicated project on every level.

By late October, I had done rough cuts on most of the acts I would be working on for the rest of the film: Crosby Stills and Nash, Joan Baez, John Sebastian and Santana. At this point we were well into developing our techniques for two- and three-screen editing. I remember sitting with Thelma, Michael, and the other editors discussing what was the best way to approach the multi-screen material. One moment with Thelma stands out where I remember discussing what looked better, making the cuts in multiple-image sequences simultaneously or sequentially. At first our instincts had been to cut all the images at the same time, but after some evaluation screenings, we came to the conclusion that in general it was better to cut first one image and then another, in order to let the viewer see both transitions and to not ovegad them with too much at once, especially on the big screen. Naturally, this didn't mean always cutting this way, for there were certainly times when I felt it was more effective to have a concussive change of all images at the same moment.

Another basic principle for me also had to do with respecting the integrity of the musical performance as presented on the stage. While I certainly did my share of flashy quick-cut editing, I felt it was important to never have the audience feel that it was being done for its own sake, that the presentation was taking precedence over the content.

When editing I always had a specific structure in mind for each act. Joan Baez sang "The Ballad of Joe Hill," a story in dialogue form between the singer and the dead labor hero. I consciously cut that song so that it had the feeling of a dialogue dramatic scene, with Joan facing one screen direction when she sang Joe's lines, and the other direction when she sang the narrator's lines. And I was sure to use some really wide shots to emphasize the ethereal nature of her voice and the spiritual aspects of the song.

Editor Stan Warnow checking sync

Cathy Hiller

My most satisfying editorial assignment would prove to be the work I did on Santana's "Soul Sacrifice," a dynamic and powerful instrumental. The piece was a natural for a different editorial approach, because it had a classic build-up opening which added one instrument at a time, an accelerating momentum throughout, several instrumental solos including a spectacular drum solo, and as a special bonus, because it was a daylight performance that had a terrific response from the audience, incredible audience-reaction shots.

In designing the opening for "Soul Sacrifice" I was able to use an idea that had been on my mind since starting the editing on the film. I was able to use shots that were

175

optically cropped and positioned to pop on as individual smaller elements against the canvas of the full screen. This made perfect sense to me because of the nature of the intro, one instrument at a time being added to the blend. And I found the ideal shot to begin with, with the camera being lifted up over the lip of the stage to reveal the bass player playing the first notes of the intro (except of course, if memory serves, I "stole" that section from later in the piece).

After a lot of consideration I decided not to show any audience reactions till later in the performance. I wanted to create in the audience's mind a question of how the crowd was reacting and tease out the answer as long as I could, and then finally explosively reveal an audience totally enraptured with the music, which in fact they were. And of course I had a fair amount of my own camera work where I knew for sure people were dancing to this exact performance, as well as lots of excellent material shot from the stage. I then came back to performance for the tour de force drum solo played by Santana's drummer, Mike Shrieve.

As the performance wound up there was a moment when the music came to a complete stop for about half a second. What to show then? It took me a little while to figure out that the best thing to present at that moment was the exact analog of the music—which was total silence. I simply cut to black and brought the images back after the pause. It turned out to be a very effective moment. There was then a quick-cut finale and the piece ended with tumultuous applause and Bill Graham coming on stage to shout something in the organist's ear. At a screening in New York I asked Bill what he had said at that moment, expecting him to relate how he had told them they had just given an historic performance that would make their career, which was definitely true on some level. But of course he told me that instead of having said anything really weighty, he had just told him to get to a mike and thank the crowd.

41

DANNY TURBEVILLE: *OUR INCREDIBLE SHIFTING SCULPTURE*

 (We were back in New York without a break. More new faces in the office now, film editors. What do you do with 30 miles of great footage? My job just sort of surfaced as we went along, like everything I'd done to this point, whatever I could do to help. I was assigned to edit the sound, given an old (pre-war?) Wollensack reel-to-reel tape deck and copies of lots of wild footage for cataloging. I also did the music rough cuts. I had to maintain continuity, all the time looking for the best possible shape to this incredible shifting sculpture.)

The now-famous director Martin Scorsese was editor and assistant director on the film. He was a generous man with his time and thoughts, a teacher at NYU and an accomplished film historian. A dozen of us would eat dinner together at neighborhood restaurants most every night and Marty would tell funny and interesting stories from Hollywood's great past.

One Monday, Wadleigh screened Ten Years After's powerful blues number "I'm Going Home." The conventional wisdom was that its 12 minutes length was too long to be considered in its entirety for the film. My task, to be finished that day, was to edit it to about 3 minutes which was the conventional radio airplay time in the sixties. With my "guess and cut" Wollensack, I spent the whole day trying out hunches and re-hunches. At last I thought my 4-minute version had everything: continuity, dynamics, color—most likely my tour de force of music editing on the film.

However, when I slipped into a seat behind Wadleigh in the screening room, I found him mesmerized by the footage. "Keep everything," he murmured. The dark velvet of the night wrapped around Alvin Lee's vigorous form and his striking red guitar was visually to die for, but we musicians (Blackstead and I) felt the music performance just would not sustain interest for 12 minutes. The finished film piece is about 9 minutes long, and I believe it was only Wadleigh's multiple-camera, split-screen and optical-effects approach which made that song work well at that length. Watching it today is like watching a fast-paced, exciting MTV clip. It makes me believe our movie was nothing short of the pioneer of the music video.

Woodstock's box-office success alerted record company executives to the increasing power of performance to sell product. I bet that for some time after, more record company money went into financing live tours than ever before.

(One the saddest stories of the entire project had to do with technology within the deal Blackstead, the music album's producer, made with Atlantic Records. The way I understood it, the deal gave him a percentage of the record rights only, which cut him completely out of earnings on cassettes and CDs. I don't think many of us had a concept of the technology of the future—videos, cassettes, CDs. And although it was his first record deal, he didn't deserve to pay that kind of dues. Can you imagine?)

My greatest disappointment was not being selected to go to California for the opticals and final assembly. I missed the camaraderie of the group. We had a lot of fun together and, from my point of view, were collectively dedicated to making the best movie about the power of music that would ever be made. I was "fed" by my association with this crew; I was no longer the loner I'd always been. The spirit of the Woodstock Nation was strong within me. I always recognize it in others.

When the crew returned from California, Eric hired me to help him sort out material for the first *Woodstock* album. I once again edited, but this time with the professional equipment at the Record Plant Studios. We worked around the clock with Tom Flye, our engineer. The documentary audio was fascinating. I collated heaps of interviews and conversations, and cataloged tons of stage announcements.

Today these would be called sound bites. Back then they were the personalities of our generation, as resounding for us as anything Walter Cronkite ever covered. "Please, it is your choice, but we suggest you not use the brown acid." . . . "Please come down from the towers, we're gonna have to sit out this rain; we don't want anyone hurt" . . . "Hey, man, the New York State Thruway's closed, isn't that far out!" . . . Hugh Romney's directive for all time: "If you have food, give some to the person next to you," and "Keep feeding each other."

42

ED GEORGE: *Short Hair and Buttoned-Down*

(Ed was one of several young men who literally walked in off the street, looking for any kind of work on our movie. Like Ken Glazebrook, Anthony Santacroce, Al Zayat and Charlie Cirigliano, they discovered their niches and helped us enormously. One of Ed's principal responsibilities was as projectionist.)

I showed up wearing a yellow shirt with a buttoned-down collar, a tie, short hair, and Dale Bell hired me as a PA anyway. What followed was a kaleidoscope of long hours, fascinating work and a musical education.

As footage started coming off the five KEMs and three Steenbecks, I became the projectionist. We had six projectors and two magna-syncs with synchronous motors, so I'd theoretically flip a switch and all eight (or however many were needed) units would crank up and run in sync. It usually worked.

Projectionist Ed George lines up a shot

Larry Johnson

At Bill Graham's Thanksgiving dinner at the Fillmore, we showed some footage using three projectors with zenon bulbs, and during Canned Heat's "Going Up Country" (Wads shot this from low angle with a 5.9) the projector jammed and Bob Hite melted on-screen. Everyone went wild. They yelled "do it again."

The climax to all this came with the three eight–hour screenings of the rough cut that we gave just before leaving New York. Michael and I would crawl through the maze of equipment in the dark, shifting the projectors to create the proper split-screen effect. The film never got any better than those three nights. It was a condensed, exhausting, exhilarating *Woodstock* experience.

43.

DALE BELL: *Ten Screening Days in October*

(Some will dispute me, but I think I remember the very first screenings of the dailies as perhaps the most exciting and thrilling of all. Every image was raw, so full of energy. It was an opportunity to relive those three days in August, but it would take us more than 10 15-hour days to see everything we had filmed.)

For the past four weeks—from mid-September to mid-October—dozens of people scurried about a 2,500-square-foot office, which under normal conditions might have housed ten or twelve people with desks and offices. The sun may come up, or set, but the activity rolls on, uninterrupted by normal routines. These people, you must observe to yourself, have a PURPOSE and a DEADLINE!

Editing tables were constantly being moved about the space as we tried to maximize every inch. So urgent were the editors that even while a table was resting in a space for a few minutes in between a move, two editors would clamor for it.

Sonya and I were always searching for equipment. Though Wads was the first to import the KEM into the country more than a year earlier, others had followed his footprints. When the importer revealed who owned them, Sonya and I began our calls. One was in Montreal. Once it was described on the phone, and endorsed by the importer, we flew one of our editors up to inspect it. That day, he rented a truck in Montreal and drove a second KEM to our offices that very night. Another was in someone's garage in Westchester County; a truck retrieved it the same day. The distributor regretted they had told us about a demo machine in California; within a day, we had coerced them into shipping it back to us in New York! In the space of ten days, we multiplied our original one machine into four.

Our luck with other machines was sometimes not so glorious. Wanting to keep the editorial troops happy day and night, Sonya and I explored a coffee machine service. The Coffee Machine Demo Man, in suit, white shirt and tie, came in with his gear not bothering to look around the space. After a short unpacking, he had coffee brewing with its fragrant aroma wafting into the nostrils of some 30 thirsty long-hairs. Silently so as not to disturb his *pitch* to us, they all stopped their editing for a moment to gather behind him. Oh, how proud he was of its percolating capacity, the varieties of coffee he could bring us, the round-the-clock service! But when he turned around to see who his clientele would be, and saw them armed with

180

Larry Johnson

"Wads" and "Ding"

their very empty mugs, he panicked. As quickly as the one demo pot was emptied, he fled our space, all equipment under his arm! Probably a scene re-enacted in many offices across the country! Examples of culture clashes.

No sooner had he left than the Water Cooler Demo Man arrived. He offered Bob and me a choice: to lease or to purchase. We looked at each other and came up with the same answer: lease. The Demo Man thrust a standard contract into our hands which Bob hastily signed. When we left for Los Angeles two months later, we discovered we had signed for ten years! They sued!

Put yourself in our place for a moment. Two months have passed since you were on-site at Max Yasgur's farm. Your exhilarating yet exhausting experience of three days and nights of filming has been completely suppressed by the night-and-day attention to every detail since. Phone calls at night because of the round-the-clock shifts of editors and assistants. Editing-room space so crowded you had barely enough room in which to wind your reels on your editing bench without striking someone else's twirling arms. Putting down a splicer for a moment while you went to the bathroom, only to return to your space and find the splicer on another bench, being used. Bins and bins of loose film being wheeled from one area to another. Repairing torn sprocket holes. Running out of white leader on which to write your reel identification information. Checking on the color codes for each performer and each day. Cataloguing thousands of edge numbers so that they—and the film they represented—could never be lost or misplaced. Saying good morning to the 8am syncing crew as you finished your own midnight-to-8am shift on their editing bench. Finding a new assistant working on your material and immediately wondering whether that person was going to replace you tomorrow. Negotiating for a three-headed Moviola instead of a single-headed one. Detail, *detail*, DETAIL. And such stress. But was it organized!

There were certain designated shelf areas which were absolutely off bounds to anyone except Mike and T. One infraction required a reprimand; two was good reason for dismissal! Some stuff just couldn't be touched!

Almost. The Vietnam moratorium demonstrations were taking place in October on Broadway outside our second-story windows. Hordes of people holding candles against the darkness were marching and milling just below us. We had to participate. But with what and how? Placing two of our biggest speakers in the open windows, we racked up Country Joe McDonald's "Gimme an F.U.C.K." cheer, cranked up the volume and watched the response with amusement. The neighborhood rocked in unison, the words echoing in the canyons of the Upper West Side. Until our speakers blew, that is, and the cops came to tell us to turn them off, whichever came first.

So here we were, looking forward to actually viewing our footage. In a way, it would be a vacation from everything else we had had to endure to arrive at this point. We would relive a collective experience in slow motion, one reel at a time, as though time were standing still. Through the beauty and versatility of film, we would be able to visit places on the farm we had only heard rumors about eight weeks earlier.

To view the footage properly, we prepared a special room. Because we had six cameramen on stage, we need a corresponding six projectors in our screening room. With three already on hand, we ordered—on Super Rush from their manufacturers in Rochester, New York (Rochester again!)—three Grafflex projectors constructed identically with heavy-duty synchronous motors to match the ones we already owned, so that each strand of performance

Jeanne Field

Larry Johnson, Michael Wadleigh, Dick Pearce and Richard Chew lining up a performance

workprint would run exactly at the same speed with every other one. Each would also have to be equipped with a lightly-pressured gate, to allow the easy passage of film spliced together with tape on only one side. Grafflex said it would take two months to adapt them. We asked: Had they read the newspapers? WE were doing that *Woodstock* Film! Warners, we assured them, would pay the overtime necessary to get the projectors into our offices within two weeks!

Because documentary (non-performance) material had been organized against an hour-by-hour, day-by-day grid of activities which spanned the original three days of peace and music, we would thread up those reels in and around the respective day's music. Our goal was to maintain accurate historical context of documentary and music sequences, to preserve the simultaneity of events as best we could. Beneath each image projected onto the freshly painted iridescent wall, we attached the responsible cameraman's name.

At 8am sharp, the screenings began with coffee and donuts. Lunch would be brought in for breaks, but as soon as a new batch of reels were threaded up, we focused on the film and ate while we watched, on into the night until about 9 or 10. Then, while some of the editors returned home, others of us went to dinner together. It was a chance to catch up on the other activities of the day.

The screening began slowly at first. A single strand of documentary material led the ten days. Green grass, rolling hills, bright sky, a pristine farm spread out in every direction to distant horizons. Cattle lowed, flowers bloomed in the field, birds flew, horses romped. Peace and harmony prevailed. We were lucky. When we were first on the site, we met these two Englishmen hired originally by Mike Lang. They had the foresight to start filming long before we'd arrived, and we asked them whether we would be able to buy their footage, since we presumed, *we* would be making the film. Of course, they resisted, but as Warner Brothers got into the act, money talked. The footage quickly found its way into our offices, then into the soup at the lab, and finally, onto the editing benches.

It was good stuff. Steady, well composed, and oh, so very green. Max Yasgur's farm would never be the same again. Certain shots just leapt out from the screen, crying to be used. Mike ("Wads") and Thelma ("T") furiously took notes, *Lightning T* capable of typing at a mere 100 words per minute, flawlessly.

When the music sequence began with Richie Havens, all work in the office stopped. Like moths to a candle, we flocked to stand in the doors of the screening room, drawn by the music and the roar of the crowd behind him. "Freedom, Freedom," he chanted, and we thrust our right fists into the air in unison. To hell with the phones for the time being! In BAM—a time Before Answering Machines— we assumed they would call back if it was important! The feeling was visceral, deep from within the groin. All our work had been worthwhile!

Entranced, we analyzed each cameraman's work. This was the first example we would see of the on-stage camera team linked together by Martie Andrews's

Richie Havens opens the show

headsets. We had no idea whether Wads's or Thelma's or Marty Scorsese's off-stage instructions were even heard by the rest of the camera team, let alone adhered to. Wads counseled everyone simply to trust their instincts. He "directed" more by example than by instruction. Each of the on-stage team was assigned a particular position; within that perimeter, they had to find the best shots they could for the kind of music, light, and group they were covering.

On Richie, Wads retained the down center stage position. He was flanked on his right and left, while two other guys were upstage, shooting the performers from behind, with the crowd in the background of their shots. On the face of a clock, Wads was at 6, while others fanned out to 4:30 and 7:30, 10:30 and 1:30. A sixth camera roamed while a tripod camera from one of the towers got the "master" shot occasionally.

Thankfully, Wads preferred the wide lenses and would generally mount the 5.9mm if he felt he could get his camera close enough to the performer. He never hesitated to push the end of his lens shade within 18 inches of the musician or the instrument, whichever presented the more engrossing shot. The detail, dimension, structure, and the expanse of the frame from his close proximity was usually the most dynamic angle of the six cameras on the screen. Though all on-stage cameramen hand-held their cameras, no one wavered. Their ability to hold this nearly 20-pound amalgamation of steel and raw stock rock-steady was a marvel to behold. (*All of this is pre-Steadicam, mind you! Yet the cameraman's use of his body and spine on the stage at Woodstock gave rise to the profligate development and use of the Steadicam-type shots soon thereafter.*)

Black leader had been inserted in the rolls by the editors and assistants to hold sync where a specific camera had shut off and the others were still running. We could easily tell which cameraman had run out of film, when, and how long it took them to slap on a new magazine. In some instances, the pauses between images were longer. At these points, Wads, or Thelma, or Larry or Marty would recall what had happened at that particular moment on stage. Maybe the song was not materializing as they expected and one or more of the cameramen had been asked, through the headset, to rest while the song developed. Maybe this was only a practice run! Maybe one of the cameramen noted a jam in their gate! There were always reasons, for one thing you always notice about cameramen: when they are shooting, or recounting the story years later, they retain indelible memories of that evolving miracle which transpires within the tiny confines of their eyepieces. The imprint on the brain echoes that of baseball players who even remember the wind velocity when they are at bat!

On the first night of the festival, Friday, August 15, it had begun to drizzle on the farm. Collecting in the dips of the plywood stage, the water created little puddles where Joan Baez was singing. Although the reflections of the blue and magenta lights on the wet stage looked entrancing, we could observe that, from time to time, when the cables connecting the headsets became so loose they trailed in the water, all cameramen would jerk in sync as they received electric jolts from little short circuits along the lines. At the time, it was both painful and disconcerting to those receiving the jolts. Here, later, in the relative safety and comfort of their director's chairs, everyone burst into uproarious laughter.

The projectionists themselves were under the gun. If one of their strands broke, all projectors would have to be shut down while an instant repair was made. Before they could start up again, a common sync point for all eight strands had to be identified and everything was re-cued. Only then could the screening continue. When the thousand feet (times the number of projectors being used!) ran out at the end of half-an-hour, the reels would have to be taken down and new material threaded. Assistants were chained to the two power rewinds during the screenings to keep pace. Pee breaks were scheduled during what we all hoped would amount to only a five-minute changeover. But sometimes frustrating occurrences prevented that kind of continuity.

All through the day and on into the night, the three days of peace and music unraveled themselves on our wall, thousands of feet at a time. Over an exhilarating period of some ten days, we viewed it all—all 350,000 feet of 16mm, all 175 hours, all 875 individual cans of raw stock.

Mike and Thelma watched everything, while Marty, Stan, Jere, Yeu-Bun and Larry would always be close at hand. Assorted people would creep in and out of the screening room, silently: people from the festival, agents and managers representing the musicians, the musicians themselves, cameramen who knew *their* material would be shown between X and Y, technicians who had to deal with the sound, the picture, or the editing machines, journalists who had wangled an invitation from one of us or another, and from time to time, Warner Brothers executives, very much out of place in these hippie surroundings. Our space was so small and so incredibly crowded, we had to insist that newcomers wait outside until a batch of people left the screening room. Almost everyone was smoking something. Seeing and breathing were difficult tasks.

Some people would show up for the screenings, then call in sick to their regular offices so they could stay hours or days longer. Our own office personnel couldn't resist the tapping of their feet to the music, which then drew them to lean on the doorjam to get a peek. The flying images were irresistible; the volume deafening.

Those who gathered for the nighttime screenings would join us all at Max's Kansas City for dinner; sometimes we were 20 strong in five taxis aiming for a raucous dinner downtown, if Tony's Italian Restaurant on 79th Street was already closed for the night.

In the course, we began the massive whittling process, the elimination of the chaff from the wheat, the search for the positive space within the mass of negative—pick your own metaphor for what was to become the most massive, complicated, intricate, and organized editing process ever known to documentary filmmaking.

From this first "screening of the dailies," our movie would now have to be reduced to about eight hours in length. Safe to say that we could never revisit that initial experience again. A pity it could not be preserved on videotape.

DALE BELL: *REDNECKS VS. LONG-HAIRS*

 (When Wadleigh-Maurice emerged as the likely candidate to be the producer of the documentary to be made about the Woodstock Festival, they quickly offered their landlord, Teletape, an opportunity to invest in the project. Teletape declined. "No, you're a bunch of long-haired creeps and we don't want to be involved with you." A mistake, perhaps, but other companies had been given similar opportunities and had not stepped up to the plate either. It was a very tough call.)

We had added gear and people, lamps, desks, chairs, editing benches, telephones, etc. Trucks would line up on the street, unload, and then, if we were fortunate, we would find a place for all this stuff. When the September rent invoice from Teletape was presented, it was curiously higher than the August 1st invoice, though we were not renting more space. "Elevator usage," the Teletape people maintained. Since the amount was only a couple of hundred dollars, we did not complain. We paid, even though we had been tipping Pete, the elevator man, deliberately, knowing we had added significantly to his load. And almost every day, one of the Teletape guys would mosey by.

When the October invoice arrived, hand-delivered by one of their "Suits," it demanded $20,000 as "key money" plus an increase of $2,000 over the previous month. They handed us a lease for five years! (Had they been talking to the Water Cooler Demo Man??) Electricity and the increased elevator usage, we were told. We had people working around the clock for several weeks, they complained. It cost more money! We were getting pissed but could do nothing with Warner Brothers breathing down our necks. (Not only was Warners demanding that we produce a single-image film by Christmas; they were also paying our bills.) Though the Teletape increase was simply absorbed, their presence in our already crowded space was becoming increasingly more irksome.

But as our October screenings subsided and we began the actual editing process, Teletape began to visit us more than once a day, putting their noses directly in our way. Towards the end of the month, they arrived with another invoice which they demanded be paid, above and beyond the increased rent. A surcharge of $2,000. We said we couldn't do it.

That night, the electricity was shut off at 6 o'clock. We thought it could have been a power failure in the neighborhood. But when it became apparent that every building surrounding us had juice, we knew it had to be Teletape. We converted to candles, stopped work, broke out some champagne, and plotted.

Tomorrow, we would be prepared. During the day, we would access the base of the outside lamppost where we could tie *our* electrical needs to the city power supply with our huge alligator clips. Hundreds of feet of "horsecock," the descriptive name given to the diameter of the electric cable necessary to draw the juice from the city, would be strung on pulleys and ropes from the street through our second-story windows where it would be downloaded into a variety of smaller receptacles and then distributed to the editing tables and machines. We would not stop. Nor would we *be* stopped by a bunch of Redneck engineering types from downstairs who could not leave us Long-hairs alone to do our work.

It was no doubt a scene acted out in countless workplaces across the country throughout the late sixties.

Promptly at 6pm the next day, the lights went out again. Within five minutes, just as the Teletape Short-hairs mounted the stairs to observe the results of their rabid sandbox game, we flicked the lights on in their faces. Were they pissed! Not simply Rednecked, they were Redfaced and furious. We told them to get out; we had work to do and they weren't going to stop us!

That night, we plotted again. We did not think we had heard the last of them. They would do something worse. We left an armed guard on our premises that night after we went to dinner. Our instructions to him: Let in no one, even if you had to scare them by firing a pistol into the air. We rehearsed him and left.

On the subsequent night, though our electricity remained on after 6, we still did not trust the Rednecks from Teletape. Once we were assured that they had left the premises, we put our new plan into action.

As the traffic on Broadway subsided after the midnight hours, we pushed our editing tables down the avenue, pausing only for pedestrians and the traffic lights. By 6 o'clock the next morning, 40 people had moved everything we owned—this burgeoning documentary which would one day refinance the Hollywood movie industry and serve as an icon for a century—ignominiously through the night, out of the clutches of the Rednecks and into the welcoming arms of another pair of New York filmmakers, Chuck Hirsch and Brian De Palma, responsible for *Greetings!* and *Hi, Mom,* who had graciously agreed to rent us their office space at reasonable rates on a moment's notice.

Such was camaraderie!

After breakfast, a few of us returned to the Teletape offices to take down some special overhead lamps we had installed. While we were on two ladders reaching for the lamp attachments, the Teletape folks arrived. Immediately, the sight of the very empty offices threw them into a fury! They knew that we had outwitted them. Now, they began to grapple with the base of the ladders. They accused us of using *their* ladders to steal *their* lamps, but *our* invoices substantiating *our* ownership proved otherwise. *We* were twenty, Teletape folks were five. Fisticuffs broke out. We brought in the fuzz to try to intercede. Finally, with our lamps and ladders in hand, we gleefully rushed downstairs and onto Broadway, free at last, free at last.

SONYA POLONSKY: *KIDNAPPING COPPOLA'S KEM*

DALE: Michael got the first KEM.

SONYA: Right, but in books it says Francis got the first one. I know that you intercepted it.

DALE: It was on its way to San Francisco. I found out that there was one on its way to Francis Ford Coppola. It was leaving Hamburg, Germany. When it stopped at JFK, we intercepted it.

SONYA: You kidnapped it.

DALE: We kidnapped it, exactly.

SONYA: We didn't tell Francis? Didn't we have some negotiations with him—did we tell him after?

DALE: No, during.

SONYA: Oh, we told him during and he said O.K.

DALE: It was a heated exchange and I asked Francis to write a piece for the book about this.

SONYA: What did he say?

DALE: He said, "I'm busy writing a screenplay. I can't be interrupted, but I remember the incident very well." As I remember it, we intercepted it; he was pissed. We told him we'd pay him. He grumbled, but I have to remind everybody that he wasn't so pissed that he ignored us completely when we got to Los Angeles, in the early December. Five or six days after we arrived, we were on airplanes to San Francisco to celebrate the opening of his new company, the American Zoetrope. A great party.

Let's go into what do you recollect about the whole post-production process, in New York. What comes to mind?

SONYA: The things that come to my mind are: sitting in that outside room with the personnel changing every day. I remember every day at six o'clock I couldn't bear it. These shifts would change. We had several shifts of people syncing. And, at six o'clock every day I would try to escape, because it would just become too much for me. But I had to stay. Because at six o'clock every day, we'd either get more Moviolas or send some of them back. Which I didn't quite understand. You were masterminding that. People would be added on; people would be laid off.

DALE BELL: *Hollywood's Longest Optical*

The last day in November. It was an auspicious day. The "Suits" were in town. Up to now, they had only caught a little glimpse of our editing. Bob had been masterful about purposefully keeping them at bay. Every time one of them would show up, the Suit would wonder out-loud what we were doing. Why didn't we get the editing done faster? Who were all these people Warners was paying for? Why did we need such exotic gear?

Get the film out by Christmas! they insisted. We've got Radio City Hall booked. December 17th! Every day for the past few weeks, Fred Weintraub had been sending telegrams: "What have you got for us today, Michael?" Bob would respond: "Nothing!" Warners kept reminding us that "the kids would just be getting out of school on their vacations! Hurry up! What did we think, they were the tooth fairy?" (Let the record show that Warners had absolutely nothing else going on that winter, or spring either, for that matter.) No wonder they wanted *Woodstock* out early—they had their stockholders to satisfy. To hell with the quality!

I remember one Bob-and-the-money scene. Bob would call the Warners money man, requesting $25,000 to repay some of the bills which had accumulated over the week. The Warners person would respond, "We won't get that to you for at least a week, if then!" Then he would hang up. Bob would call someone else at Warners and tell him that we needed $50,000 and receive a similar response. Bob would turn to us with that twinkle. Then he would pick up the phone again, talk to someone new, presumably higher up, and say we needed $100,000 that very afternoon. Fred Weintraub would then call back to find out what's the problem. Bob's reply would be something like, "Do you want to continue to send telegrams or do you want us to stop editing the movie? Send the $100,000 this afternoon." In a couple of hours, a meek man with a check for $100,000 would arrive. And although it sounds funny now, at the time it was very painful for all of us, particularly for Bob, who had to adopt a "drop-a-keg-of-nails" personality in order to succeed on behalf of all of us.

Now, today, all day, we were finally going to show the "Suits" our work.

After lunch, we stuffed about 40 of them into our compact and very makeshift screening room, then turned out the lights. Crammed together expectantly in the darkness were Fred Weintraub and John Calley, producer of *Catch-22*, as well as various other promotional types. Significantly absent was Chairman of Warner Brothers, Ted Ashley, who had let Weintraub shepherd the picture.

For this rough-cut screening, we had edited 350,000 feet of 16mm film down to approximately 30,000, once you counted all the multiple images. Or to put it in its true historic context, we had cut 165 hours of running time down to eight and a half hours. And it wasn't finished yet. There was no physical, practical, mechanical way we could release the picture by this Christmas holiday. ("Maybe by spring break?" Bob suggested with a twinkle in his eye.)

Thelma was still bent over her KEM, chop! whack! splat! putting the last touches on one of the latter reels which wouldn't be up for a couple of hours.

The configuration of the screening room was designed to create the effect of multiple images for the audience. Wads and Larry would choreograph the projectionists so that, at appropriate times while the film was still running, they would grab a couple of the stands, and move the images on the wall to a different position. Thus, we could create between one and five overlapping images. In that darkness and among the spinning noise of all these machines, Wads, Larry, and the editors were designing, through trial and error, how the final film would look. When he could, Larry adjusted the pots to even out the sound track.

This screening lasted well into the middle of the night. Reel changes, a food interlude, a warm batch of Alice B. Toklas brownies, and breakdowns contributed to the delay. The retention power of the Suits was becoming a little blurred after midnight.

At one reel break, they were so overwhelmed, they called a halt. The sound of the machines, coupled with the sometimes deafening sounds of the music, was enough to numb the senses. Monitoring the multiple images dancing on the wall, the lack of fresh air, collective body odor, all contributed to a sensory overload! When Wads checked the carefully stacked and numbered reels awaiting their respective projectors, he determined that we still had almost two hours to go! It was decided that the screening would continue the following morning at 10am. We had already spent more than ten hours in the screening room, the Suits on chairs, everyone else on cushions scattered about the floor, coiled among the legs of the projector stands.

The following morning, the Suits accumulated again, but this time there was a new arrival. Fred Weintraub had invited his Chairman to view the end of the movie with him. Bob, however, designed a different opening scenario over coffee and donuts. Wrapping his burly frame around the diminutive Ted Ashley, who had come dressed like a bellboy in spats, Bob whisked him away from Weintraub. "Hi, Ted, how are ya?" Ted's response: "Understand you got a good picture here!" Out of earshot, Bob told Ashley he would have to see the film from the very beginning. Ashley, Bob insisted, could not rely on Weintraub to interpret the film for him. Weintraub was causing all of the filmmakers too much *souris*. Masterfully, Bob was excising Weintraub out of the picture forever, even as Weintraub stomped angrily around the office, bemoaning his fate, yelling to me to "Stop him! Stop him!"

Almost alone, Bob walked Ted into the screening room and started the film at its very beginning, with Sidney Westerfeldt's prologue (much to the astonishment of the projectionists who had to hustle to catch up!). I think the Warners' business and legal guru, Sid Kiwitt, was in the room, too. All other tall people, like me, were kept out of the screening room so as not to overpower Ted. It marked the end of Fred and the inception of our relationship with Sid Kiwitt, for better or for worse.

The screening of *Woodstock* culminated with the searing rendition of the "Star Bangled Banner" anthem, as reconstructed by Jimi Hendrix. His finale at the end of the festival would mark the end of our movie, played over the debris and devastation left behind by 500,000 festival participants on Max Yasgur's hillside. Overwhelmed by the totality of the movie, the Suits retired to their downtown offices to reconnoiter. Many of their best-laid plans would have to change. No Christmas at Radio City Music Hall. (Steve McQueen's movie could get back in there!) Yes, they would lose all those kids home for the holidays. Yes, more money would be spent to complete the movie. More hemorrhaging, possibly. No quick solution to the irascible hippies they were in bed with!

And Bob, who had originally committed to Warner Brothers for a December delivery date to induce them to back the movie, was ultimately relieved that the Suits would accept the film later without recriminations. He always admitted it had been a dumb but necessary decision, bred of a combination of naivete and negotiation.

All along we had known that only the West Coast had the technological knowhow to realize Michael and Thelma's creative decisions in post-production. We were going to have to move to L.A. for the mix, the optical and the printing, and lock the final cut there. Our task, once we got to Hollywood, would be to translate our on-the-fly projection technique to 35mm Cinemascope, a term most of us had heard simply as moviegoers, not as producer/editors. We had no idea of the problems we were going to bring with us.

Yet at the same time, the press began to visit us, eager to do a story before we fled New York for Hollywood. Warners wanted to get the word out one way or the other. Today, you'd call it "spin" or putting on the "buzz."

This had been only the first of four screenings scheduled before we were to depart for Hollywood. After the Suits left, we invited people who had worked on the film to come by, as well as critics and friends. Some would come by early in the morning, catch a few reels before work, and then return to view the middle of the movie during their lunch break. One screening started in the evening and went through the entire night, finishing early in the morning: this to accommodate those who could not take time off from their normal work. It was like a floating crap game in New York: you could float in and out of the movie on your own schedule! It was on a continuous loop!

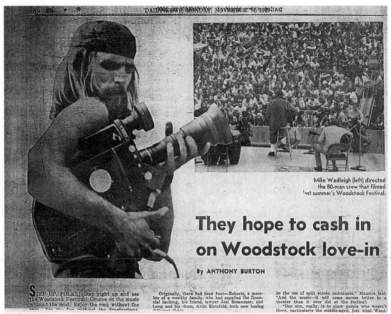

During these last few days, we were able to pack up everything not needed specifically for the screening to ready it for the trek across country. One U-Haul truck would carry the furniture, editing tables and the bulky, uncartonable equipment. The two who drove the truck were told they would have jobs in California, if they arrived safely. Otherwise, . . .

One incident comes to mind. Wads had long ago purchased a motorcycle which never ran. He decided it needed a new home in California. As the truck was being loaded, we decided we would put the cycle in the back of the truck. But there was no key; the cycle was locked. And Wads was asleep by this time. Not to be deterred, we took the cycle down to the street in the elevator. Five of us were carrying it to the truck on Broadway that night when—you guessed it—we were accosted by the fuzz. "Hey you guys, what are you up to? Are you stealing this motorcycle? Whose motorcycle is this?" I answered the last of the questions. "It actually belongs to a guy upstairs who is sleeping and we don't want to disturb him, so . . ." Of course, the cops wouldn't let me finish. What a line! Herding us together while one of them stayed on the street with the cycle and the truck, the other cops accompanied the rest of us to the fifth floor.

Wads is asleep on the screening room mattresses. Bob tries to mollify the cops: "Michael had bought the cycle in Italy," he began. "We don't have the registration. It has 'Roma' license plates on it, you know." Bob was going nowhere fast. The cops were getting more frustrated. Wads heard the commotion, emerged sleepy-eyed from the screening room, asking, "What's going on?" The cops asked him to identify himself. But then one of them said, "Hey, aren't you the guy in the *Daily News*? Aren't you making a movie? About freaks? Didn't I see your picture in the *Daily News*?" Wads acknowledged, explained that it was his cycle and that it was on its way to California. The cops shook hands all around and helped us complete the loading! A cultural gap had been bridged.

Crates were built to contain the sensitive gear we would ship by air. Some of the edited workprint was copied just in case it got lost or broken in shipment. Special cardboard boxes, filled with insulating material, would transport the gold—the 350,000 feet (70 miles worth of film spooled around itself!) of 16mm negative which would eventually serve as the basis for constructing the multiple images on the West Coast. Nothing was more valuable than the negatives. Even the gear could be replaced, but there was no way to go back and reshoot!

At one point during the syncing process, we were up to some 50 or so employees, working three eight-hour shifts. It was at this time that we completed the whittling down of the staff. These days were called "Bloody Fridays" when I would have to invite people into my desk area—offices did not exist—and let them know we could not continue them into the next week. When they saw me coming, and heard me announce their name in a mournful tone, they knew their days were numbered. It was sad for both of us.

But now there loomed the Final Cut—the time we would pick those who would accompany us to Hollywood. Bob, Wads, T and I had determined that we would take only 17 people. I had the dubious distinction of letting everyone know their destiny. It was not a kind task, but someone had to do it.

To this day, I do not recall exactly what I said to Marty Scorsese, who was not part of the "finishing team." I still feel awkward about it. It was difficult for both of us. Thankfully, we overcame it. (When he had *Mean Streets* and *The Italian Americans* to do two years later, he called me both times and I joined him again, absolutely thrilled to be in his creative company.)

We had truly become a very large, devoted family. The intensity of the work, the historic nature of the project, the symbol we began to represent, our visibility, all had bound us together in a sort of eternal camaraderie which would extend far beyond the confines of work. Though there were many disappointments and some tears, it was replaced with a great deal of understanding and spirituality over the years. Those who had been designated part of the finishing team in Hollywood were given their first days off in three months. Actual days off they weren't; for everyone had to pack, say good-bye, while preparing themselves mentally for an even more intense period of learning new technology, disseminating information to a new team of professionals, and much reworking of the sequences.

These were our guidelines to those who would come to Hollywood:

1. You are coming for an indefinite period of time. We cannot predict now how long we will need you.

2. We will pay your round-trip transportation.

3. Effective Monday, 11/10 and thereafter, through California, there will be no payments for overtime. Your salary will remain as is.

4. We will pay each individual $70 per week in per diems (including Saturday and Sunday), which you do not have to account for. This is to cover your food, laundry, etc. [This was 1969 and we would generally pick up a communal dinner! Remember that this money is not taxed.]

5. The housing accommodations present a problem and we would like some answers as soon as possible so that we can firm up our temporary arrangements. There are two options: private houses, seven bedrooms each, or the motel route. From an economic standpoint, we cannot afford to provide more than the private house. The cost to the company is $40 per week per room. Due to the close proximity of these accommodations, and the fact that seven people will have to share private bathrooms, kitchen, etc., we do not feel we can provide space here for spouses or friends. Therefore, for those of you in the latter category, we would like opinions: if we provide a room at a cost-to-use of $40 per week per person, and you want other kinds of accommodations, will you pay the difference between this $40 and the price of other accommodations you may desire in a neighboring motel? Our estimates on motels booking for a length of time comes to about $80 per week per room. If we arrange these kinds of accommodations for those of you desiring them, we feel you should pay the additional cost. Okay?

The truck left at dawn on a Wednesday with an ETA in Hollywood of Saturday. It would take the southern route to avoid possible bad weather across the country. By pre-arrangement, Ed George and Ken Glazebrook, the two drivers, would call in every night to assure us of their progress.

Finally, Saturday, December 6—the day before Pearl Harbor Day—arrived. In the early morning, just hours after the last screening, we loaded another truck with all the gear, negative, and workprints which would be taken to JFK for air shipment to Los Angeles. So fearful were we of losing something, or of an airplane crash, that we had created a system whereby we would ship only part of the negative of a certain musical group on one airplane. We would put the other portion on a second flight. Nor would we ship the workprint of one group with the negative for that group, just in case we would have to replicate the editing from the workprint. We were paranoiac about it. With the gear, we followed the same procedure, shipping only one KEM on a pallet, under a net, per airplane. Four KEMs, two Steenbecks, six Grafflex projectors, two Magna Tech playback machines, and more than a hundred separate boxes of negative and workprint, carefully numbered and labelled, were slipping from our primary custody, entrusted into the hands of others for the first time since mid-August. The surrender factor was difficult to grasp!

Larry Johnson

Editor Yeu-Bun Yee protecting his stack of edited sequences

From about 10 in the morning until late that evening, we used more than 15 separate flights to ensure that everything would arrive safely. Cross-checking with Lewis Teague, our newly-hired production manager in L.A. (and the guy who had originally introduced Bob and Mike), assured us that the flights were arriving with their predetermined loads. Lewis and the two drivers then transported everything to our new offices on Yucca and Vine. Sunday, they set up the office and the cutting rooms.

The team flew over the weekend, picked up their cars at the Los Angeles airport, and spread out among the three houses Lewis had rented for the duration of our stay. Wads and I stayed behind for several hours more, checking and cross-checking our plan for Hollywood. And finally, as the sun set in New York, we boarded our flight to L.A.

Airplane rides are often ethereal experiences. Purchased by Warner Brothers travel people, our tickets entitled us to first-class seats. But neither Wads nor I ever felt comfortable there. Within a few minutes, we took our drinks and spread out in the relatively empty coach section. It represented our first pause from 18-hour days in almost five months. The process had been unforgiving. And here we were floating in space for the first time, very detached from life itself, or so it appeared.

I looked over at him. My foolhardiness had almost killed him, John Binder, and me on our first job together, outside Chicago years earlier. Now, here we were together again. . . .

When Antoine de Saint-Exupéry wrote his monumental work *Night Flight*, he was metaphorically describing filmmakers bound together by their camaraderie, facing the very uncertain forces at work in society, trying to set them straight. Filmmaking had become confrontational, and in some instances, a life-and-death struggle. It put you on the front lines between good and evil. More than any other place in America, New York represented a thriving cauldron of concern and passion. And what allies we had all become: Bob Drew and his associates had started the Sixties with a bang. Their revolutionary use of the new technology astounded television viewers. Add to this mix Al and David Maysles, Ricky Leacock, Don Pennebaker, Fred Wiseman, Amram Novak and his cohorts David Hoffman and Harry Wiland, Beryl Fox, Bob Elfstrom, Bill Jersey, Al Perlmutter, Bob Squier, Irving Gitlin, Arthur Zegart, John O'Toole, Ofra Bikel, Jack Willis—and these were just some of the documentarians. Think of Arthur Penn, Phil D'Antonio, Kenny Utt, Gordon Parks as dramatic filmmakers and you have a sense that New York was precisely—and only!—where the action was. And now, here we were, on our way to Tinsel Town with a picture born in that New York City foment.

Bob Maurice had been such a logical person to fill the role of barrier between us and the Warner Brothers types. Crafty, wily, cunning, smart, outrageous, a brilliant debator, insensitive and callous when necessary, enormously kind and generous at an instant's provocation, Bob had been successful in holding those "Suits" out of our way in spite of his instincts to be a burly Teddy Bear. (He was also a marvelous maker of omelettes!) All he and Wads had argued for with Warner Brothers had been artistic freedom: *to make the picture their way.* As the plane took off, Wads and I knew we were halfway to the finish line. Soon both of us were asleep.

Our drive into Hollywood from LAX took us down Sunset Boulevard. From our vantage point in the rented white convertible, California did not have truly black nights, even at four in the morning. Grey, hazy, like aurora borealis, a glow glimmered all along the route. The boulevard was empty. What a heady feeling as we wound beneath the swaying palm trees! We were coming to town with the hopes of setting it on its ear. Little did we know what awaited us.

After a little reconnoitering, we found our place on Orlando Street and settled in. It did have a pool with a slide, and a good kitchen. For the next several months, Orlando was our communal home and the center of our team's social life.

Monday morning brought everyone back together again at our new offices. Our workprints were stacked in the editors' respective rooms. The screening prints were in the newly designed central screening room, complete with its six projectors, playback machines and speakers. Much of the foam rubber used to line the crates transporting the equipment had been tacked to the walls and ceiling so that the sound would not disturb our neighboring tenants. Our precious negative was carefully delivered to Ed Richards, our chosen negative cutter, under contract to us. Everything was accounted for. A miracle of planning, or luck. We were ready to work again and it was only Monday noon. Plans were discussed. Some initial deadlines were set.

The arrival of the ABDick copying machine caused a slight diversion. As soon as we realized that, in addition to paper, it could also copy a hand, for example, everyone decided that we should have a little contest: insert other body parts into the scanning device. The only way to ensure fairness was to sequester the ABDick copying machine in a room of its own. There, in private of course, a participant could expose whichever body part(s) s/he wanted, place it—or them—on the cold glass with the help of a nearby chair, if necessary, and push the Print button. Amidst a constant stream of giggles and laughter, each participant would emerge from the ABDick room with their printed results hidden from everyone else. After each had printed everything s/he wanted to, the black-and-white portraits were discreetly inserted and shuffled in a leftover moving box.

Then, the goal of the contest was to try to determine the owner of a particular private body part! One picture at a time was drawn from the box and held up to view. Guesses were made. Such knurled and matted shapes! More laughter and high-pitched shrieks of delight and horror. But the rules dictated that no one could be forced to acknowledge their own part(s) unless they wanted to. Many actually denied ownership! The individual portraits were pinned to a wall as inducement for future contestants. Group initiation complete. The ABDick copying people were thrilled at our inventive use of their gear. Warner Brothers was aghast! Our new-technology work in Hollywood had begun! After all, weren't we in the picture business?

Tuesday morning, we began in earnest the process which would consume us for the next four months: making the longest optical yet devised by man.

We had filmed the festival in 16mm. To project a movie in theaters, we needed to create a 35mm print from our original. In short, we had to enlarge, or blow up, our original negative or color reversal to another negative, from which we could make a print. It was a tall order. Almost impossible, as we were about to experience. No one had ever done it before.

Calculate for a moment with me. Assume that our edited film would run about four hours in length. Since 16 mm film runs at 36 feet per minute, or 2,160 feet per hour, in four hours you have 8,640 feet. At 24 frames per second, times 60 seconds, times 60 minutes, times four hours, you have 345,600 individual frames to blow up and crop, lay out and shoot—if you are releasing only a single, non-multiple-image film. We were not. Many of our sequences would contain two, three, four, and sometimes five images on the screen simultaneously. Let's say, for example, that we had at least twice as many images as a single-image picture, or 691,200 frames; maybe we had more. I don't know the answer, even today. Regardless, a helluva lot of frames to deal with!

Pacific Title Company, owned by Shirley and Gordon Hubbard, was one of the optical companies recommended to Bob, Mike, and T on their initial visit to Hollywood.

Gordon and his technical wizard, Dick Bond, became our first visitors on Tuesday. Now understand something. No one in Hollywood had ever seen a KEM editing machine up close and personal, unless at a trade show in some distant city. There were NONE in the film capital of the world until we brought our four and set them up in our editing rooms. Consider as well that we were not at all the well-manicured, short-haired people represented by our first visitors. To them, we must have appeared very strange, even though we were able to keep up with them in the *vision-and-technology* department.

To produce the opticals we illustrated with a screening, Dick had recommended that we employ a two-perforation techniscope process. In an optical camera, loaded with 35mm internegative film, they would photograph our original 16mm negative through especially designed stationary mattes that would conform to our desired combinations of images, but instead of using four perforations, they would use only two perforations per 35mm frame. A four-perforation squeezed print would be made from the two-perf negative. Technicolor Labs would handle all the processing. The cinemascope look we wanted would then be accomplished by equipping the projectors in the theaters with anamorphic lenses, which would unsqueeze the print.

Meanwhile, we met the people from Warner Brothers we would be working with: Rudy Fehr, an émigré from Germany, now the head of post-production; his associate, Fred Talmadge, an ex–film editor who would be our daily point man; Dan Wallin, a staff music mixer who would be in charge of our mixing board and guide our sound team of Larry Johnson, Eric Blackstead, Lee Osborne, and Danny Turbeville in the processing of the music and production tracks; George Groves, an Englishman now running the WB Sound Department whose claim to fame had been as mixer of the first talkie, *The Jazz Singer,* in 1927, more than 40 years earlier; and Graham Mahin, our jump-suited Dubbing Supervisor, who would work closely with T and the editors in the technical preparation of the edited sequences for the mix. An interesting group!

They had to come to our offices. The screening room was our bastion. And like the Pacific Title group who had preceded them, they were blown away with our mastery of the technology and by the power of the film itself. We didn't, we *couldn't* show them everything. So we cherry-picked our way through some of the sequences, trying to offer them a taste of things to come. One single panel, a double, a triple, and so forth. Some doc. Some music. None of them had any conception about how we had done it, or indeed, what we would have to do to complete it!

So in spite of the Long-hair/Short-hair bit, we recognized we had a massive job to do and we'd simply better get down to work.

The next day, we were given a guided tour of the Technicolor laboratory on Romaine Street. Again, the Short-hair/Long-hair issue cropped up but was quickly dispensed with. Walking down their hallways decorated with legendary movie posters everywhere, gawking in wonder, we felt like time-travelers. Just a few years ago, we had been simply moviegoers. Now, we were filmmakers in our own right, and walking through the hallowed halls of Technicolor! Soon, they might install our poster alongside that of *Gone with the Wind* and others, ensuring our place in the historical annals. Although we were selected only through the improbability of happenstance and by a willingness to risk everything for a cause, we felt we were speaking for an entire generation of Americans. It was a heavy responsibility.

The Technicolor people readily accepted us as their customer. We signed their papers describing our relationship to them. Forewarned by Warner Brothers, they knew this would be a massive project. Yes, they said, they were looking forward to servicing our requests. At one point on the exhaustive tour of the plant, their chief executive told me that, in rare instances, they were even able to move huge pieces of machinery and equipment from floor to floor to accommodate special situations. I silently stored some of these public relations tidbits I was gleaning.

Back in our editing rooms, our editors—Thelma, Stan Warnow, Jere Huggins, and Yeu-Bun Yee—and their assistants, had to learn a whole new language. We were already designing film mattes for single, double and triple images. When special circumstances arose, we would design special mattes.

Beyond learning this new language of opticals, the editors also had to reduce the length of some of their sequences while cleaning up all of their edits. After all, we left New York with an eight-and-a-half-hour film. Music comprised about five hours, documentary about three and a half. While T was concentrating her attention on the many documentary sequences, she and Michael would give guidance and recommendations to each of the editors as they began to hone their music segments. These sequences that could not be edited quickly were dropped, under pressure of time.

Within a couple of days, we determined that one single optical house could not possibly handle this movie. Calling on Warner Brothers' Fred Talmadge to help us, we invited four other houses to our screening room for a "war room" conference. Dick Bond laid out the technical dilemmas. We then looked at a calendar. Too many sequences, too few days.

Deja Vu all over again: we would have to repeat the 24-hour cycle of September, October, and November.

If we were successful in processing our primitive sound tracks so that our vision of full wrap–around sound in the theaters could be achieved, we might be able to make an innovative mark there. Larry, Michael and Thelma had always envisioned that the sound would travel from speaker to speaker to match the ever-changing picture.

Recorded under very primitive conditions, where the voices and instruments frequently landed on the same tracks, the sound processing was going to need a lot of work. Larry and his team spent more than a month at the Record Plant, attempting to separate and enhance both music and documentary tracks.

We thought we were presenting the optical people with a simple prescription: we were not asking for wipes, travelling mattes, spinning images or strobes, just lay-out and blow-up. We would submit to them ten minutes of new material each day, beginning January 5, and we would deliver all the edited footage in one month's time. We expected that one week later the optical work would be completed by all hands. The schedule we were working on dictated that we have optical prints available to work with in the mix, which had to begin in February. Suddenly the optical houses realized that they were dealing with high-speed New Yorkers. The laid-back hippie image had been misleading.

Four days after giving the optical houses our first sequence, our problems popped up. Mysteriously, a black speck appeared in the center of the projected image. It was in the techniscope internegative. It had been photographed as part of the solid matte, the frame around the image.

Since some of the performance sequences required as much as twenty five hours on the optical bench the first time they were photographed, the optical men dreaded going back through that material for pickups. Dirt, color balancing, positioning, size, sync—all contributed to re-do's. First they would photograph the right side, re-wind the entire negative without scratching it, then photograph the center section, or the left side onto the negative. It is a mind–blowing procedure requiring much skill and patience.

The alarm of early January. I am going over the invoices from Technicolor, preparing them for payment by Warner Brothers. I notice Technicolor is billing us for two prints, not the single one I always request when I send in the purchase order. *We* only receive one print. What happens to the second one if it is delivered? Or where is it delivered?? Bob and I talk about it. I naively ask the Tech people about this apparent mistake, since we only get one copy. They tell me it is not a mistake. It is standard with them to bill for two copies. We get one and Warner Brothers gets one. It is sent overnight to New York for their viewing. I quietly acknowledge that this might be standard operating procedure and hang up. Bob and I talk again.

Warners is watching our movie in New York!!!! Who is? Who ordered it? What right do they have? They are looking at all the mistakes, too. Nothing in the contract between Wadleigh-Maurice Productions, Ltd. and Warner Brothers permits

Warners a look-see at our material until we are ready to show it to them ourselves. We are the client of record with Technicolor! We submit our purchase orders, not Warner Brothers. If Technicolor is doing stuff without our permission, behind our back, they have a problem! Perhaps a big one.

Bob calls an attorney. Within hours, in New York City and Hollywood, we have slapped an injunction on Warners and Technicolor, the accomplice in this subterfuge. Unless the practice is halted immediately, he tells them, we will stop editing the movie. We will not submit any more workprint to the optical houses. The whole process will stop dead in its tracks!

Technicolor is immediately apologetic though it maintains Warners has always received copies of dailies from other pictures; they don't see why this situation is any different. But Warners is intransigent as Bob argues with them on the phone. They have the right to see what we are doing, they insist. After all, they are paying for the picture. The contract is repeatedly brought out; language is read. Nowhere does Warners have the right to look.

Bob decides he has to go to New York to present our case. He is protecting our right to make the movie our way. Besides, he has not yet agreed on an opening date or cities. The promotion has to be designed. All this has to be dealt with at the same time, he reasons.

A day passes. The clock is ticking towards the deadline: the opening of the movie.

Before Bob departs, we develop a strategy. Very carefully, so as not to cause alarm among the Warners staff editing people who are helping us, we will pull back one sequence at a time. We will claim that someting is wrong, a segment is out of sync, a new piece has to be re-edited, anything to recall our material into our own shop. We use the same approach with the optical houses.

Bob leaves for New York, promising he will only stay three days.

Over these days, we systematically withdraw all our work from Warners and from the optical houses. It is stacked in our offices on Yucca and Vine. We hire a series of armed guards who protect everything at our command. No stranger is allowed in. We continue to work, unbeknownst to everyone on the outside.

Warner Brothers and the optical houses confer, discovering that they are both in the same situation: they have nothing to work on as the hours tick by.

In our screening room, the telephone is connected to the speakers. When Bob calls in from New York to report on his progress, or more specifically, his lack of it, he is piped in to the screening room where everyone gathers to hear his rendition of the talks. He is getting nowhere but he receives cheers from all of us for his fortitude.

As the days pass unproductively in New York, we continue our editorial work but do not let the Warners people know of our ongoing progress. On the third day, we take a truck to Ed Richards, our negative matcher, and pull out all of the negative, very carefully. This action triggers another phone call to Warners. They discover that they are paralyzed.

The negotiations, according to Bob on the speakerphone, begin to change. He is beginning to get concessions. "We've got this point," he says in the screening room, and we cheer. "We've got this, too," and we cheer again. We know we have the upper hand. Piece by piece, the film finds it way back to its original spot, on the Warners lot, in the optical house, inside the negative matcher's vault. Bob has won all his points and then some. The project is resuming its speed. Artistic integrity is restored. He returns from New York triumphant. It's a "Villa Capri" night! (The restaurant is now defunct.)

Warners has backed down, but in the process, they dispatch Sidney Kiwitt, the attorney we had met in New York, to our team. At first he deals only with Bob and Wads, to finally negotiate Warners out of this snafu of their own making. Soon, all of us immediately befriend Sidney, whose sense of fairness, honesty, and ability to forget that he is a "Suit" make him unique among the Warners personnel. Without Sidney as our interface, I doubt the movie ever would have been completed.

Our original film had by this time gone through a number of passes in the attempts to produce acceptable material. In the rehandling, it acquired hairline scratches which, when enlarged in a cinemascope image, looked like railroad tracks. We had to use liquid gate. The only type available in the houses we were using was an applicator type. It reduced scratches, eliminating them completely in some of the material. But because a coating had been put on our original film by some of the New York labs which did the processing months ago, the liquid gate dissolved it into globs on the original. Fine for the Rain sequence, perhaps, but! We needed a special immersion-type liquid gate.

At Hal Shieb's Cinema Research, one of the five optical houses, we located an immersion-type liquid gate. But they didn't have a techniscope camera. Scouring throughout Hollywood, we found one the next day and put Cinema Research to work. There, Jack Glass and his team pre-shot all our mattes, then bi-packed them with the negatives. Quickly mastering this innovative technique, they shared it with the other houses, accelerating our process.

Four weeks into opticals, however, it became clear that we would not meet our deadline. After we asked the optical people to work 24-hour shifts, we demanded that they find more techniscope cameras. Since we had hired an engineer to service our KEMs at night, we told the houses to retain an emergency technician. The very next night, he prevented a major loss.

Because we were under such pressure, we couldn't spare daily sequences for viewing by the optical people or others. As soon as Technicolor gave us a print we rushed it out to Warners Brothers for the mix. Now we did order two copies of every daily—one for the mix and the other for us to look at. Warners still received nothing.

It was not infrequent that one of us would get a call in the middle of the night from an optical cameraman, questioning a particular piece of information or instruction. On occasion, one of us would have to get dressed, drive to the house and work with the technician to sort out the problem.

No one had ever conceived of an optical four hours long. No producer had ever before worked with five optical houses simultaneously. We were asking them to stop everything else, delay their regular clients, turn themselves inside out for us.

Every time we thought we had a decent enough picture and its respective sound track even roughly mixed, we would put out the word to the artists to see whether they wanted to come by the screening room to take a look at themselves.

In some instances, we wanted the artists to "approve" their sequence so that they would sign their contract with Warner Brothers allowing us to include their segment in the movie. For some mysterious reason, for example, the Jefferson Airplane refused to sign, citing creative differences between what they envisioned and what they saw and heard. Or maybe they wanted more money. On the other hand, Alvin Lee, vocalist for Ten Years After, dropped by Warner Brothers and plunked himself down in the darkened theater.

47

ALVIN LEE: *PLAY IT AGAIN!*

(Alvin was the vocalist for the band Ten Years After.)

DALE: I was there and I remember what you said.

ALVIN: I was hoping you would remember. You tell me first because I . . . [laughs] I only remember a little bit. But how I got there or who I was with, . . . I just remember being there. And Bob Maurice and Michael Wadleigh were there. Where's Michael these days? What's he up to?

DALE: He's up in New Hampshire. He's living on a farm with a woman named Cleo. It's a several-hundred-year-old farm, and I was up there in September. They've got about 200 acres that have been in her family, not in his, for some 200 years.

ALVIN: Oh he's a father now, is he?

DALE: He's not a father, . . . no no no, he *is* a father, but he was a father long ago.

ALVIN: No, I meant a *farmer!*

DALE: No, he's not a farmer. He is a motorcycle rider. He did something like six thousand miles in India alone, back in August, I hear—

ALVIN: All right! Good, man! OK, . . . so what did I say then, at that screening?

DALE: Well I remember what you said because I was sitting right behind you. And what you said was, something like "Oh my God, that's absolutely so pretty" (or "so stunning," or something else). But then you said, "If that weren't me up there on that screen, I'd bloody well wish it would have been!"

ALVIN: [laughs hard] That's a good one!

DALE: And then you said, "Could we play it again please?"

ALVIN: Huh, yeah!

DALE: And of course we did and we played it and we played it, of course.

ALVIN: Oh, yeah, I was really knocked out with it, that it came out so well. I was quite nervous, wondering of course what it'd be like. But, it was great. I remember that. I wish I could remember more, but I actually remember you. I remember sit-

OK, WHERE'S THE MOVIE?

ting in the seat; I've got a mental picture of it; I can almost run it frame by frame in my mind. And I was a bit embarrassed at the time, and a bit sort of apprehensive, wondering if it was going to turn out all right, and then tremendous relief when I realized it was a cracker.

DALE: Had you heard anything in advance, about what your sequence might look like?

ALVIN: Not at all. I think Michael had told me it was really good, but that's a very relative kind of thing to say. I really didn't know what to expect. Yeah, I

Vocalist Alvin Lee of Ten Years After

was really pleased.

DALE: Yeah, it was marvelous actually. I mean it was so sensational, it was the only time that we ever used that technique of mirror-image printing.

ALVIN: Well, let me tell you my story of this, because it kinda happened after that screening. Michael then told me all the problems he'd had with Warner Brothers, said they'd wanted it to be an hour and a half long. And I think he showed me a telegram he'd got saying that "if

"Goin' Home"

you don't cut it, we'll cut it." And there was a big hurrah going on and they'd had guards on the film cans. And I remember one night Michael took a car out with loads of empty film cans in the back so that the guards would stop him, just to be a nuisance, you know? But, what he told me was that all the artists, Janis and Jimi and all those guys, were all getting together and sending telegrams to Warner Brothers, saying, "You're not allowed to cut this movie. It's got to be left as it is."

So I got on to my manager—at the time it was Dee Anthony—and I was very enthused by this "artists all pulling together" business, and I told him this, and I said, "We've got to send a telegram." And so he composed the telegrams saying "you're not allowed to cut any of this, any of our music out." And I think he signed it "Long Live Artistic Integrity." And the next morning he got a call from Warner Brothers and the first thing they said was, "You're out of the movie!" But they got the hump about that [meaning they were sullen]. And we were the only band that sent the telegram! . . . [big laughs] . . . I don't know if it was a kind of perverted joke of Michael's, but I don't think so, . . . I think he was serious. I think everyone else just chickened out, you know?

DALE: I think everybody was serious, and I know damn well he was, because we were having to pull that kind of a ploy with Warner Brothers every other day.

ALVIN: That's right. Yeah. Anyhow, we sent the telegram and the first thing they said was, "You're out the movie," but as it happened, Dee Anthony was also managing Joe Cocker. And they got down to that "well, ok, if they're out the movie, then Joe Cocker's out of the movie too," and they managed to come to some compromise. But it wasn't a compromise; I think we were really lucky to have such a long jam without being cut. But the trouble is it's very difficult to cut Ten Years After because the tempos change all the while. And once you cut a bit out, you got to find another bit the same tempo to get back in; that's tricky.

DALE: Well that's exactly what happened, I mean we tried. We had a couple of expert music editors, trying to make an incision here and there in order to get it down to around eight minutes. And in the end, we capitulated to the music itself.

ALVIN: Great! I'm glad you failed!

48

JEANNE FIELD: *First Film = Academy Award: Easy!*

Larry Johnson had become Assistant to the Director and Head of Sound and was working long hours. I began to work with him after I put in the time for Bob, watching and learning as he laid in "Wooden Ships" and edited the lyrical opening section of the film.

Paradigm had now become Wadleigh-Maurice Productions. One of the perks of being part of the company was attention from the managers and bands who had been in the festival.

Many of them came by the office to see their footage and give comments on which piece they preferred. CSNY, Joe Cocker, Alvin Lee came over. Other perks were great seats at Steve Paul's Scene for the Jerry Lee Lewis show.

Larry Johnson and Jeanne Field took care of the sound tracks

When it was announced that Warner Brothers was moving a crew to L.A. for the rest of post-production, I went to Bob. He would not hear of my going. So, I quit my distribution gig and went with Larry as his girlfriend, bringing our cat, Woodstock, along.

This move pushed me into a realm of tension that began to seep into the production in several areas.

It's not news that when something big is happening, people's egos get bruised and they begin to change. Bob was under immense pressure. He had never produced before, but he was loyal to Michael and he was smart and tough. He wrote me off and I was not usually welcome in the Yucca Street office. This was okay because Larry was doing most of his work at the Record Plant logging tracks, mixing down, and I was able to continue working with him.

I lived at the Orlando Avenue house with Wads, Dale, Yeu-Bun Yee and Thelma, and on occasion made sure they had dinner waiting and the house in order (this meant making sure the packing crates that served as furniture were cleaned once a week). Bob seldom visited there, and less after he careened into our driveway and ran over Woodstock the cat. Bob and I eventually called a truce when he and I agreed that we wouldn't backbite each other in favor of the health of the production.

Warner Brothers sent a limo to Topanga to pick us up when Larry was nominated for an Academy Award for Best Sound. But it was the year that *Patton* swept, and he and Thelma, who was nominated for Editing, lost. The film won for Best Documentary and remains one of the most financially successful films ever made.

I thought, how easy—work on a first film and it wins the Academy Award. Easy.

49

STAN WARNOW: *From Student to the Warner Brothers Lot*

After driving across country for three days, I found my way to our new offices and edit rooms on Yucca Street—"Mecca." I had the slightly surreal feeling of irrational dislocation, caused I guess by all those grueling hours on the road and then seeing the very same people I had left behind in New York. Within a few minutes I had taken a brief look at the editing rooms, and was on my way to the house on Genesee Street in Hollywood where most of the editors were going to live communally for the duration of our West Coast stay. This was one aspect of the experience that I liked a whole lot; it was only fitting in the spirit of the sixties for us to have our own little commune. Within a few days we had settled into a comfortable familial rhythm. We would usually all breakfast together and then drive to work, go out for lunch together, work till late in the evening, and go home exhausted to sleep the sleep of the just.

While at work, it seemed that every day brought a visit by at least one famous or infamous member of young, hip Hollywood. Our film was definitely a high-profile project among Hollywood's young elite. There was a subtle satisfaction in knowing that a group of documentary-oriented outsiders were working on what was clearly a major project of the season in the film capital. I doubt that a documentary has had such a profile there before or since.

I became totally immersed in the musical performances of the Woodstock Festival. Although the material was roughed out, there was still a lot to be done. The first cut is often more of a draft, subject to radical revision, than something close to a finished product. I often feel when I'm editing that the real work begins after I can sit down and view a complete first cut. It is only then that a full picture of the strengths and weaknesses of the work begin to emerge.

I particularly remember screening my much-revised version of "Soul Sacrifice" for Mike just before we finally locked, and him telling me, "It just keeps getting better and better," which I naturally found very satisfying.

As we began to lock up the final versions of our cuts, we were faced with the reality of transforming them from up to three individual strips of film to one combined version that would exist on a single anamorphic 35mm print for theatrical projection. This was done using a layout grid on which each editor would sketch the locations of each image exactly as he or she wanted them, then work very closely with the optical house personnel to ensure that the opticals came out as planned. It was an extremely detailed and exacting procedure, involving many hours of preparation before submission to the optical house.

Around the time that we were locking picture, we moved the editing rooms from the Yucca Street location to the Warner Brothers lot in Burbank. This was another milestone for me, as I suddenly found myself working inside of a major studio. Eighteen months earlier I had been a film student, and now I was working at Warner Brothers. For the first several days there was a definite thrill just driving through the security gate and knowing I was part of a privileged group of industry insiders. As we were a group of non-union kids from New York, we had to have union standbys for every one of us who was actually editing, and I got to meet and work alongside Hollywood veteran editors, and see how they did things, which was certainly revealing. Our main liaison to the whole editing infrastructure at Warners was Fred Talmage. Even though he may have thought we were a bunch of wild-eyed radicals on some level, he was unfailingly supportive and friendly.

Stan Warrow

I particularly enjoyed the proximity to the Warners backlot, and began to see it on a certain level as my own personal theme park. On my lunch breaks I would often pick up a sandwich from the commissary and go exploring among the various unused standing outdoor sets. One day I might eat lunch in Victorian New York, on another in Dodge City in 1870 and so on. It was an intriguing combination of the fanciful and mundane.

A few months later the film opened to universal acclaim, which was of course very satisfying. Then came our Academy Award nominations, another gratifying moment. The film was nominated for Best Documentary, Best Sound, and Best Film Editing. But this was a bittersweet moment because despite all my work on the film, I was

Editor Jere Huggins in the stacks.

not personally nominated, nor were Yeu-Bun Yee and Jere Huggins. At the time, I didn't think that much of it, having a "sixties" attitude that it was really only the work that was important, and the Establishment recognition in the form of awards and such really didn't mean much on the cosmic level. So I didn't object.

Now I know better, that an Academy Award nomination may not mean much cosmically but it means a hell of a lot in building a career. If I found myself in that situation today, I'd make damn sure my work was recognized, because those things do count, like it or not. *Woodstock* will always remain as a wonderful work experience for me, but if I had to list a regret, it would be my failure to fight for what I deserved.

DALE BELL: *Ping-Pong on the Dubbing Stage*

Technicians have measured that the sound contributes about 75% of what we perceive and *feel* about movies. On the dubbing stage is where the magic which captivates us is created, with its innuendo and its orchestration of all the sounds—and silences. In the darkness of the theater, the combination of image and sound transports us out of our own world and into that of the movie.

One of the goals of our movie was to let the audience feel that they had become the actual center of all the activity. Sound would be our tool. Larry Johnson, Dan Wallin and their team would be the guides.

We had the Stage A at Warners. Why not? Nothing else was happening on the lot. In fact, I don't think any renovations had been implemented in this particular room since the head of Warners' sound, George Groves, won an Oscar for the sound he mixed in this very room for *The Jazz Singer* more than 40 years earlier. Let's just say, it appeared—and performed—that way.

George had to be in his sixties, or beyond. White-haired, clipped mustache, British upper-crust tongue. "Dyed in the wool," one might say. George had his way of doing things in his studio. It seemed to involve intimidation. Once he accepted our looks (he never got over them!), he had one basic word for us: "Don't!" Early on, I lost count of the number of ways he told us we were foolish, time-wasters, unorthodox. He had the most difficulty with our proposed use of the surround speakers. Time and again, he would deny us access to them by scolding us in front of his own men. "No," he kept saying, "you can't put primary information into those surrounds. They're just for background noise."

The men who were assigned to help us through this arduous task of cleansing and manipulating the dozens of sound tracks we had accumulated in our production were kind and helpful enough, but the gear itself seemed out of an earlier era. To create a signal path from one track to another, a technician had to "re-patch" the channels, creating a link between hitherto unconnected modules. Once, this sound console with its myriad of dials and pots might have been able to accomplish innovations beyond compare, but that time had long since passed. Re-patching became a nightmare.

One option: We could have abandoned our dream. George was trying to encourage us to do just that every day. Whenever we asked that a sound or group of sounds be patched into the surround speakers behind the audience, for example, George would protest, then rush off to complain to Ted Ashley that we didn't know what we were doing. Or conversely, that it would require too much time for us to achieve our effects.

Bored by the delay of patching, repairing, and re-patching our cables, I bought, had delivered, and then installed a full-size ping pong table on the dubbing stage one evening. When everyone arrived the following morning, there we were with paddles in hand, playing a rip-roaring game as George came in for his morning visit. In clipped tones, he asked "What the hell is that doing here? Is that for sound effects?" I guess I hadn't thought that the pinging and the ponging might have a practical use, so his question took me a little aback. "Well, George," I said, "we plan to play ping pong in between the roll backs and the takes." He said: "What do you mean? Our men are working terribly fast!" "Well, George," I replied, "apparently they're not working fast enough because they want to play ping pong with us. They are waiting for the men to come to make repairs on the gear." George was extremely frustrated, and flustered. "Well," he said, "we've never done this before. You freaks come out here and mess up our stage! Don't you know, we try to run this as a very tough business. We're going to have to fix this mess after you've left! All this re-patching!"

George stalked out to tell Ted Ashley again about how we were disrupting his mixing stage.

We discovered quickly that the technical people on our dubbing stage were fast becoming our friends. We called them by their first names, instead of "Hey you!" Mostly Short-hairs from old-school Hollywood, they addressed us as Mr. this and Mr. that. "Mr. Bell, we would like an additional ten minutes for lunch today. Would that be all right?" We had never been treated that way before. It was entirely out of character. We agreed to no "Misters"; we all agreed to first names; and we granted them longer lunches as they needed so long as the work got done on schedule. Of course, we discovered that our management style received instant rewards. Respect, camaraderie and friendliness bound us all together much closer. And as a symbol of our new personal and business relationship, we shared our Ping-Pong table.

It was not long before we brought the table outdoors to get some rays. On one vacant patch of green lay our green table, not far from the croquet court we had also installed onto the lot for diversion. Everything was taking a good deal longer than we had ever expected, from a Hollywood that was far from the technological capital of moviemaking.

Larry Johnson was trying to impress us with the need to take the tracks, re-record them onto a fresh tape, and isolate or split them apart by equalization and filtering. This was the only way to produce clean tracks to work with. For this, he would have to take the original tapes to a music recording studio before we even tried to mix at Warners, because he knew it would be impossible to clean these tracks on vintage machinery with a vintage mixer.

Larry and I had this "foxtail" joke going. He would walk up to me and calmly announce that he had to have this or that piece of fancy equipment, or three weeks of time at a music studio. None of this was in the budget and was more expensive than a string of polo ponies. I told him these items were like *foxtails* on the handle-bars of a bike: great stuff but totally without function. Undaunted, he started to avoid exact descriptions of what it was he needed: "Dale, I have to have a 'humma humma' before we can split the tracks." And "humma humma" soon assumed universal meaning for the entire sound team when referencing anything at all! "Humma humma" was verb, noun, adjective—an all-inclusive code word.

I simply could not believe that he could spend so much time—at hundreds of dollars an hour even from dusk to dawn, the cheapest time period—with his pals at the Record Plant on Santa Monica Boulevard. But as I was later to learn, it was also very necessary. The original tracks were a den of snakes, each trying to consume the other. And there was no precedent for this kind of technology in Hollywood, so we had to invent again.

After more than a month of playing with his "foxtails," Larry brought his multiple, re-mixed 24 tracks into the dubbing stage. If the new processed tracks did not seem as "alive" as the original—maybe too muddy from all the EQ—Danny Wallin would try to clean up the originals by using the many pots and tweaks available on the mixing board. Comparison would be made by A–B'ing the two sounds. A vote conducted between Dan, Larry, Michael and Thelma would determine which source would eventually be used.

To clean up the "tape noise" which had accumulated on the re-processed 24 tracks, we discovered a new process—or foxtail—which might eliminate some of the noise buildup. Standard today in movie theaters throughout the world, Dolby sound was in its infancy in 1970. It was used only in making records. The Dolby noise reduction could be added at the end of the chain to the mix stems: the final four mixed-down channels, used for the print master. At the last minute Larry had convinced all of us that this was absolutely necessary. We believed him. So I ordered four Dolby units from Wally Heider.

I thought Larry meant that this little filter thing would fit on the end of a patch cord somewhere. But when the truck pulled into the loading bay at the back of the dubbing stage, I knew I had miscalculated Larry's foxtails again. A forklift unloaded these huge black-box processors as big as refrigerators, and positioned them on the floor of the stage. I couldn't believe what we were getting into, particularly when Wally, who spoke loudly and stammered mercilessly, brought me the invoices for the rental of these little boxes. At first I thought, Larry had won again. And I was the dupe.

Probably the least technical member of the team, I nevertheless had to admit that my lay ears noticed a perceptible difference between the sound pre-Wally and post-Wally. Larry was crafting a very complex tapestry of sound.

All in all, pretty complicated. And very necessary to put the audience in the center of the experience. More invention, without precedent. No wonder Larry and Dan would later be nominated by the Motion Picture Academy for Best Sound! And Larry still wasn't shaving!

Music mixer Dan Wallin celebrated his birthday during our mix. Since nothing we were doing was ordinary, the singing of "Happy Birthday" required some extraordinary effort. In one idle moment, we had quickly edited together a sequence which featured John Wayne (who had visited our dubbing stage a week or two earlier and laced through us with comments about our looks!), Sly and the Family Stone, and the traditional "Happy Birthday" song. I think the editors were able to make Sly sing "Happy Birthday," topped off by John Wayne's sardonic remarks! Whatever happened was hilarious, I recall, probably because it was accompanied by cake and champagne for one of the many brilliant Warner Brothers staff people who really got our film.

51

DAN WALLIN: *THE MAKING OF THE SOUND TRACK*

(As told to John Rotondi.)

The making of the sound track for the documentary concert film
Woodstock *posed numerous technical and logistical challenges to the staff of the*
Warner Brothers Sound Department. Its completion marked a turning point in
the development of sound-for-picture. Up until this time, feature film post-pro-
duction was a staid and proper affair. The Sound Director of Warner Brothers
was a formal English gentleman by the name of George Groves. Mr. Groves did
not know what to make of the "hippie" film crew, so he gladly turned the project
over to the department's youngest mixer—the 40-year-old Dan Wallin. Dan's
experience as a Music Scoring Mixer, along with his big-band and rock-and-roll
mixing background, made him the most qualified person in the Department to
handle the sound for such a production, both in abilities and temperament. As
Dan reflects: "The film's Director, Michael Wadleigh, and Supervising Picture
Editor, T. Schoonmaker, drove the Department mercilessly, dragging them into
the 20th century, in search of perfection." For Dan Wallin, this would be a great
experience, and a welcome advance in the state of the art as it stood at Warner
Brothers.

My first viewing of the partially edited and assembled film took place in Hollywood.
The screening room was at Ivar and Vine, not far from the famous Capitol Records
building. This first screening utilized three 16mm projectors running in sync on a
split screen. This was very exciting and impressive new technology for 1969. The
screening gave me a glimpse of what Director Michael Wadleigh was striving for—to
capture on film the energy and scope of this one-time happening, this amazing experience. The whole spectacle—the music, hippies, and various "characters" involved—
proved to be an amazing revelation to a me, a guy from the big-band era. The scope
of the event—cars locked in for miles, and the mountains of garbage in the fields
afterwards—was beyond belief!

When the editing crew moved onto the Warners lot, they brought with them four
KEM flatbed editing tables. This was my first time seeing such a device, as all edit-
ing was done on upright Moviolas at that time. Ed Shied, Warner Brothers' Senior
Effects Editor, seeing these editing tables for the first time, stood there with his
hands on his hips saying, "What the hell is THAT? It'll never take the place of a
Moviola!"

The first part of the process undertaken was the mixing of the location music tracks. These were recorded on 8-track 1" analog audiotape, possibly on a Stephens or 3M machine, as there was no capstan. Sync to picture was maintained by resolving the 60Hz pilot sync tone recorded on track 8, the remaining 7 tracks containing the music. Larry Johnson, the location sound supervisor, was very helpful in providing information on the recorded tracks, and insight into the sound of the actual venue, so this could be recreated during the dub.

Artistically, the music and performances were great—but those great performances were often plagued with technical problems in the original sound recording. I knew it would be a hell of a job to attain the standards sought by the Director, and I hoped I was up to it.

The music mixdown was made from an Ampex MM1000, and made to 4-track magnetic sound film in the Cinemascope format—3 front channels and 1 rear (surround) channel. In this format, the release print itself was striped with magnetic tracks, which allowed a full-fidelity, discrete sound track to be presented—a welcome improvement over the mono optical sound tracks of the time. An important note was that, *for the first time ever in the production of a feature film sound track, Dolby Type-A noise reduction* was utilized on the magnetic sound elements to reduce the magnetic oxide noise build-up that accumulates with successive generations of transfers and mixing.

In the case of the tracks for Alvin Lee and Ten Years After, the drums were not picked up on tape, so these tracks could not be used. I enlisted studio percussionist Larry Bunker to "foley in" the drums. This was done on the Warner Brothers Scoring Stage. The good location tracks were mixed to magnetic sound film, so they could be played back as a guide track. An interlocked 3-

Music mixer Danny Wallin

track mag recorder was used for recording the new drum track. Mr. Bunker played along with these tracks while watching the picture, maintaining sync with the visuals. Alvin Lee personally approved of the final music mix.

During Joan Baez's rendition of the hymnal "Swing Low, Sweet Chariot," the tracks were played out through the Scoring Stage speakers, and picked up with Neumann U67 tube microphones. This use of the large stage as a live acoustic chamber added great warmth and dimension to this poignant moment.

Jimi Hendrix's now-historic rendition of "The Star Spangled Banner" was much too long to be presented in its entirety in the context of the current cut of the film. His improvisational virtuosity was quite complex, and posed a challenge to edit down. Composer Dominic Frontieri, who was working on the Warners lot at the time, was brought in to help edit the piece, and was able to do so while maintaining its musical integrity.

The film was dubbed (final mixed) on an RCA tube console, with 12 rotary pots, plus an additional 6 outboard faders. This console consisted of groups of rotary Daven "tri-pots"—each pot being linked mechanically to 3 channels (left, center, and right) of audio signals. I was joined in this process by Dialogue Mixer Gordon Davis and Effects Mixer Fran Shied.

Generally, the tracks were balanced and equalized for proper perspective to the action on the screen. Vocal dynamics were sometimes controlled using an RCA tube compressor to smooth things out. During the dub, Senior Effects Editor Ed Shied suggested adding rolling thunder to the big rain sequences, but the production team rejected this, wanting to maintain accuracy in the manner of "cinema verité." However, upon revisiting this scene, it was decided that the addition of thunder would add life to a scene which might have played weakly otherwise.

During the screening of the completed film, Sound Director George Groves was very puzzled by the wonderful performance of Joe Cocker, asking, "Is he spastic or something?" and "What's wrong with his voice?" Mr. Groves' limit of tolerance was reached during Country Joe McDonald's "Fish Cheer" sequence! Upon hearing the chant "Give me an F, give me a U...," Mr. Groves turned a ghostly white, and left the screening in a speechless flabbergast, never to return!

This groundbreaking project's sound track was done in about 18 weeks *[Less than that, Dan!]*, and was ultimately honored by being nominated for an Academy Award for Best Sound. The passion of its production team in striving for excellence shows, as this film is regarded as a classic of its genre. I was honored to be able to participate in this creative endeavor.

52

COUNTRY JOE McDONALD: THE LEGACY OF *"GIMME AN F!"*

(In the early confusion on stage, John Morris pressed Vietnam veteran Joe McDonald into service to appease the crowds. Armed only with his acoustic guitar, Country Joe McDonald, echoing Kennedy's inaugural speech of "Ask not . . . ," tried to grab their attention with a song which invited them to volunteer for their Army. But his mockery of our involvement in the Southeast Asian war became another anthem, like Jimi Hendrix's "Star Spangled Banner.")

DALE: Joe, when you first saw yourself in the movie, what was your reaction, please?

JOE: I was . . . awe, I would say. Stunned. Stunned. I was totally unprepared to see it. I was there by myself, in a viewing room with Michael [Wadleigh]. And I was blown away. Blown away.

DALE: Did we have the titles on at the time we showed you that?

JOE: Yes, and he told me he wanted to put the "FUCK" on the screen and they had said no, but they had the bouncing ball and the whole thing. Yeah, that's what I saw, yeah.

I don't think I realized that there was even a movie, or that I was going to be in the movie. And Michael didn't really tell me anything. He said, "I want to show you something. And when I saw it, it was just like, "*Fuck!*" I didn't even make a rational decision, now when I look with hindsight. Because that appearance totally changed my life; it had an unbelievable effect upon Joe McDonald's musical career. But that never occurred to me at the time. We never had a discussion—I think he might have said, "Well, do you like it?" and I said, like, "*Wh-huhhh!*" I don't remember saying I liked it or I didn't like it. I was just blown away. Because of course I was . . . *large.* You know? Larger than life.

DALE: That was a big screen.

JOE: Yeah. I wasn't prepared, to see myself that way. And then the bouncing ball was just so cute and clever; I realized also that my harangue in the middle, because of the audience not singing, was untrue. I could see their mouths moving and I heard them; when I saw the movie, it was obvious to me that they were all singing along and they knew the song very well.

DALE: As well as you did.

JOE: That's right. The vast majority of the audience knew the song as well as I did, and the cheer in front of it too. And I wasn't aware of that because the sound was going *up*, you see, and outside it goes up and you can't hear it; inside, it bounces around, you hear it on stage; but outside, you have to learn from experience that the audience *is* singing, and, you know, don't yell at them!

So, what the hell. I mean, up to that point I was a little bit scared, needless to say, performing in front of that many people, solo acoustic. You don't see in the film that I had been on stage 25 minutes before that, and no one paid any attention to me. But when I actually realized that no one was paying any attention, and they were all having a good time talking to each other, then I went, "Gimme an F!" And then, it seemed to me as though every single person in that audience stopped talking, looked at me and yelled, "F!"

Country Joe McDonald leading the F.U.C.K. Cheer

Bill Pierce

And you know, I thought to myself, "It's too late to stop now; fuck! Here we go, here we go ..." And I completely forgot that there were cameras around. I don't remember cameras *being* around me when I was doing that solo thing at all. That's why, when Michael said he wanted to show me something, I had no idea what he was going to show me.

DALE: How did it change your life?

JOE: There are many, many, many reasons. First off, it established me as being Country Joe McDonald, a solo act, which I never was before. There was a group called Country Joe and the Fish, and I guess I was Country Joe; but with the release of that film, and that image of me singing that song, after that I was definitely Country Joe McDonald. A solo act, singing that song. I wrote "Fixin-to-Die Rag" in '65, and this was 1969; so the song was an underground hit. Even Pete Seeger recorded it in '72 and no one would sell it, it was so controversial—just the lyrics themselves, not with the cheer in front of it at all. But when I put the "FUCK Cheer" in front of it, which we had invented months before and we were used to doing it then, it guaranteed that it was unplayable. Absolutely unplayable. Absolutely unplayable.

So you combine this lyric, which was blasphemous because it was, from a military point of view, essentially demanding the right to be empowered and make a decision on whether you're going to lose your life or not, and it dissed everybody that was important—Wall Street, the Commander-in-Chief, the generals, everybody— just in general all the fuckin' leaders, it dissed in the song, and not the rank and file at all, and so it made all the leaders mad, right? Of course.

It made the left wing mad as hell; they didn't really know what to do with this song because of the satire in it anyway. The Anti-War Movement, they loved it, the rank and file. But the leaders, the left-wing leaders themselves, who were very puritanical actually, in a left-wing way—when I put the "FUCK Cheer" in front of it and it came out on film and millions of people saw it, I mean, that just guaranteed that I would never be a left-wing darling in my life. Never. Never. Which means that the right wing hated me now, and the left wing also hated me.

The Establishment didn't know what the fuck to do. I saw Bowser from Sha-Na-Na like ten, fifteen years after the film came out, and he came up to interview me for some rock-and-roll thing he was doing. And he said that Sha-Na-Na, the whole group, thought that I was nonexistent. That someone had created a Country Joe McDonald, and it was an *act*. You see? It was like a Tiny Tim act or something, like a shocking kind of a "Country Joe" suit that I put on and I came out there . . . It made Country Joe like, *I don't know* . . . like a living legend. So it made me unbelievably famous. I mean I had the number one hit song, for the Vietnam War era. The number one hit song as far as the Woodstock Festival was concerned. People have now said that one of the greatest highlights of the film was yelling "FUCK!"

But it also made me an asshole as far as the business was concerned. So to this day I haven't sold quadruple-platinum copies of "Fixing-to-Die Rag." Today you don't hear it. So it just stuck me in a larger-than-life weird place that forced me in the long run to deal with my role in the Vietnam War and my military background and my political background, in a way that no one else from the Festival or the Generation has had to cope with. I have become a living symbol of the Vietnam War, and now I'm a living symbol of not only the resistance to the Vietnam War, but of the veterans themselves. And almost all the veterans have come to love that song.

And so it's still today. Here we are, it's 1999, and the song is really not—the *Woodstock* version of that song is really not playable. In an era of Dr. Dre and Snoop Doggy Dog,... [laughs from both] it's unbelievable that Country Joe still strikes fear into the heart of program directors. Many who are thirty-something now have never even heard the "FUCK Cheer." Maybe. But they just know the reputation of Country Joe McDonald. And well, I can laugh about it now, but at times, it was a real albatross around my neck, and that's why I said that if I had thought about it from a box-office point of view,...

DALE: We gave you a premiere on Broadway at 80th Street, when we were editing. We put two big huge speakers out the windows of the second floor, on 81st and Broadway, just down the road from Zabars, and put on the "FUCK Cheer" outside. There was a march going on.

JOE: End the War march, Probably.

DALE: Yeah, probably. And we had pande-fuckin'-monium for about three blocks, from about 79th Street up to 81st Street. 'Cause we kept re-playing and re-playing and re-playing the song. Finally we were busted.

JOE: Oh, really?

DALE: It was sensational. Just classic.

JOE: And to this day, it's cutting edge. Even to this day, I mean, it makes a hell of a lot of people nervous. That performance, that little excerpt there, you know? There's some parts of the film that just make people nervous as hell, and the pre-frontal nudity [sic] is one of them, and Country Joe, I mean, singing that thing.

Richard Nixon was in office, right? And he must have said, "What the hell is going on up in New York?" you know? And they said, "Oh, well, there's like,... they closed the freeway down ..." This is stuff I imagine in my mind, because the FBI had been watching my family and they were watching me, and I know they were really aware of what the fuck I was doing, anti-war and all that. There must have been a point where they said, [Nixon-esque voice] "W-hell, what happened? Tell me." "Well, Mr. President, the whole audience just yelled 'FUCK!' and sang a song that essentially said, 'Fuck you, we're not going to Vietnam.'"

And I just always thought, "Whoa, what did he say, 'Get that guy!'" or something, 'cause it must have made him really pissed. It must have made a lot of people really, really pissed off. You know? That that was in there. And even to this day, I still can't get played on the radio. I'll tell you that. "Aw, Country Joe. He's the guy that invented the word 'fuck' and made everybody say it." No, no no, it's not my fault, man.

And on the record, didn't they know that they had this monster hit that couldn't be played on the air? Because, you know I was with DJs and we were on the radio live, and we used to play a joke on them. They'd say, "What do you want us to play?" And we'd say, "Oh, why don't you play this track." And we wouldn't tell 'em, right, and they'd just drop the needle on there and they'd turn the volume down 'cause we'd engage them in a conversation so they wouldn't hear that they were pumping the "FUCK Cheer" out over the *airwaves*, and then we'd leave, you know? And then the shit would hit the fan. General Manager'd call in and say, "What the hell's going on?" And the guy'd get fired. He never knew what happened.

53

BILL BELMONT: *The Distribution of Wealth*

(Working with John Morris on-site, Bill was the one who negotiated contracts with the artists, and then witnessed the subsequent inequities.)

The idea of a film was just another bother—but not a really big one.

By 1969 many groups had gotten intelligent about not signing away film and TV rights. But for the most part, a vast majority of all of the participants had agreed to be filmed. It was mostly a "wait and see" prospect. As soon as it became evident that the Festival was going to be a worldwide media event, the documentary of the event became of paramount importance.

Instead of viewing the film as an impediment, an afterthought, many of the performers began to view the film as a living entity. Once the film became a possible reality and editing was taking place, the bands participating became an integral part of the process. Most were invited to view the footage as edited, most agreed in the approach that Wadleigh took: his use of multiple-screen images, stop action and other not-commonly-used editorial techniques.

Some of the performers insisted that their performances were extremely important to the film, and held out for substantial additional payments.

So as the film became a reality, and the "buzz" about it increased: the nonchalant, "*It's just a 'small film'*" attitude metamorphosed into "*This is going to be a big deal? How can I make this worthwhile?*" Many of the agreements were renegotiated by Peter Knecht of Warner Brothers Films who, as he later described to me, "got all the rights he possibly could for least effort and money." This in itself brings up some interesting questions.

The idea of "home video" devices was at best a possibility for the future, not a real consideration at the time. So when artists went with the original participation agreement or signed the revised agreement, the only rights they felt they were giving up were theatrical release and television. Oh, it did say *all rights*, but Warners has used the "television" aspect in the film agreements for the most part.

Warners later refused to pay any of the artists for home video sales. And when a number of the Festival's "ad hoc" MCs approached Warner Brothers and Atlantic Records about payments for the "voice announcements" made throughout, those companies took the position that since they were employees of the Festival, it was "work for hire"—though no one had really originally expected Chip Monck, John Morris and Wavy Gravy to actually introduce the performers. As with the rest of the show, things just sort of—happened.

So the inequities of the "distribution of wealth" remain. It seems inconsistent with contemporary practice that Warner Brothers would have continued to take a no-pay-for-home-video position so long after the existence of the music video format. Unfortunately, not many of the artists considered it financially viable to "go after" the film company. For the most part, no synchronization licenses were obtained either; Warners relied on the film's sync for the video release.

54.

DALE BELL: *FINAL CUT, FINAL BATTLE*

Early March. Three weeks to go before we were to open in eight cities: Los Angeles, New York, Washington, Boston, Chicago, San Francisco, Dallas, and Toronto. Bob Maurice had been so successful in keeping the "Suits" at bay that no one from Warners, except Sid Kiwitt, the sound-mixing people, the staff editors and the projectionists, had seen anything of the movie, with or without sound. Even *we* had not seen the entire movie strung together; only individual pieces out of order as they came from the dubbing stage and Technicolor.

Warners wanted a screening. What did we think, they were going to promote this movie without having seen it through even once? Only 25 of their executives would see the film, they promised. Use the big screening room where the screen and speakers had already been adapted to our movie. They wanted their way in two days.

Bob protested. How could their Suits get a true sense of our movie, sitting in the back row, talking among themselves? We wanted to invite some of our friends from L.A. How many? they asked. Twice as many people as *they* brought, we countered.

Bob Maurice and Michael Wadleigh preparing for the final battle

228

No, said Warners. They wanted to look at it by themselves, come to their own judgment. We wanted to invite some members from UCLA, USC, and other neighboring universities who were studying film. We wanted a theater-type atmosphere. Warners bristled at the idea. We countered. We had already invited them: "Come sit on the floor and watch the picture." More than a hundred would show up. On March 15, they would be appearing at the guard gate, demanding entrance. What would Warners do then? Risk the bad publicity? We warned them we would alert TV stations!

Warners maintained that the screening room wouldn't hold more than a hundred people. We demanded the building specs, to check them out with an attorney and the building inspector. But according to some Warners staffers, the screening room had received larger crowds before. We argued some more. Finally, they relented. I'm sure Sid Kiwitt intervened. Only one hundred, they insisted.

Larry and Dan finished our sound mix on Saturday night, just in time to prepare the tracks for the screening.

At the designated time, 1pm on Sunday March 15, the film students lined up at the gates. Long-hairs almost exclusively. More than one hundred.

When the executives arrived, they were astonished. They had to step over all the seated and sprawling bodies that littered the chairs and the floor. Students were leaning up against the walls, against each other's knees. Those way down front had to lie down to get a view of the screen. Already, smoke was in the air. As soon as the "Suits" were seated in the few remaining seats in the back, we began to roll. And rock and roll we did!

The screening would last four hours without intermission. The atmosphere in that room was so vibrant, so electric as a result of the "sardine" effect, that its pulse rate could never be measured or duplicated. It was the very first time any one of us had ever seen—experienced—the overwhelming power of what we had wrought. Superlatives are inadequate to describe the synergy that bound everyone together for those four hours. It was a once-in-a-lifetime experience. Literally. There were acts and documentary footage in this cut which would never again be seen, not even in the Director's Cut issued at the 25th Anniversary.

Little snickers curled to full laughter and cheers. When the students knew the words to a tune, they sang along. As the stereo sound traveled around and around the screening room, behind and in front of them, their heads turned to follow it. As the music modulated on the shock cut from a single panel to twin panels heralding the arrival of the crowds, there was an audible gasp from our audience. After each act, they applauded and shouted. When Country Joe McDonald asked for an "F" in the "F.U.C.K. Cheer," the students obliged in unison, adding their voices to those on-screen in front of them and those they heard behind them. The bouncing ball was greeted with hilarious cheers. And the Port-O-San Man received an ovation from our audience, the first of many he would motivate around the globe.

Even some of the Suits began to get into the mood, irresistibly drawn into the atmosphere. I frankly think they were very pleased, though perhaps silently, that we had invited the students. How sterile it might have been to watch alone! The screening went off without a hitch.

As the executives left, we agreed to a meeting in Ted Ashley's office the following morning at 9am for notes. We met in his "Alice in Wonderland" world where the furniture was designed to increase *his* height to the level of other, normal-sized people. Specific chairs were designated for specific Warners executives. There were five of us: Wads, Bob, Thelma, Larry, and me. Warners presented an equal number.

It would be a lie not to say that the atmosphere was extremely tense. The movie was to open ten days hence, on March 26. One day was needed for the shipping of the prints to the respective theaters. Calculate eight days in which to take their "notes," translate them into changes if we agreed, remix and/or re-opticalize, make prints in Technicolor, pack and ship. Very frightening.

"We want a movie which is only two hours and forty-five minutes long," Ted began. Not accommodating, we thought. We began discussing the end of the movie, with the Jimi Hendrix sequence which had played at almost 15 minutes in length. Bob opened by saying we were not going to cut it. Ted said they were going to cut it for us. Bob said they couldn't do it, by contract. Ted: "Yes, we can, and we will! We want it cut to three and a half minutes! At its present length, it makes the ending of the movie too dark."

Representing the demands of their exhibitors, Warners wanted the movie to turn around at least four times per day in each theater. At its current length, their income would be reduced by one-fourth. Vision be damned! Money was their motivation. They didn't care about our film.

It was a short meeting. Amid much anger, name-calling, and frustration, we got up and left and went back to work. During and after the screening, we had made our own "notes" and had a lot left to do to meet the deadline, without this silliness. But we were scared.

In another cutting room, sequestered somewhere on the Warners lot, we felt there was another editing team, headed by John Calley who had really not been very much involved in our picture. Unbeknown to us, we feared, Calley was re-editing— or truncating, or whittling, or chopping—our film down to the size Ted Ashley dictated. If Calley was at work behind our backs, where did he get his prints from, and his sound tracks?

The next day, we had a second early meeting with Ted Ashley and his people. Apparently, some critical picture and sound elements were missing from the editing and the mixing rooms. "Did we know anything about it?" he demanded. "No," we said, "we knew nothing about the missing elements." "What about Hendrix?" Ted Ashley asked. "We're not going to cut it down to three and a half minutes," Bob said. Ted repeated that we would or that they would cut it for us. We reminded him that nothing could be cut without the sound, and they (Warners) apparently couldn't find it. Had they looked everywhere?

We talked some more, but the renegotiation did not work.

On Wednesday, we held our third meeting since the screening. Ted wasn't there at this one. More accusations were thrown at us about material missing from the lot. Everything had stalled with the opening dates just days away. We were told that we should edit the Hendrix sequence down to a size that we thought was "manageable, but a maximum of around five minutes." We replied that we would edit, but that its length would be longer than five, and Warners would have to live with it. They said, "In other words, we're going to have to chop it?"

Returning to our editing rooms, Michael and Thelma edited Jimi down to eight and a half minutes. Warners accepted the new length. The next day, as though miraculously, all the missing material reappeared on the lot again as though nothing had happened.

Throughout these frantic days, we had other "notes" to implement. Though we liked the Canned Heat sequence, its boogie-woogie music did not wield a huge effect on the students. We decided to drop it. (Twenty-five years later, it resurfaced thankfully in the Director's Cut. Watch it carefully. There is not a cut in it for 11 minutes, the entire length of a 16mm magazine, frame to frame. Wads's camera work, weaving in and out of the performers with his wide-angle lens, is nothing short of astounding in its spontaneity, responsiveness and ingenuity. Listen to the sound, too. As Wads weaves in and out of the performers, the perspective of the sound changes to conform with the visual. Credit Danny Wallin, Larry Johnson and the sound-mixing team; it did take a great deal of time and patience to achieve such revolutionary effects for the time.)

Johnny Winter and Leslie ("Mountain") West succumbed to Warners' request for a shorter film. Jefferson Airplane did not want in. Tim Hardin's and Janis Joplin's performances were so inebriated, we felt we could save them embarrassment by not subjecting them to further, eternal visibility. The Grateful Dead's footage was so dark it was invisible anyway. Coupled with these "notes" were certain short documentary sequences which did not seem to work in their present context. All this was dropped. (Much of this original four-hour cut was restored in the Director's Cut issued in 1994 under Larry Johnson's and Michael's supervision.)

Now we were at length, plus or minus three hours, without credits. Already, we had determined who would get what credit and the order in which they would appear. Yet many other people had helped us throughout the movie; we wanted to thank all of them. (If we inadvertently left someone off, please forgive us!) Pablo Ferro, brought in by Warners, created some overblown designs for the opening titles that just didn't fit. This immediately confirmed another simple concept: no opening title at all. Let Sidney Westerfeld, the man standing on the stairs of the inn in White Lake, invite the people into the Garden.

CHARLES CIRIGLIANO: *END CREDITS*

(Son of an artist, Charlie found his way to our offices in New York and discovered he could service all of our complicated editing equipment. But it was in the last weeks of the project, when Bob Maurice asked him to design the final credits for the movie, that Charlie exceeded all expectations for diligence.)

One night I got a call from my friend, Winn Tucker, to get my ass up to 80th Street and Broadway ASAP and ask to see Dale Bell. Upon completing my job interview with Dale, I was hired, and two things were made clear to me: #1, predictably, were the things he deemed most important in an employee, and #2, that Dale Bell was a he, not a she; having seen too many Roy Rogers movies, I had asked to see *Miss Dale Bell*.

After this auspicious start, my next meeting was with Thelma Schoonmaker who, hugging her ever-present clipboard, succinctly informed me of my duties: "Fix anything mechanical that breaks, get anything the editors request, and give the editors no creative input."

It was from that moment that I knew I had a shot in putting my mark on this film. The KEMs were to guarantee my tenure on this project. I learned the mechanics of them inside and out. Literally, they were all mine; well, me and Wolfgang, the world head of KEM. With Wolfgang at my ear on

Graphic artist Charlie Cirigliano designs the end credits

233

the phone, guiding me from West Germany, only I was allowed to open the beast, the automaton with three heads that consumed film. "Consumed" means that the machines' torque motors were so powerful and the tolerances were so sensitive and the machine ran through film so fast that if the splices were off-kilter or the editor was working in too much of a hurry, the gears would "eat" all the sprocket-holes, or slit the print right down the middle, for 40 or 50 feet. This could really mess up your day.

The climax of this whole endeavor for me was crafting the logo and the end title sequence. Bob Maurice came to me to ask a favor: make a "W" for the logo because the Warner Brothers designer couldn't get past the "Woody Woodpecker" look.

So all I did was to create a "W" that logically looked like Barry Scholnick's famous dove on a guitar with the inscription "3 Days of Peace & Music." Bob liked my "W" and now he wanted the whole word, "Woodstock," which was easy. Then he loved the "Woodstock" I came up with and wanted me to do all the titles. Now the work began. We had mere days left until the release date.

From those 12 letter-specimens, the numeral 3, and the ampersand, I designed 26 uppercase and 26 lowercase, and 9 numerals. I had to go through all the outtakes and movie footage, selecting those shots that most went with the group or situation, and choosing the sound to overlay on it.

Counting from the day Bob Maurice asked me to make a "W," to me handing him the finished Main Title and End Credit reels at the door of the jet that was to propel him to the NYC premiere, eight days had passed. Well, those titles were first viewed sight unseen at the premiere, to rousing applause. My denouement was hearing this news. This final act of mine took eight 20-hour days, preceded by the six months of continuous work.

Wow, that was filmmaking!

🎥 56.

DALE BELL: *Th-Th-Th-That's All, Folks!*

The final burden for meeting the deadline set by Warners fell on Technicolor. Five days to go before opening nights, three days to go before press screenings. Already Bob and Mike were approving newspaper, radio and television advertisements. There was no turning back. Technicolor said they couldn't do it. I remember saying to them: change! You've got to do things differently! They told me that one piece of gear was on the 10th floor, the other on the 3rd. Remembering what I had heard in our original tour with their chief executive, I reminded them that the gear could be moved closer together in order to obtain greater efficiency. Twice as fast, I remember hearing. "But it will cost you $20,000 to make that move," they replied. "Make the move," I said. "Do it." This whole deadline business had just cost another $75,000 in the course of one telephone conversation. But in light of the embarrassment of not having prints at theaters on time, this was a small price to pay.

As the hours ticked away Saturday and

Bob Maurice and Michael Wadleigh happy it's over

Stan Warnow

235

Sunday, and more overtime began to aggregate, the weekend bill at Technicolor mounted to $150,000 to produce ten full-length prints with wraparound sound tracks. On Monday, March 23, Warner Brothers executives hand-carried one print each to the major cities, except New York and Los Angeles, for the opening the next day.

On Monday evening, I took one print to New York, by hand, just in time for the press screening on Tuesday at the Trans-Lux East.

Made it.

AFTER:
5 YEARS, IO YEARS,
30 YEARS AFTER

DALE BELL: *WHAT IF?*

Afterglow about "Woodstock—The Movie That Almost Didn't Get Made"

Just before the Woodstock Festival, Mike spent a well-paid month in the Wind River Canyons of Wyoming to shoot *Thirty Days to Survival* with Paul Petzoldt's National Outdoor Leadership School. Filming in the rugged back-country of Wyoming, Woodstock was no doubt the farthest thing from Mike's mind. Or was it?

When he returned to New York City at the very end of July, his only thought was to buy some good tickets to this music festival in upstate New York he had heard about. Larry and Jeanne inspired that idea. Larry was far more into the music than anyone else. Together, they would lie on the grass and hang out! After all, he needed a rest from the rigors of backpacking the past 30 days.

I don't believe Bob Maurice or Mike Wadleigh even began to take the notion of filming the concert seriously until the Maysles brothers and Porter Bibb came to our Broadway offices during that first week in August to try to build a coalition: They had not tied up anything: not Warners, not another financing studio, not the festival, not the musicians, and apparently, they did not have enough money in their own bank to finance the project independently. The dark abyss was opened. The Ten Days of August began.

No film would be made unless we did it. Into this power vacuum we plunged, relying solely on adrenaline and our own skills. *Carpe diem.* A challenge of immense proportions. The lure of the unknown . . .

Though no one knew then that this historic concert would attract hundreds of thousands of young people seeking community, it did promise to be the greatest assemblage of musicians ever gathered in one place. Both Bob and Mike had a strong pulse with music, though Bob's love for jazz was very dissimilar to Mike's connection with folk and rock.

Mike had just set records climbing mountains; the ordeals had taught him a good deal about himself as a human being. Bob had other records to his credit: for devouring courses in history, psychology, philosophy and religion at CCNY without receiving a diploma. Mike had given up medicine to conquer films; Bob financed his fascination with philosophy by balancing as close to heaven as steel construction girders would allow. Both men were daring beyond compare, though both had afflictions they were able to hold in check: As in Dostoevsky's *The Idiot*, each retained a clarity of thought, and manipulation, not to be duplicated.

Both men saw the concert as an opportunity to create a venue for Mike's experiments with multiscreen filming of music concerts, where others would be the producers.

Both felt passionately that the war in Vietnam was wrong. Preserving this concert on film might at least let the message carried in the music and the lyric of the sixties reverberate more than once. Serving as director on some Richard Nixon presidential spots in 1968 allowed Mike to flirt with an eerie sense of power, but he also was able to turn his back on it. That work might have actually served as motivation to make the movie.

Both were rebels with a cause. Consorting with authority, to learn from it only to defy it, was standard operating procedure for both of them, just as scaling heights to defy gravity was also common to both.

When they began their exploration of the abyss, and brought others of us along, no one knew where the journey would take us. Yet all of us were intensely aware of the yawning chasm before us.

With a documentary, you cannot control the events; by every rule, silent or carved in stone, you are forbidden to even try. Your job is to be prepared to go with the flow, to film what interests you and to turn off when you lose interest. You have to be in shape, physically, mentally, and psychologically, and to be armed with the right equipment so you can follow your subject wherever he/she/it takes you.

Much like climbing mountains without a rope, freestyle, you had to be willing to fall or to climb. Within the last 12 months, Mike had done nothing but climb to great altitudes. Bob had tiptoed across girders suspended over city streets. Neither was about to fall here.

John Roberts of Woodstock Ventures turned down Bob's offer to own the movie rights 100% if Michael and all of us would be allowed to make the movie with full editorial control, *on spec*. Though this decision changed John's life forever, he simply didn't have the cash. This forced Grappling Bob Maurice to search out a way to make the movie, *because no one else was going to*. Pounding on every New York/Hollywood studio door: Columbia, Paramount, and Warner Brothers, produced only echoes of negativism. No one got it!

Within those frenetic couple of days in August, Bob scoured about, trying to put a deal together. That's when Artie Kornfeld worked over Fred Weintraub. That's when I called Jules Winarick. That's when Eric Blackstead called Alex Brooks. Full press scramble. And Bob brought home the bacon. His reward? He then had to deal with all those Suits and keep them away from us so the original vision could be fulfilled. Thank you, Bob. THANK YOU! It was a role you didn't want, but it was a job only you could do.

Why? If Everest is there, climb it. Trust your gut. Lash yourself to the mast and keep going forward. Do not allow yourself to be overwhelmed by the totality of the undertaking for it will intimidate you. Break it down into manageable parts. Determine what you can say "Yes" to, and implement those as you move on to others. Rely on your training. Fight for what you believe in.

"Impossible?" Yes. Looking back, very much so. Yet there's the film, brought into being by ordinary, caring, funny, creative and ingenious people who "Just Did It."

Los Angeles Times critic Charles Champlin, writing in March 1970, would say:

"The unifying characteristic of the Hollywood films of the 1970s was boldness. Sometimes, oftentimes, it was a boldness with a cynical eye to profits. In other and more enduring instances, it was artistic boldness—daring to do what had not been done before on the same scale or with the same candor and depth. *Woodstock* with its twenty cameramen deployed to record an epic musical gathering, became itself an epic.

"The Woodstock Rock Festival of August 1969 started out to be a nice, simple, king-sized money-making weekend. It ended up as an historic togetherness of crisis proportions ... The Woodstock gathering has now been recorded in what I think is an historic piece of film, *Woodstock: Three Days of Peace and Music.* ... Wadleigh and his platoon of film editors have made superb use of the split screen—have in fact made clear that the split screen is an urgent part of the grammar of film and not an amusing gimmick. The reverberations of the electronically driven music find their shimmering images on the screen ... Sound and images echo. Sometimes there are two disparate but related images; a song of children and children in the crowd. It is all ebullient and astonishing.

"The use of film technique is conscious and artful, but there is no sense of technique for its own sake, as a plaything. The multiple images, the wild sound tracks, the faces gone lavender or green under the flood lights in the dark night, the sometimes deafening music, all come as close as film can to recapture the essence of a unique and remarkable moment in time.

"*Woodstock* is a record, not an analysis. There is no narration and no real attempt to examine society or a generation of musical history or of American affluence, to learn how it was that nearly a half-million young people showed up, stayed through three cloudbursts in three days and cheerfully endured hardships that would have evoked instant mutiny in any army camp on earth.

"Let the analysis come later. This is source material, brilliantly compiled. It is aimed primarily at the audience that was there—or would have been there if it had been humanly possible to get there ...

"Michael Wadleigh's stunning film, produced by Bob Maurice and financed by Warner Brothers to the tune of a reported $600,000 [actually more than a million], raises true concerns about how responsive our society is to this generation. Yet in its affable optimism, *Woodstock* also suggests that we're not without a considerable and defiant hope."

New York film critic Judith Crist would write:

"*Woodstock's* distinction is in its camera work and editing. Rock groups and personalities lend themselves to theatricality, and this film's gifted makers have used split screens, stop motion and freezes to brilliant and striking effect, with subtle variations in the size and shape of the frame. The Richie Havens sequence for starters is joltingly beautiful—and toward the end, the freeze of Sly is a work of art in itself."

A *Time* magazine said:

"It is happening all over again. Woodstock, last summer's "three days of love and peace," has just been re-created in a joyous, volcanic new film that will make those who missed the festival feel as if they were there ... But *Woodstock* is far more than a sound-and-light souvenir of a long weekend concert. Purely as a piece of cinema, it is one of the finest documentaries ever made in the United States."

What might have happened had there been no movie?

XXIII° FESTIVAL INTERNATIONAL DU FILM
CANNES 1970

SAMEDI 9 MAI, à 18 h. 30
PALAIS DES FESTIVALS

WOODSTOCK

réalisé par
MICHAEL WADLEIGH

INVITATION   CORBEILLE

At the 23rd Cannes Film Festival in May 1970 (the movie had played in the States for six weeks to packed and passionate audiences), Warner Brothers scheduled our three-hour movie as one of the five American films in the main festival. One day earlier, as Bob, Mike, Larry, Thelma and I were having lunch at a restaurant on the beach opposite the Carlton Hotel, I noticed a newspaper headline at an adjoining table. In French, it screamed that several students had been killed by militia at Kent State University in Ohio, Mike's home state.

Shocked by the news, we immediately bought papers in French and English and began to figure out what we might have to do to symbolize this horror at the Cannes festival. Indeed, had the passions aroused by our movie contributed even indirectly to these traumatic events? Certainly there were redneck short-hairs in the National Guard in Ohio! Among the many plans we discussed emerged one: find some black cloth, create black armbands in the hundreds, and distribute them among those who would come to screen our film. It would take us most of the night and the next day.

We had written a short speech, which I had translated into French, and we would deliver it in both languages before the running of the movie. In part it said:

"We filmmakers want to dedicate this film to the four American students killed by the militia in the United States, students who were demonstrating against the war in Vietnam and Cambodia. We also dedicate this film to all those who will die for the cause of peace throughout the world and the struggle against domestic oppression. We completely oppose the wars in Vietnam and Cambodia. We support completely the struggle of students and the efforts of blacks and other minorities to overcome their oppression.

"At the end of this film, if you also oppose the wars in Vietnam and Cambodia, please join us and wear the black armband throughout the remainder of the festival."

Vincent Canby of the *New York Times* would comment that, though the film was well received as a "political" film, Warners' high-pressure publicity created a lot of unfavorable comment.

But had the power and symbolism of the movie already had its frightening impact in Ohio, and was it spreading? Were we responsible?

THELMA SCHOONMAKER: *HAVE TO HAVE A HONDA*

It was wonderful to be able to go around Europe with *Woodstock*. The press didn't know what to make of it, but the young people were responding to it as strongly as young people back home in the States. It was really great to see that, after such a long hard battle to get the film put out in its original length.

But at the Cannes Film Festival I got a nasty shock. Someone at Warner Brothers had had a secretary on the lot transcribe everything said or sung in the movie for use by foreign translators. It turned out she didn't know much about the youth culture of the time, and had some difficulty with the song lyrics. I realized the enormity of it when I looked at the French subtitled print at Cannes and saw Sly and the Family Stone saying in French, "I have to have a Honda, I have to have a Honda" instead of "I want to take you higher!" Then I noticed that many things were translated incorrectly. It was an awful feeling to know that all around the world people were mis-translating the film into Indonesian, Japanese and Czechoslovakian.

From that point on I have personally supervised the transcribing of all Scorsese films. Even the best-intentioned transcriber can sometimes misunderstand dialogue, or convey the wrong intent. All along the way, when you are making a film, you have to guard against it being whittled away by well-meaning people.

ELEN ORSON: *GRAB YOUR OWN MOVEMENT!*

Woodstock went on to win the Oscar, and The Film Industry discovered what a huge market there could be for films about the counterculture. The next wave brought such films as *Midnight Cowboy, Joe, Butch Cassidy, M.A.S.H.* and *Little Big Man.* Then TV gave us *The Brady Bunch, The Partridge Family* and *Mod Squad*, and America ate it up; everyone wanted to be regarded as hip. Not like the angry hip demonstrators in Chicago, but like the beautiful hip people they had seen in *Woodstock*. Bankers and stockbrokers began to wear bell-bottoms and wear their hair "long" and search for inner meaning. And that was pretty much it, for the youth movement as it had been. You're no longer unique when everyone is trying to look just like you.

There is almost no way to trace the million and one imprints that the film has made on society and film culture. When you watch a drama on TV now, and it's shot with a hand-held camera panning and swinging around, that's *Woodstock* invading the cultural subconscious. When you watch the beautiful nature documentaries of National Geographic, that's *Woodstock* too; many of the crew members went on to work at WQED Pittsburgh and brought their sensibilities with them, along with their sense of adventure. No retrospective of the sixties would be complete without footage from the festival. Our film is the dominant popular image of the festival, and gave it its place it in history.

The youth movement finally grew up. We now find ourselves trying to lend sage advice to teenagers who roll their eyes as the Old Ones speak. I'd like to think that we did change the world, for the better, and I am secretly pleased when I see kids in bell-bottoms and tie-dyed shirts. (Ah, the classics.) I never get offended by outrageous hair. I guess it's a phase everyone should go through. But I don't want them to be just like us; they should go find their own movement and grab it. Run with it. Don't imitate us, or especially our mistakes!

We got clobbered and tear-gassed and arrested, to admit self-expression into the culture. And I get upset when I see it wasted on self-indulgent bull, and I get upset when I see teens leaning on their parents, expecting everything to be handed over to them for free. How is it that we have swung all the way from student peace to students with guns on campus? We blew open many doors; we gifted them with a world where at last they could have their own power, go after their dreams, and make it on their own, in peace. Sometimes I think these kids don't appreciate the sacrifices we made!

SONYA POLONSKY: *Is Optimism Gone?*

SONYA: There was a whole spate of music performance documentaries afterwards, for almost ten years, that I believe imitated it and badly. I think they thought it was an easy formula to success. And they missed the wonderfulness of the film itself. And the painstaking care that was taken with the performances and the way they were optically presented. And I think also a lot of television music was shot for several generations and possibly still is, in an imitation of the form that was probably basically developed on *Woodstock*: the three cameras moving a lot and jumping around, which they do very mechanistically and sort of perfunctorily on television, but which in *Woodstock* was really beautiful and really meant something.

DALE: You teach, and you teach film history and film editing to younger people. What kind of reaction did they have to the film?

SONYA: When I was watching the opening with my class, it felt very optimistic to me. I think that it makes me feel sad, and possibly—but maybe I'm just imagining— it might make people my students' age feel bored. That kind of optimism they think is sappy, I think. They're about 20—19, 20.

DALE: Optimism is sappy?

SONYA: I think so. 'Cause they're into irony and being cool. And they only like things that are obviously satirical. They don't like displays of emotion; they think it's sentimental. There wasn't any emotional display in that opening of *Woodstock,* it was just all these beautiful young people riding around, and everything kind of golden and nice, and this nice country blues song. So it made me sad, because I felt like it was a feeling of optimism that seems to be gone.

DALE: Gone in the present generation.

SONYA: And gone in life.

61.

LISA LAW: *The Hog Farm Lives*

(Lisa's perceptions as a Hog Farmer with Wavy Gravy are a part of her "Flashing on the Sixties" book and video.)

Lisa Law and son on the Hog Farm in New Mexico

Woodstock was the first music festival I attended where there were more of us than them (not forgetting the smaller Fantasy Fair and Monterey Pop festivals preceding it). We (the Hog Farm) were in charge for a while, with the blessings of Michael Lang, and it was heaven. We knew what to do because our communal experiences had taught us how to share and care and feed large numbers. Only this time, there were 400,000 on the grounds and 2,000,000 trying to get there. The cops collaborated with us and the result was three days of peace and music. We set up trip tents for those who'd taken too many drugs, helped in the medical tents, and fed 160,000 hungry people. I know that's how many people we fed because that's how many plates, cups, spoons and forks we bought with the $6,000 I got from the promoters to go into town for supplies. (The food concessions had sold out on the first day.)

The participants of the concert know what went on in those fields in Bethel, New York, because they were there—experiencing the rain, the music, the mud and the oneness of it all. But the film *Woodstock,* documented by over 50 dedicated cameramen and women, brought those harrowing moments to the screen so

Wavy Gravy and Hog Farmers arriving at JFK on their way to Woodstock in 1969

hundreds of thousands of people could share in the joy, the passion, the one mind, and the birth of a nation.

The spirit of that weekend, the vibe that created the Woodstock Nation, still lives today in people all over the world. It's the elevated consciousness that drives us to save the planet, to make things right for native cultures, and to revere all species of animals and plants. These concepts weren't born there, but they came together there, and dispersed from there to all parts of the world, spawning a new generation of mindful youth.

🎥 62.

MARTIN ANDREWS: *Drop Back In*

After all that was done at Woodstock, and all that has been said about it in 30 years, what does it all mean?

The pendulum of history perpetually swings movements in and out of vogue. After some very bad economic times at the end of the 19th century, World War I and the lifting of the stupid Prohibition, our fathers (swells) cut loose and boozed it up to hot jazz with our mothers (flappers) in the Roaring Twenties. Fashion, style, language and music were revolutionary quantum leaps away from the Stephen Foster, square dance, church socials that had preceded them. Their party was suddenly shattered by the Crash of '29 and the Great Depression.

For us, the energetic American accomplishments (settling the land, industrialization, etc.) engendered by free private enterprise had been perverted into the free private avarice of mindless consumerism and the military/industrial complex. It was time to have some fun, and we "kicked out the jams." It couldn't last—and it didn't. Nixon's criminality, the killing of King and his dream, the killing of Bobby Kennedy, buried the white dreams. Our party was ended as definitively and abruptly as the Depression had ended our parents' party.

Martie Andrews, Mike Wadleigh, and Dale Bell on Cleo's New Hampshire farm, September 1998

Our parents' party had no agenda. Ours did. We were politically savvy: we got our country out of a war in which it did not belong. If that wasn't a historical first, it's certainly the greatest example of one.

If you are hip (a hippie), then, by definition, you can see through the shams imposed upon you by the Establishment. Once you're hip you can't become unhip. You can sell out to the Establishment to support your family in the Reagan (ray gun) years, but you don't become unhip. You are just completing the forgotten part of Timothy Leary's dictum: "Drop out, turn on, tune in, drop back in."

We will have to see if our survival instincts are sufficient to make the human intelligence experiment a success here on this planet. I'm telling my sons (22, 18 and 12) that only Bucky Fuller had the right answers. His philosophy was simple: If you don't bring the bottom up, the bottom will bring the top down. Bucky lucidly explains how we can bring the bottom up and make the world work by doing more with less, by advantaging everybody at the expense of nobody.

Perhaps our kids will hate us for the mess we're leaving them. But they can discover the wealth of Bucky's wisdom and wise us up with a Woodstock of their own.

63

MIKE LANG: *A Worldwide Phenomenon*

DALE: Did the release of this movie change how the Establishment dealt with young people? With music business, with the record business, was this a watershed?

MIKE: Well I'll tell you one thing: that every place we go, we are known because that film brought the festival to the rest of the world in a very real sense. I mean, whatever happened in the microcosm up there was brought very viscerally to the rest of the world, and it became a generational high point for every country on the planet, because of the film.

I've worked in Europe a lot over the years ever since the mid-seventies. Woodstock is so well known everywhere. You take a poll in America and you ask how many people came, were at the event, and probably 5 million people will say that they were there. A similar phenomenon happens around the world; they felt so close to the event and it brought it so much into their reality that they felt that they'd experienced it, through the film. And so I think, beyond it becoming an American phenomenon, it became a worldwide phenomenon because of the movie.

DALE: You've used the words, thank goodness, that I would use. There were only 350 or 500 thousand people there. They served as a "microcosm."

MIKE: Yes, absolutely.

DALE: What did the film hammer home?

MIKE: The power of . . . music. That culture. The fact that there was this community that existed in America, that was tied together, and that was so large and so strong and so positive. I don't think that anybody realized the extent of all of that before the film was actually released. And I think it brought home to people that it was not just these sort of radical groups that were spread around here and there in the East Village and Haight-Ashbury, but this was everybody's son and daughter who was involved here.

You look at that crowd, you don't see half a million long-haired Freaks, you see kids with crew-cuts, you see kids from every walk of life. I've always looked at *Woodstock* as a way for anybody who was a young person during that whole era who didn't smoke pot and wasn't interested in politics and wasn't a music fanatic and sort of missed the ride through the sixties—that it's instant access to that generation. You

Woodstock crowd of EveryKid enjoying three days of peace and music

Amalie Rothschild

came, you were in, you had it all. It was an open door for everybody, and I think that the film spread that even further. And I think that that may have been its—the festival's—biggest cultural impact, at that point.

DALE: Did it change business?

MIKE: [rapidly, assertively] It changed the music business radically. Because I don't think anybody'd realized the potential, and the power of bands to bring people into a concert. And right after Woodstock, it went from a cottage industry to a real industry. The amount of money that bands demanded from their performance [laughs] skyrocketed! Instantly! I think the day after! I paid Hendrix $15,000, which was the top; I think we paid him two shows. But the top fee was $15,000 an act, and three weeks later I think he was getting $150,000 at the Isle of Wight. It just instantly skyrocketed the price of bands and events, 'cause they realized that the bands were really capable of generating that kind of draw and that kind of income.

DALE: Did it change culture? How did it change, let's say, communications? VH1, MTV, the way commercials were shot, the style . . .

MIKE: I think it changed the way America viewed the power of Youth, and their style, their attitudes, their interests. And their commercial viability, for industry.

Because suddenly you saw this huge marketplace out there, that was a lot bigger than anybody had previously thought. Madison Avenue suddenly came out of the fifties, [laughs] and into the sixties and seventies, realizing that this was their future. And things had to start appealing to this culture and these kids, or they weren't going to survive through the seventies. And I think that was true pretty much across the boards, y'know?

DALE: Yeah. The music. The Establishment co-opted it. You know we designed the movie so that it would never be seen on television, and kids—audiences—would be required to go to a theater and Warner Brothers would then be required to distribute it in theaters. We never thought that you'd be able to scan this wide-screen format, and collapse it to your TV back home. We didn't want that to happen; that was one of the big reasons for making it anamorphic. It's so frustrating, you know, to try and keep it isolated, to keep it away from all that corruption.

MIKE: I'll tell you, the strongest impact that I saw was traveling through the rest of the world, even East Germany. Even behind the Iron Curtain, as it was then, Woodstock was such a legend, because of the film, that everybody identified with it. Even some of these guys who were very hard-liners in the government warmed to it, because of the film. So the effect that it had politically as well as emotionally around the world was amazingly strong.

There's a Polish artist who told me some story of the sound track being played, and he was listening to it in a Russian tank. [Laughs] I mean, if you talk to some of the people from Europe, especially behind the Iron Curtain, I think you'd be amazed because for them it really became their link to freedom, and connected them with the Youth Culture here. They became bonded through the film and through the record.

DALE: Talk about *Gimme Shelter* [the movie made by Al and David Maysles about the Rolling Stones tour in the fall of 1969 and early 1970].

MIKE: I think that *Gimme Shelter* kind of shows the dark side of what can happen within . . . given the same group of people. And for me it maybe showed something different than it showed to anybody else. Because Altamont did not have to be the horror that it was. It was because of a lack of preparation—something that I always believed, and in preparing Woodstock I went to every festival that year where there were a lot of problems.

In Denver and other places there were riots and people crashing gates and confrontations with police, a lot of tear gas at some, and it occurred to me that they were always caused by the attitude of the planners.

When we planned Woodstock, we planned free kitchens, free campgrounds, we had a free stage, we had speakers set up in the free camping areas so that if people came—and had we had gates, which of course we didn't, people who didn't buy tickets wouldn't just be confronted, they'd be taken in, and taken care of.

The problems at Altamont were caused by little or no planning, and bad decisions. Having the Hell's Angels as security, for example, was a monumental . . . fuck-up. And it comes out of the fact that the people who planned this were from London, didn't really understand what the Angels were, or how that functioned. And so you placed a group who was pretty paranoid anyway—'cause of the attitudes of the public toward them—between the stage and 100,000 people, and they're there to defend it, that's what they're going to do. There was more acid eaten that day than anyplace else that I've ever seen in my life. And . . . had it gone any other way, it would have truly been a miracle.

So to me, as I say, it just means that you have a huge responsibility when you put a crowd like that together. You can't just expect it to work and function on its own and think its way through this. You have to at least provide an environment that lets it happen the right way.

In terms of the lasting effect, I think that Altamont was looked at as a local phenomenon, you know, a California kind of madness. It did not have the penetration that *Woodstock* had anywhere in the world, and didn't really represent a dark side of that culture so much as just a bad incident.

DALE: In *Woodstock* did we glorify the drugs too much?

MIKE: I think it would have been hard not to because a lot of it was so humorous and so charming, in a way. And so much a part of the culture anyway. I think maybe we highlighted it a bit too much, and so it became sort of the overriding theme, in a way, with everybody being high. But I don't think that was even the case at Woodstock. It was just the idea that if you were getting high and sharing it with people, that was the essence of it. I don't think that the drug culture per se is what that was all about. I think it was youth culture, not drug culture.

It was peace and it was a coming together of people in very much a real community spirit. And people opening up to each other I think that was the essence of it, that everybody came and found each other. And opened up to each other in a positive way.

And the truth of the matter is, no matter how much security you have, you cannot control a crowd of half a million people, or 400,000 or 300,000, with security. They have to do that themselves. And you have to create the attitude and the environment for them to do that. And to be able to do that, that's the trick.

64

AL MAYSLES: *The Dumbing of America*

(After losing the rights to film the Woodstock Festival in August 1969, Al and his brother David went on to make "Gimme Shelter," with Porter Bibb producing.)

DALE: When you talk about your filmmaking technique, elaborate a little bit on what you mean.

AL: Well, I guess as most people know from the films we've made, there's probably not many people making documentary films that are as purist as we are about music and narration and script and research. We don't use narration in our films; we don't script it. We don't get people to repeat things; we forgo interviewing people. Just as you go to church and God is your guide, in documentary filmmaking the controlling element—the guiding hand, if you will—is reality. And we leave that powerful force to give us what we get, so we don't ask anything of anybody and certainly don't interview them. In a word, it's totally uncontrolled cinema.

Now, of course, when you get into the editing room you have to put it together into some sort of structure. I suppose if you follow the philosophy to its brutal end, then all you do is show the 40 hours of footage, but no one has the patience to see that.

DALE: What was your reaction when you saw *Woodstock*, this film you might have made?

AL: We were put off. I didn't know how much of the film we saw. We were put off by the fact that there were interviews. And especially the way the interviews were constructed. All the questions seemed to be designed to answer the "Well isn't this wonderful; we've got the flower generation and everything is just hunky-dory." Even if they had to use interviews, which we felt they shouldn't have in terms of filmmaking technique, then open the answers. It would be more revealing and less "point of view." So, that put us off and I can't say we stormed out, but we slipped out from the audience.

I react strongly against the so-called "point of view" documentary because I think that it limits the outcome to the point of view that you start out with, no matter what that is. Maybe you can agree with the politics of the one point of view over the politics of another, but I feel that in a documentary film, which has one obligation above all, it has to be factual. For me, it has a second obligation, that is, to be fair so if there's a judgment to be made, it should come from the viewer. And, the viewer should have a good deal of information from which to make that judgment.

DALE: Well you found yourself in a quandary at Altamont filming *Gimme Shelter* there, when you discovered what had happened right in front of your stage.

AL: Well, what you mean, in that—the question of people being beaten up and so forth. Maybe to drop a camera and take and defend those that are being hurt or something, is that what you mean?

DALE: Isn't that or doesn't that enigma pass through you at some point?

AL: It didn't happen to me, in my case, because I was on the stage. And getting off the stage and getting into the thick of the battle, so to speak, I would have lost what I think we really needed, which was the point of view from the stage. And of course, we had other cameramen as well. The killing itself, I didn't get that. My brother, at that point, was above me on the scaffolding above the stage. Brian, who was the cameraman with him, got it, and in fact, they weren't even quite sure having gotten it because of the quickness with which everything happened. But of course, we discovered later on that it was. There are instances, I'm sure, where something is happening where a moral decision has to be made as to whether it's more important to intercede when someone is being hurt and stop filming, even though what you're filming is an essential or nearly essential part of the story. But I wasn't faced with that.

DALE: Do you think the *Gimme Shelter* factor is still at work in our society today, and how does it compare with a *Woodstock* factor?

AL: Let's see, we have different demons, I guess. For most of all these years, and even now, if I look at *Gimme Shelter,* I walk away from that film. There's one impression that I have, most of all—that is, oh my god, look at these kids with all that promise, with all that idealism that's lurking somewhere in there. You know, drugs, and whatever else, the energy just can't seem to express itself. I think also that the elements of repression in our society were there then, but it's diverted now. The energy has been diverted into diversion.

Whereas that music and the kids of that time, the music was a very engaging kind of music. There's a lot of history behind it. If you take the word "entertainment," there was entertainment going on, but it was an engaging kind. Whereas now the entertainment is all diversion, and actually it expresses itself in the very way movies are made now and television is constructed now. It's all little pieces of five minutes here and 20 seconds there. Commercials are made up of maybe 30 shots instead of three or four, and it's all dumbing America. Those kids weren't dumb at that time. They were being dumbed by drugs, but the process hadn't been so complete as to dumb them completely.

Now, the fact is that people—kids and older people too—watch 6, 8, 10, 15 hours of this stuff a day, and all of it is diversionary. None of it is inspired insight, or gives you pause to contribute to your meditative, contemplative faculties. It's the dumbing of America and I think it's quite a different scene. I'm very disappointed in what's going on right now. It's reaching a point where it's practically prohibited to show anything good.

DALE: When you walk around the streets and you see skinheads and tattoo people and outrageous garb or decoration or body piercing or denigration of body—which of course, also must have some effect on soul and spirit—do you think that comes out of or is symbolic of, let's say, *Gimme Shelter* or *Woodstock* or films?

AL: Those things are so severe that I'm hopeful that kids who do that—it's a rite of passage. But these other elements—the cutting down of our attention span through the way the media forms itself now, without any content and all style—that's the danger that I see which is so pervasive and so destructive.

65.

MICHAEL WADLEIGH: *FROM COUNTERCULTURE TO COMMERCECULTURE*

(This interview was conducted in the spring of 1994 while Mike, Larry Johnson, Jere Huggins and others were completing the reprocessing of the images and the remixing of the sound track in the expanded version of the original movie, which would eventually become the Director's Cut. The re-release was timed to coincide with the 25th Anniversary celebration, Woodstock II, financed by Polygram.)

Q: 25th Anniversary—big thing? Why not 15th Anniversary?

MIKE: Timing. That's the secret to great comedy. I had no interest in doing this maybe until Polygram started all this anniversary shit, where there became a need to remind people what the real Woodstock was really all about. Because in the absence of this movie, what are they going to think? They're going to think it's all about the Pepsi generation.

And then Warners Home Video called me about three months ago. And the pitch was—Hey, Wadleigh. Why don't we do this? (Obviously in the hopes of making some money, from Warner Brothers' point of view.)

Q: Did you realize, when you started this, that the other was going to be so commercial?

MIKE: Yeah. When I first heard about the plans—the moving it from counterculture to commerceculture—I was very upset, because I know how powerful the media is. And MTV is giving it live coverage, and it's Pay Per View, and it's going to be seen all over the world. And I thought—well, wait a minute, this is really radically changing what counterculture is all about. You're going to have a situation where it's so formulized and corporatized and cutting away to commercials, one could hardly think about it. Can you imagine? We wouldn't have permitted it. If Pay Per View were possible then, with commercial interruptions, I can guarantee you that none of us would have allowed it. That would have been making us cannon fodder—dollar fodder for the mill. That's why I thought it was important to make a clear distinction—have this product out there, so you can see what the real thing is.

Q: What was comforting to see again and what was unsettling? The people who are gone now, for instance.

MIKE: Yeah. That was the single most dismaying thing. It's still dismaying. You hear Janis sing, and as my daughter says, you don't hear people sing like that anymore. You just don't. What a loss. That's the starter. There's Janis, there's Jimi Hendrix, there's Bob Hite in Canned Heat, Adam Wilson, Canned Heat, Keith Moon from The Who, Richard Manual from The Band. Abbie Hoffman is gone,

Director Michael Wadleigh, curious about the outcome

Larry Johnson

Pigpen is gone, Bill Graham is gone—these people were my friends. They weren't good friends, but I knew them all. It wasn't just that they were in the movie. We hung out sometimes together. Then you kick into selfish gear, and you say—these are some of the greatest musicians there ever were, and now I tune in MTV and what do I get? Are these the people who are really upholding this kind of incredible performing ability and songwriting ability and interpreting ability that these Woodstock performers represent?

Q: Was there something different about those times, those people, that allowed that to happen?

MIKE: I definitely think so. There's a generalized loss of innocence, a generalized instant communication and also a general feeling that the sixties have been lost—that altruism didn't work, that alternativism doesn't work, that it's the end of history. There's one ideology left—free market democracy and a kind of central conservatism. If you're in that kind of atmosphere, like we are today—as opposed to "question everything, let's look at all the alternatives"—then of course, the atmosphere isn't conducive to putting on an event like the original Woodstock. It's more conducive to putting on a Polystock.

Q: Do you think this generation is looking for their Woodstock?

MIKE: I think so. I think they're afraid they're never gonna have it. They're never gonna find it. And that's what I meant about cynicism, pragmatism and a sense of hypocrisy. I think they feel that opportunities are so closed on them that the possibility of getting something on that is theirs and that has a real decency just ain't gonna happen. And they protect themselves with cynicism.

Richie Havens starts the music while cameramen Michael Wadleigh, Dick Pearce, and Don Lenzer prepare, with assistant Anne Bell

Amalie Rothschild

Q: You have a daughter of that generation—what do you kind of see and hear?

MIKE: My daughter's an interesting case in point because she left college and went into marketing. She went to work for BUM Sporting Goods—where as she said, "In Taiwan we make the sweatshirts for $3 and sell them here for $60." And she found the whole rag trade and marketing to be exhausting and debilitating. She said she came home from work at the end of the day and she didn't feel good about herself. She felt dirty. She made a lot of money, but then she'd try to spend the money by going out on the Upper East Side of New York so she'd feel better—compensating. In the end, it didn't work. She said she got more and more cynical, and finally she said, "Okay. Lend me money. I want to go back to school and get my master's degree in education." And ever since she's done this, she's never been so happy. The pay is less, but you feel better about yourself. Now if that isn't Woodstockian, I don't know what is.

Q: What about the idea that all the people that were at Woodstock are the population that has ended up on Madison Avenue?

MIKE: Rock and roll has gone from rock and roll to Rock and Roll Inc. So no more can you get these great bands with these great sounds. You get people who have programmed music to get to the chart positions.

Are they selling out? I have mixed feelings about it. I think the seventies were very hard on people and the eighties weren't much better. "Hard" meaning economic realities, facing, earning a living.

I don't spend a lot of money. Maybe what I've retained of the sixties ideal is that this is about all I need to wear. I don't equate materialism with happiness. It doesn't make me happy. You know what makes me happy? Making a CD-ROM, writing something, making a good film. Making things. Creating things. Bringing things to life. But consuming things is destruction basically. I don't think people are really made happy by destruction. I think they're really made happy when they're gardening, when they're making a little toy, writing a poem for their girlfriend, whatever—honestly, I think those are the highest forms of happiness. All of which are antithetical to Madison Avenue's "Hey, buy it and you'll be happy."

66

ARLO GUTHRIE: *IT ENDED ONE ERA AND BEGAN ANOTHER*

DALE: How do you think the movie affected the music business? Up to that point, I'm not sure that the record companies really understood what kind of an audience they might have.

ARLO: No, I think you're absolutely right, and I think that was the end of it, in terms of the fun we were having and the free-for-all and the fact that nobody up until that moment really thought that this was marketable. And I think after *Woodstock* everything became part of the market economy. The next day, we were—there was soap named after Woodstock, you know what I mean? Blue jeans named after Woodstock, I mean, the Next Day.

I think corporate America realized, "We can sell this." And so we started seeing pictures of sort of natural women washing their hair in streams, you know what I mean? And it has not gone back, I mean, since that day. We have sort of wrapped it up and been buying it and selling the image in various ways for the last 30 years. Which is a shame.

DALE: How does that affect our society?

ARLO: Well in the long run, I don't think it will mean much. It's only in the short run right now that people have bought into it, because frankly, it was only a minority, a very small minority of people who did anything in the sixties. And yet everyone who was alive gets the credit for it. So, you know, I think that's just the way it works out historically. In the same sense that the American Revolution was probably endorsed by only a few people actually living here, and yet the whole country gets the credit for having thought it up.

DALE: Where do you think it's going?

ARLO: Well you know, in fact it is still going on, because Woodstock was not a single, unique moment in and of itself. In the context of the times, it was maybe the highlight, but there were a lot of other things going on simultaneously around the world in those few years. It wasn't just the people that went to Woodstock, because there were people overseas in Holland, in Amsterdam and in Denmark, in Kristiania and other places. And some of it is still going on in places around the world where some of the communities and some of the people who were involved in these things are still there, their descendants carrying on some of the traditions of free thought.

I would suggest that what made Woodstock so important is that it ended an era. And it began another one. People now would have no concept of the idea that at the time, we were living in a country where anytime more than 50 people with hair over their ears were gathered, was cause for a police action. There were people actually shot and killed on the streets. Simply for having, for expressing ideas, whether it was about a war, or it was about civil rights, or it was about one thing or another thing. And we were being told that the people who were participating in all of these were dangerous, they were anarchists.

The same people who were at Woodstock were in Selma. And the same people who were involved in the Civil Rights Movement were involved in the Environmental Movement and the Anti-War Movement and the Ban the Bomb Movement, and the Educational Movement, and the Power to the People Movement. This whole world is different because it was the same people involved in all of these movements, which we tend to separate in terms of what they were actually about, instead of who participated. And it probably is just a footnote in the history of what was going on, but these people changed the entire world.

And I tend to view this—I don't want to get too long-winded on you here, but I view this as the Woodstock Generation being the first generation in the history of the world who had the occasion of dealing with instant global annihilation. And that's not to say that the Aztecs or the Greeks or the Romans or the Incas or the Chinese or the Egyptians or the Atlanteans or the Vikings or all these people didn't have a lot of fun, raping and pillaging. But no one of them, and as a matter of fact, even all together, none of them had the destructive power available that was not only in front of us in the years of the Woodstock Generation, but had actually already been used.

So it wasn't a question of whether we were going to use this destructive power. The question was: Were we going to continue historically in the same way that our ancestors had gone, or were we going to do something differently, and stop what we saw as an inevitable race toward the destruction of humankind? And maybe other kinds. And we did that.

We changed the course of history. I want to take full credit [laughs] for the fact that we are still here, for the end of not just the Cold War but of all the sort of major difficulties. And I think in some of the struggles we've been seeing overseas even now recently, are kids who are caught up in the same spirit that we were caught up in Woodstock 30 years ago, working for peace whether it's in China or Tibet or Jakarta or in Bosnia. I can name all the conflict flash points around the world, and there are generally some kids out on the streets somewhere, reminiscent of what we were going through 30 years ago, who are trying to do things differently so that they can enjoy life.

And that's what we were doing. Thirty years in global time is nothing. So in historic time I think we're still living in that moment, it's just that we're through with it over here and we're on to the next thing,

It was the last great moment when we were all in the same boat. It was after that we all decided it would be better off to be in separate boats, so that we could get our act together or reevaluate our own uniqueness, or any of the fancy words they use today; but that was the last time we were all in the same boat. Didn't matter if you were black, white, yellow, red or tan; didn't matter if you were man, women, clothed, naked, rich, poor, this or that, everybody was in the same boat at Woodstock.

And the fact that we all not only got along, but had a hell of a party, it disproved beyond a shadow of a doubt the theories by the same idiots who proposed the Domino Theory: who told us that if we didn't go over to Vietnam, there were going to be Chinese Communists in New Jersey within two weeks. As if they could have found their way around New Jersey! And we were told by these same people that if those hippies get in control of things, there's going to be stealing, and murder, and injustice, and the American way of life is going to fall apart. And everybody bought into it!

But all of a sudden, when you have a half a million people not only all getting along, but getting along under the worst conditions imaginable, and everybody going home smiling anyway, this is not just historic, this is of Biblical proportion. And I don't mean that lightly. I think there was a great spirit that moved everything at that time, and really not only protected us but gave us the right attitude to deal with it.

I'm so pleased to have been a part of that. Yeah, it would have been nice to have been able to be more eloquent on stage, or take advantage of the moment, but I've had years to do that now, so I'm not complaining too much.

67.

MIKE SHRIEVE: *The Power of Music*

There's no getting around the fact that the power of music is great, and truly, I think that music has the power to heal. I believe to change, to take hate out of people's hearts. And contribute, in a way, to turning negative situations into positive situations.

Mike Shrieve and the Santana Band filmed by Michael Wadleigh

The power of music is like no other power. What I call it is *invisible architecture.* Music is invisible, but what other forms are there that affect you so much emotionally as soon as you walk into it? You can't see it, you can't touch it, you can't smell it or anything, but it creates this place. Depending on what the music is, it can transport you into different areas emotionally. It can change your life.

I think if you see the power of music, then you have a responsibility to use the music in a way that is uplifting and unifying. I think that you would want to do that.

68

MARTIN ANDREWS: *IN MEMORIAM: TED CHURCHILL (1944–1995)*

(Ted's work on the Woodstock stage was one factor which propelled him into his innovative work with the StediCam. Years later, on the stage of the Opera House at the John F. Kennedy Center in Washington, D.C., Ted (accompanied by his StediCam) and I worked over the Dance Theater of Harlem's ballet troupe performing Stravinsky's "Firebird." It was the first time formal dance had availed itself of this new technology. Proudly, the one-hour special triggered the Peabody Award for my "Kennedy Center Tonight" series.)

My relationship with Ted Churchill goes back to before he was born. His uncle (mother's brother), Chippy Chase, was a celebrated woodcarver of bird statuary who grew up with my father in Wiscasset, Maine. My mother was Ted's godmother, just as he became the godfather of my first son, Hilary Buckminster.

I had grown up with Ted and his dominant twin brother, Jack (also in the business but not on Wadleigh's team because he was ducking the draft in Sweden), during summers in Wiscasset. Wiscasset was small enough to force kids within a 10-12 year age range to play together, dress up in old clothes from the attic for birthday parties and be driven around in my parents' 1930 Ford Roadster.

I actually lost track of them for a decade until Ted resurfaced in the New York film scene, and Jack had fled to Sweden to avoid the draft.

As youngsters, the identical twins were considered as a unit: the twins. They looked alike and they acted alike; they were always together. They were nonstop fireballs of enthusiasm, energy, competition and noisy activity. To the discerning, Jack had a huskier voice and was more dominant in initiating their incessant antics of fierce competition. To those who only knew Ted, it was inconceivable that he could be dominated by anyone or anything. He took that competitive compulsion and administered it to everyone and everything with the same exuberant frenzy he had developed with his brother.

Ted and I took part in Ed Lynch's (another *Woodstock* veteran) foundation of AIVF—the Foundation for Independent Video and Film. Those initial meetings at Ed's place featured our realization that we were onto something radical and new, in contrast to the moribund and exclusive union scene. Ted's enthusiasm and intelligence helped shape our vision of bringing something new, technically and aesthetically, to East Coast filmmaking.

While Ted lent his enthusiastic support to all of our "trips," he was pursuing a hand-held and fluidly mobile trip of his own. In contrast to our out-of-control wackiness, Ted, though not always exactly sober, exhibited a characteristic, intelligent, self-aware coherence that was unique. He was destined to be and very conscientiously developed himself as the ultimate human fluid "head" camera bi-ped/pod. We were all into hand-holding the camera in order to give it unrestricted mobility. The inherent instability of hand-holding was a problem. I tried to solve this with multiple exposures and the fluidity of the fades and dissolves.

Ted really worked on his technique to keep the camera steady no matter what direction a shot might take. He was much more thoughtful and disciplined than we. He would really think about a shot before executing it. The rest of us were more likely to just "go with the flow." Ted saw the virtue of this flow and was able to fold it into his obsession for control by becoming the king of single-frame shooting. He would take one frame at a time with his Bolex and choreograph the most elaborate and jazzy studies of stop signs, stoplights, unusual cars, etc. He would circle and move in and out on his subject with a phenomenal sense of control, varying the rhythm of his move by how many shots he would take, ever mindful of the exact effect he was after and fully cognizant of how to achieve it.

Ted was very mechanical. He made a gadget to clamp his Bolex to his bicycle frame. He then fired off his shots with a shutter-release cable led up to the handlebars. He shot the most extraordinary scenes of his travels around New York. The background was ever changing and you could see the front wheel steering the bike in the foreground. What really made the shots, though, was a constant, which was the part of the bike that held the front wheel fork. This bike frame element provided an unchanging frame of reference that aesthetically legitimizes the pixilated wildness of the shot. Ted was fully aware of this and I was there as he made adjustments to maximize the effect.

Later in his career, his design modifications to his Steadicam and firearms became so complex that he had to hire a machinist to execute them.

Ted made a 30-minute documentary portrait of me called *Hoboken*. The film, shown on PBS, was a portrait of a Greenwich Village hippie and how gaffer tape held my apartment and my life together. It is something of a masterpiece in its bravura, camera work and highly intelligent editing. He was a major cameraman on *Woodstock* as well on *Sidewalks of New England*. Ted became king of the single-frame symphony of animated reality.

Ted took a classic shot of me at Woodstock stripping a piece of insulation off the end of a wire with my teeth, with the result that a piece of my tooth broke off and flew across the screen in dazzling backlit glory out of the frame. This shot was such a favorite at screenings that the projector had to be run in reverse and back again so many times that the workprint got totally chewed up. Somehow the original could not be found and the shot couldn't be used in the film.

Ted took up roller-skating and dance to perfect his mobile hand-held technique. Later he moved up to the Steadicam, developed many custom modifications and was second only to Garrett Brown (its inventor) as its greatest master. His distinguished career was cut short by his tragic suicide in 1997, induced by many factors, not least of which was his being betrayed by some whom he had really loved and trusted. This is my (our) tribute to a unique and fabulous person, an outstanding humorist whose vision extended into the highest technological realization of voyeurism, a key cameraman on the Wadleigh team—a true legend in his own lifetime. Thank you, Ted. May God bless and keep you.

Cameraman Ted Churchill beginning a move on the Santana Band

Bill Pierce

69

WHERE WE ARE TODAY . . .

MARTIN ANDREWS:

Woodstock and Martie parted company when the gang moved out West. His upbringing and genetic makeup prevent him from being a hustler in a hustler's game. Every summer, when the work action heats up, he has taken his three sons to Maine to get them (and himself) off the mean city streets. He's left the business three times. He has managed to dip in and out of the business as a technician. Once in NABET, he got turned on by the members, attended electric department meetings, became active on the testing committees, and eventually became head of the department from 1986 to 1990. He stepped down when his father died and he had to take care of his mother in Maine. Slowly he has resigned himself to the fact that his three sons, with his wife, Lizzie, are his real "motion picture productions."

ANNE BELL (TIRANA):

When Anne and Dale parted, she remarried to Bardyl Tirana, a Washington attorney. They now live in Washington and New York City. Anne has been able to reconnect with her passion for painting. She recently had her second one-woman show in Washington, while tending to our three grandchildren by our three sons Jonathan, David (architect and painter), and Andrew (attorney).

DALE BELL:

After *Woodstock,* Dale went on to make two more feature films (*Mean Streets* and *The Groove Tube*), two *National Geographic Specials*, a series of award-winning PBS performance specials entitled *Kennedy Center Tonight, WonderWorks* movies for PBS, and is now a writer/producer of specials and series for cable, network, and PBS. He has a fourth son, Reavely Bell, and shares the three grandchildren with Anne.

JONATHAN DALE BELL:

Jonathan graduated from Sarah Lawrence College in music and film. With his wife, Anita, he has returned to Grand View on the Hudson where they became recent parents of Belinda. Anita is the author of four books, while Jonathan divides his professional time between filming/videoing, running his production company, and composing music for films. The Tappan Zee is their playground.

PORTER BIBB:

Porter went on to produce *Gimme Shelter,* the film about the Altamont concert and tour of the Rolling Stones, with the Maysles Brothers. After producing other films, he has since left the business and is now raising capital for a new technology company in New York.

JOHN BINDER:

John was educated at Kenyon College in literature and theater. He studied acting and playwriting at HB Studios in New York, then attended NYU Film School with Michael Wadleigh, Marty Scorsese, and Thelma Schoonmaker. With Wadleigh he formed Paradigm Films, which dissolved in 1969. In the 1970s, John became a full-time screen and television writer in Los Angeles. He wrote and directed a feature film, *UFOria,* in 1981, and is still writing and directing in Los Angeles. John's oldest son, Joshua, is also a screenwriter and assistant director. Younger son, John Henry, an actor, is also opening a restaurant in L.A. John Binder has been married to Jeanne Field for five years. They met in 1969 when Jeanne worked in distribution at Paradigm Films.

ALEX BROOKS:

Alex has returned to Mexico with his trusty trust fund intact.

CHARLES CIRIGLIANO:

Charlie's extraordinary design capability led him into the union as a carpenter, an inventor, and a remodeler of old houses, many of which are on Nantucket. He has a college-age son, Jed.

MIRIAM EGER:

Five years after being in the States, Jeff and Miriam moved to Israel where they had their own production company. The move and two children changed their life dramatically. After seven years, they moved back to America for economic reasons. Three decades later and a world away, Miriam is now a successful real-estate agent.

AHMET ERTEGUN:

Ahmet is now Chairman of Atlantic Records, the company he founded with his brother, Nesui.

JEANNE FIELD:

Two years after working on *Woodstock,* her first Academy Award–winning film, Jeanne—with Larry Johnson, Dave Myers and John Binder—worked on *Marjoe,* which won again for Best Documentary. She continues to work in the film and video business, now as an agent representing writers primarily. She and John Binder were married a few years ago.

ED GEORGE:

After graduating from Paul Petzoldt's National Outdoor Leadership School, Ed received a fellowship for an MFA in film from Carnegie-Mellon University where he was reunited with Dale and briefly with Thelma. He finished in 1976, moved to

Jackson, Wyoming, then to a small town in rural Virginia and on to Flagstaff, Arizona where he lives with his wife, Liz, son and daughter in their handmade house in the woods. Along the way he worked on commercials, TV movies and features as diverse as *Dune* and *A River Runs Through It.* "I think I've finally found my niche shooting documentaries from South America to Mongolia to Italy," he says, "celebrating diversity, our interaction with the natural world and hopefully, along the way, cajoling some to be more caring stewards of the earth."

ARLO GUTHRIE:

Arlo continues to live in the Western Berkshires of Massachusetts, his base for forays on television and on stages throughout the world. He recently talked and sang on a PBS special. He and his family have bought the Church, made famous as part of *Alice's Restaurant*.

TINA HIRSCH:

Tina quickly became an editor in her own right, in film and video, and has numerous feature and television credits, including *Dante's Peak* and the recent *Behind the Mask*. She and husband Karl Epstein continue to live in Los Angeles.

MICHAEL LANG:

Mike has produced a number of major concert events all over the world, beginning with the Miami Pop Festival in 1968. Known as the founding producer of the Woodstock Music and Art Fair, he later owned and operated Just Sunshine Records, and managed the career of Joe Cocker for 16 years. He has staged concerts in Berlin and Dresden, including Fall of the Berlin Wall in 1989. He operates Better Music, an entertainment management and production company and lives in Woodstock, New York.

LISA LAW:

Lisa's photography and cinematography at Woodstock culminated in her book and video, both entitled *Flashing on the Sixties.* She continues to live in New Mexico.

ALVIN LEE:

Alvin now makes his home in Barcelona where he visits Gaudi architecture on a regular basis and speaks Catalan.

DON LENZER:

Don continues his career as cinematographer and videographer on projects scattered all over the world. Now he is adding writing and producing to his skills. He and his wife, Bettina, live with their daughter, Antonia, on Long Island.

CHUCK LEVEY:

A few years after Woodstock, he and Karen were divorced, but he tried to remain as close to their two girls as he could. Brooke is 32 and lives in Lincoln, Nebraska.

She's the head of curriculum for environmental studies at the University of Nebraska. Jessie will be 31. She is married, living in Brooklyn with her husband and little girl, 2. She teaches dance and is an Artist in Residence in a teaching program run by Lincoln Center. In 1973, Chuck met Carla Bauer. In 1977, he found out that he had a brain tumor. He came through the operation pretty well, but deaf in his left ear. Four years later, the tumor had grown back. The operation was not so easy that time. He lost most of the sight in his left eye, the left side of his face was paralyzed, and balance was something that he had to learn again. He and Carla married in 1987. They have two kids, Nicholas and Annie. Of the two films he shot that have been nominated for Academy Awards, one won. Four TV shows won Emmys. Personally nominated for an Emmy in Cinematography nine times, he has won four.

AL MAYSLES:

After producing and filming *Salesman*, Al and his brother David made *Gimme Shelter*, which followed a Rolling Stones concert tour to Altamont, California. Since then, the Maysles brothers have gone on to make other notable films, among them *Grey Gardens*.

COUNTRY JOE MCDONALD:

Still an advocate for the Vietnam veterans, Joe is releasing a new album, *Country Joe and the Bevis Frond*, playing Country Joe and the Fish music. His website, *countryjoe.com*, features his current activities as well as his continuing research into the life of Florence Nightingale. Joe lives in Berkeley, California, surrounded by a large family.

MUFFIE MEYER:

With *Woodstock* on her resume, Muffie had a fairly easy time getting editing jobs. She cut a number of music films and documentaries, followed by a couple of feature films, including *The Groove Tube* ("Thank you, Dale!"), and *The Lords of Flatbush* ("echoes of Sha-Na-Na"). She worked with David and Albert Maysles on several films, and in 1976 directed (with the Maysles and Ellen Hovde) the theatrically released documentary *Grey Gardens*. With Ellen, she then formed Middlemarch Films, and together they have produced and directed over 150 documentaries, series and specials for television (and a couple of dramas). Her most recent work, *Liberty*!, a six-hour series for public television about the American Revolution, just won a Peabody. And on many of these films, she has continued to work with people whom she met during the making of *Woodstock*. She is married and has one daughter.

JOHN MORRIS:

After launching several music productions, John left the music business. Now he devotes his time to his first love, Native American Indian art, creating traveling shows that tour the Southwest. He lives in Santa Fe and Malibu with Luzann Fernandez, a labor attorney.

DAVID MYERS:

Life after *Woodstock* invited Dave into more rock-and-roll films, feature films (*THX 1138* and *Welcome to L.A.*), and a continuing diet of documentaries and music specials. He lives with his wife, Barbara, a painter of primitive scenes, in Marin County, California.

ELEN ORSON:

Elen reports, "My work is my life and *Woodstock* had a profound effect on my work relationships: my co-workers usually become like family to me, and I'm kind of picky about 'redeeming social values' in the projects I choose. This makes me a pain in the ass. I have been Writer, Editor, or Associate Producer (and grunt) on over 650 productions, also worked in Music Recording, and Live Theatre production. I was Managing Editor for the Walt Disney TV Animation Editorial Department for six years. I work on an Avid (a digital Moviola of sorts) now and I never want to splice film for a living again, unless it's something special. In 1994, with my husband Christopher Carysfort, I co-founded a non-profit, Foundation of the Arts for Cultures and the Environment (FACE), which works to promote and publicize successful solutions to environmental problems. Still in the Garden ..."

CHARLES PECK:

Charles Peck graduated The Rhode Island School of Design in 1965 and was a staff designer at New York's public broadcasting station when Binder and Wadleigh lured him away to the Cinema Verité lifestyle. In the year prior to *Woodstock*, he worked as Wadleigh's assistant cameraman and soundman. In the decades that followed, he teamed up with *Woodstock* cameraman Chuck Levey as a partner in a successful documentary production company. Now in his fifties, CHARLIE prefers the art direction and design work he left thirty years Ago. He says, "It's a less glamorous career, but it's always nice and warm in here. I guess I'm getting old."

HART PERRY:

No one hired Hart as an abstract filmmaker, but he did get hired as a cinema verité cameraman. He filmed *Harlan County, U.S.A.* for his former wife, Barbara Kopple, and then *American Dream*. Both films won Academy Awards. He stopped working as a cameraman 15 years ago and concentrated on directing, although he continues to shoot his own films and films for friends. This year he directed *Motown 40*, a four-hour ABC special and he is currently directing two one-hour documentaries on paramedics. He has two children and lives in Manhattan with his wife, Devin.

SONYA POLONSKY:

Sonya finally got her wish. She became an editor, working with Thelma Schoonmaker and such directors as John Sayles on *Matewan*. She now teaches documentary films and editing at the University of Florida in Tallahassee.

JOHN ROBERTS:

With partners Michael Lang, Art Kornfeld and Joel Rosenman, John Roberts created Woodstock Ventures to finance and produce the 1994 anniversary celebration of the original Woodstock Festival. They have plans for a 1999 30th anniversary—a festival in Rome, New York.

THELMA SCHOONMAKER:

Though Thelma was nominated for an Academy Award for Best Editing on *Woodstock,* she did not win the award until she completed *Raging Bull* for director Martin Scorsese. *Raging Bull* went on to win many other awards, including the BAFTA (Oscar equivalent) for Best Editing. Since 1975, Thelma has edited and collaborated with him on all of his movies. She also married British director Michael Powell and helped him to write and edit two volumes of his autobiography, *My Life in Movies.*

MICHAEL SHRIEVE:

Since Woodstock, Mike has made seven solo albums and is working on his eighth. His collaborators have included a Who's Who of popular music: Mick Jagger, Pete Townshend, Steve Winwood, Jaco Pastorius, Bill Frisell, and Andy Sommers, among many. He lives with his wife, Cindy, and their two children in Seattle, where he continues his life in music. He also served as mentor to Jonathan Bell in Grand View, N.Y.

PHYLLIS SMITH:

Phyllis now lives in Los Angeles where she works at Paramount Studios.

JANET SWANSON:

Janet now lives in Los Angeles where she is an editor of documentary films.

LEWIS TEAGUE:

Lewis went on to become a director of feature films (*Cujo, The Jewel of the Nile, Collision Course*) and television series (*Op Center, Navy SEALs*). He lives with his wife, Elizabeth, in Beverly Hills.

DAN TURBEVILLE:

The *Woodstock* album finished, Dan worked in the recording industry until he walked out onto a carnival midway and was hooked. Hi-hi hee-hee, the carny life for him! And so in 1982 he became Captain Tattoo, painting temporary body art at fairs in the U.S. and Canada. In 1993 he married the artist Joyce Kingsbury. She, her daughter Rio, now 13, and son Logan, now 9, came to live with him and a year later Raskal Jack Turbeville was born. They live in Ojai, California and New York City now. Two years ago, they responded to the popularity of henna arts in America and created a small company of friends which sends high-quality temporary body-art henna products to all parts of the world. They think the thing to do is to "keep feeding each other."

MICHAEL WADLEIGH:

After directing the innovative *Wolfen,* Mike wrote several screenplays and is now producing and writing CD-ROMs. He lives in New Hampshire with Cleo Higgins, his collaborator in CD-ROM design, on her 200-year-old farm.

DAN WALLIN:

Dan has continued his award-winning career as a freelance Music Mixer of feature films. He and his wife, Gaye, live in Los Angeles.

STAN WARNOW:

After *Woodstock,* Stan has taken his editing skills to both coasts, working on dramatic and documentary films in New York and Los Angeles.

AL WERTHEIMER:

Al has given up filming, and running an editorial equipment company, to return to his first love, still photography. The photographs of Elvis Presley he took over a 12-month period in the late 1950s fill most of his waking hours. He lives on the Upper West Side of Manhattan.

🐦 ACKNOWLEDGEMENTS

The trail of breadcrumbs towards the publication of this book begins with Peter Pilafian. His introduction to Michael Tobias led me to publisher Michael Wiese and his encouraging staff of Ken Lee, Michele Chong, and Parthena Simone. Thank you all immensely for the opportunity and the encouragement. It represents the fulfillment of a dream born 30 years ago.

Of course, nothing could have been written at all had there not been a movie. For his perseverance, we thank Bob Maurice, producer; for his encompassing vision, we thank Mike Wadleigh, director. But as they have readily admitted, the making of this historic movie was nothing but a group effort, requiring the superhuman involvement of so many people from exhausted and hungry assistants ankle deep in mud at the site to optical house, laboratory and dubbing stage technicians working round the clock in Hollywood, months later. As we now know, each person's hands and ingenuity forged an icon for generations to come. Our extended family is vast. Each member is deserving.

Many people helped me in the writing and editing of this collection of remembrances. All of the contributors and their respective spouses (Liz Andrews and Liz George) can now relax; I will not bug you anymore. Thank you all for your efforts on behalf of our tiny piece of history. Our on-paper reunion is complete for this anniversary.

Others who helped include Chick Churchill and Andy Godfrey, who coaxed Alvin Lee to the telephone from Barcelona; Lela Logan and Anne Weldon at Atlantic ensured Ahmet Ertegun's participation; Jackie and Annie Guthrie found time in Arlo Guthrie's busy schedule; Ray Neapolitan for Joe Cocker; Kitsaun King for Michael Shrieve; Bill Belmont for Country Joe McDonald; Jerry Hughes for Charles Champlin; Julie Brennan and Gretchen Campbell for Martin Scorsese and Thelma Schoonmaker; Bob Kosberg and Charlie Mercer for Merv Griffin; and Patti Zarnowski in Richie Havens's office for her persistence which almost led to Richie becoming an actual part of the book, though his spirit infuses it.

Patti Fela may still be looking through the Port-O-San personnel records with a flashlight, trying to find Tom Taggart, the Port-O-San Man. Thank you.

Without the eager gifts of transcribing services provided through Pi Ware and the Filmmakers' Alliance, the insights and stories obtained through interview would never have left the can. I thank Robin Rindner (who traded her bowling shoes for two tickets to the original Woodstock Festival), Larry Oliver of Post Scripts, and

Nancy Williams (who attended Altamont, not Woodstock). In Pittsburgh, Dorothy Hanna and her niece, Cinda Perla, transcribed some of my own recollections from 1970. All gave willingly of their time and skill.

Elen Orson, from our original crew, answered the call for "all hands on deck" just as she had in August '69. Many thanks to her husband Christopher for letting me kidnap her for the duration. After transcribing many of the first interviews, she then lent her considerable editorial skills to reading and commenting on possible items to improve the work in progress. She spent long days with me whittling; I could not have done this without her. The combination of her moral and technical support were both necessary and invaluable.

Photographs leapt out at me from Henry Diltz, Amalie Rothschild, Larry Johnson, Martie Andrews, Charlie Peck, Chuck Levey, Steve Cotler, Stan Warnow, and finally, from my summer-stock friend who appeared on-site 30 years ago, Bill Pierce. Thank you, Marcy Gensic, for getting Larry's photos to me.

Larry Johnson's vital spirit is reflected in every aspect of the original movie as well as in the Director's Cut 25 years later. I hope that some of his vision emerges from this book.

David Frank, my partner from San Rafael, believed so much in the project that he and his partner, Margaret Wendt, offered to try to sell it as television.

Jeanne Field and her husband, John Binder, listened attentively to my progress, and provided encouragement even as we were trying to develop a series on Los Angeles Jazz and Cultural History with Branden Chapman of Vista Vision Entertainment.

John Andrews, my colleague on The Shakespeare Guild, offered advice in the early stages of organization.

My niece, Holly Scribner, and my daughter-in-law, Ting Bell, solved many computer problems as my laptop became over-saturated with *Woodstockiana.*

Linda Reavely provided a solid, nourishing home for our son, Reave, during the writing.

Ted Strauss and the Brueggemann family always provided inspiration.

For their musical and spiritual fellowship, as well as shelter during the last months of my work, I want to thank Larry and Virginia Keene, Bill Thomas, David Loeb, Irving and Gladys Cousino, and the Church of the Valley choir and congregation.

For her understanding and patience, I thank Brandette Anderson at Campbell Hall School.

To Di Nelson, my life-partner who grew up distanced from these tumultuous events, I offer this book as a bridge to another culture which contributed mightily to who I have become. My warm thanks to you for standing by me throughout every phase of this, my first book project.

To my first three sons, Jonathan, David, and Andrew, to Anne, your ever-compassionate Mom, and to your respective spouses and children, I offer my thanks for your continuing love and my apologies for any pain I have caused you as a result of my being caught up in this fervor.

To my fourth son, Reave, I offer the hope that, through this book and other media, you will come to understand the impact the sixties had on us as individuals, compelling us to set down our recollections and perceptions for generations to come— you and yours!

Perhaps, you as well as all of our extended families of children can "*Keep Feeding Each Other!*" Perhaps you can heed Martin Scorsese's vision in the Foreword that there may yet be another Woodstock, imbued with the same passion and spirit. It, and the healing power of music, can maintain the *Woodstock Factor* in all of our lives. There is still much to be done! *Find your own Woodstock.*

And to Henry Friedman, Bob Koslow, Jill Duffy, Cecelia Billingslea, Jay Shanker, Mel Shapiro, and Jeanne Paynter, my thanks for continuing to feed me.

Lastly, the errors are mine.

Grateful Dead at Fillmore East, January 2, 1970   ©Amalie R. Rothschild

Rock Music Photo Archive 1968–'74
Wide range of groups and musicians, venues include:
Fillmore East, Woodstock, Tanglewood, Newport,
Madison Square Garden and Isle of Wight '69

For general information contact

Amalie R. Rothschild
a.rothschild@agora.stm.it
Tel & Fax 011-39-06-687-9072

For fine art print sales and viewing:

SoHo Triad Fine Arts Gallery
107 Grand Street
New York, NY 10013
212-965-9500
SohoTriad@msn.com

STEALING FIRE FROM THE GODS
A Dynamic New Story Model for Writers and Filmmakers

James Bonnet

STEALING FIRE will take readers beyond classical story structure to an extraordinary new story model that can demonstrate how to create contemporary stories, novels, and films that are significantly more powerful, successful, and real. James Bonnet reveals the link between great stories and a treasury of wisdom hidden deep within our creative unconscious selves — a wisdom so potent it can unlock the secrets of the human mind.

Great stories are created by powerful and mysterious inner processes. The stories are designed to guide us to our full potential and are as necessary to our well-being as fresh air. Understanding great stories means understanding these inner processes can lead to a profound understanding of ourselves and the world.

This book introduces two important new models:

• The Golden Paradigm — discovery of a new psychological model brought to light by the intriguing patterns hidden within great stories.
• The Storywheel — a cosmological view of story that brings all of the different types of story together into one grand design.

Movie Entertainment Book Club Selection
JAMES BONNET, founder of Astoria Filmwrights, is a successful Hollywood screen and television writer. He has acted in or written more than 40 television shows and features including *Kojak*, *Barney Miller*, and two cult film classics, *The Blob*, and *The Cross and the Switchblade*.

$26.95, 300 pages, 6 x 9
ISBN 0-941188-65-5
Order # 38RLS

Available
September 1999
Advance Orders

THE WRITER'S JOURNEY
MYTHIC STRUCTURE FOR WRITERS - 2ND EDITION
Christopher Vogler

This new edition provides fresh insights and observations from Vogler's ongoing work with mythology's influence on stories, movies, and humankind itself.

Learn why thousands of professional writers have made THE WRITER'S JOURNEY a best-seller and why it is considered required reading by many of Hollywood's top studios! Learn how master storytellers have used mythic structure to create powerful stories that tap into the mythological core which exists in us all.

Writers of both fiction and non-fiction will discover a set of useful myth-inspired storytelling paradigms (e.g., The Hero's Journey) and step-by-step guidelines to plot and character development. Based on the work of Joseph Campbell, THE WRITER'S JOURNEY is a must for writers of all kinds.

New analyses of box office blockbusters such as Titanic, The Lion King, The Full Monty, Pulp Fiction, and Star Wars.

• A foreword describing the worldwide reaction to the first edition and the continued influence of The Hero's Journey model.

• Vogler's new observations on the adaptability of THE WRITER'S JOURNEY for international markets, and the changing profile of the audience.

• The latest observations and techniques for using the mythic model to enhance modern storytelling.

• New subject index and filmography.

• How to apply THE WRITER'S JOURNEY paradigm to your own life.

Book-of-the-Month Club Selection • Writer's Digest Book Club Selection
Movie Entertainment Book Club Selection

$22.95, 300 pages, 6 x 9
ISBN 0-941188-70-1
Order # 2598RLS

Michael Wiese Productions

11288 Ventura Blvd., Suite 821
Studio City, CA 91604
1-818-379-8799
kenlee@earthlink.net
www.mwp.com

Write or Fax
for a
free catalog.

Please send me the following
books:

Title   Order Number (#RLS___)   Amount

_____ _____

_____ _____

_____ _____

_____ _____

SHIPPING   _____

California Tax (8.25%)   _____

TOTAL ENCLOSED _____

Please make check or money order payable to
Michael Wiese Productions

(Check one) ___ Master Card ___ Visa ___ Amex

Credit Card Number_____

Expiration Date_____

Cardholder's Name_____

Cardholder's Signature_____

SHIP TO:

Name_____

Address_____

City_____State_____Zip_____